SECRET SOCIETIES IN CHINA
Jean Chesneaux

SECRET SOCIETIES
IN CHINA

In the Nineteenth and Twentieth Centuries

JEAN CHESNEAUX

Translated by
Gillian Nettle

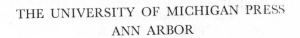

THE UNIVERSITY OF MICHIGAN PRESS
ANN ARBOR

ISBN 0-472-08207-8
Library of Congress Catalog Card No. 76-124425

Published in the United States of America by
The University of Michigan Press
Printed in Hong Kong

Foreword

It is not without some diffidence that I venture to write a foreword to Professor Chesneaux's book. There is no need for me to introduce Jean Chesneaux because he is already an internationally-recognised scholar. As this book, however, is really meant for the general reader just as much as scholars of Chinese sociology and history, perhaps a few words of introduction by way of providing a setting for the fascinating book he has written may not be out of place.

Furthermore, I feel I owe this courtesy to Professor Chesneaux. I first came into contact with him, albeit indirectly, some years ago through my first wife, Han Suyin, when she lent him one or two books from my Chinese library dealing with Chinese secret societies, although I did not actually have the pleasure of meeting him until a few months ago at the 28th International Congress of Orientalists held at the Australian National University, Canberra, A.C.T.

However, two or three years before we met, he had asked me to contribute a chapter to another book he was editing on Chinese secret societies. Unfortunately, I was never able to get round to this not because of any slothfulness or indifference on my part but simply because of pressure of work. I have been stretched to the full since 1963 in establishing the Far Eastern subsidiary company of Heinemann Educational Books, which now has its headquarters in Hong Kong, branch offices in Singapore and Kuala Lumpur, and agencies in Tokyo, Seoul, Manila and Bangkok. In fact, this book is being published under the imprint of our Hong Kong company.

By way of a general setting for Professor Chesneaux's book, I should say that Chinese secret societies have always played an extremely important part in the life of the Chinese but by their nature very little has been known about them. Their influence was nevertheless widespread — and still is among the overseas Chinese — and their ramifications extended to every branch of

v

Chinese life, especially politics, religion, commerce, trade unions and the criminal underworld.

Their activities in China have included the organisation of opposition to the government; the stirring up of anti-foreign feeling; the formation of self-protection units against robber gangs; 'protection' of, and extortion of money from hawkers, shopkeepers, hotel-keepers, prostitutes, labourers, transport undertakings, opium and gambling dens; kidnapping for ransom, and the operation of criminal rings and rackets. However, there is good reason to believe that many of them were originally founded as benevolent associations for laudable and unobjectionable purposes, something akin to Freemasonary in the West.

Secret societies are mainly significant, in my opinion, because they are associated with frontier conditions or with shortcomings in the social and political structure of government. In China, many peasants undoubtedly joined secret societies because the writ of constitutional authority did not readily reach the villages situated at a distance from the seat of government, and they banded together to counteract the power of local officials and gentry, and to protect their own economic and social interests.

The arcana of Chinese secret societies include nocturnal initiation ceremonies, secret signs, symbols and passwords, and the taking of an oath of blood brotherhood which binds a member to absolute loyalty to his society. Those who lightly break this oath are put to death. To a secret society member the laws of his society supersede the ordinary laws of the land, and, in this way, secret societies have come to exercise what has rightly been called by many authors an *imperium in imperio*, a state of affairs which clearly cannot be tolerated by any self-respecting government.

Although legislation has been passed against Chinese secret societies in many countries, their eradication cannot be brought about by the mere passing of a law, and history has demonstrated that not only are they able to withstand persecution but they even thrive on it. As far as Chinese secret societies are concerned, this is not surprising when one thinks that they can be dated back to the former Han dynasty (206 B. C. – A. D. 23), and possibly even before that, as some Chinese scholars have taken the famous quotation, 'All men within the four seas are brothers' from *The Analects* to mean that Confucius was really referring to the universal brotherhood of secret societies.

The names used by Chinese secret societies are confusing to the extreme, perhaps purposely so in order to confound the authorities. A list of their more important and exotic names in Chinese history would have to include the Red Eyebrow, Copper Horse, White Lotus, Yellow and Red Turbans, Heaven and Earth, Three Dots, Triad, Eight Trigrams, Small Sword, Righteous Harmony, Red Beards, Black Flags, Two Dragons and a Tiger, Elder Brothers, Mutual Progress, not forgetting the notorious Green and Red Band Societies in Shanghai of the 1920's and 1930's, which was then the Chicago of China.

The most vigorous period of Chinese secret society activity was undoubtedly the Ch'ing dynasty (A.D. 1644 – 1911) when they constituted a dangerous underground revolutionary movement aimed at the overthrow of the Manchu Government. What part they played in the T'ai P'ing movement of 1850, which lasted fifteen years, devastated one-third of China, and almost brought the Manchu Government to subjection has always been a moot point with sinologists. Anyway, it now seems to be generally accepted that at least there was some connection at the beginning. The Boxer Uprising of 1900 was also an anti-Manchu secret society movement which was cleverly turned by Empress Tz'u Hsi into an anti-foreign movement against the Western powers and Japan. The 1911 Chinese Revolution, engineered by Dr. Sun Yat-sen was yet another anti-dynastic movement which was aided greatly throughout by secret societies and finally brought about the overthrow of the Manchu monarchy and the establishment of a Republic in its stead.

Incidentally, Dr. Sun himself became a secret society member in Canton in 1893, and he is known to have joined the Chi Kung Tang (an overseas Chinese secret society first formed in the U.S.A.), with the rank of Red Staff in 1902 in Honolulu.

It is interesting to reflect that the part played by secret societies in the defeat of the Kuomintang Government by the Chinese Communists in 1949 and, indeed, the connection between traditional secret societies in China and the Chinese Communist Party, have still to be fully evaluated.

As Professor Chesneaux points out, General Chu Teh, Commander-in-Chief of the Chinese People's Army, was a member of the Elder Brothers Society — in fact, secret societies have always had a strong following in the Chinese army — and Wu Yu-chang, a member of the Central Committee of the Chinese Communist Party, was at one time a secret society member.

It is known, too, that from his youth, Chairman Mao Tse-tung has admired the bandit leaders and glorified the exploits of the peasant rebels portrayed in the famous Chinese novel, *Shui Hu Chuan,* which was translated rather loosely into English under the title *All Men Are Brothers* by Pearl S. Buck. Many scholars (including Professor Chesneaux) believe that Chinese secret societies owe a lot to this story and that it has provided them with a source of imagery and inspiration — certainly it is evident that many of the names used by them for office-bearers and symbolic articles used in their rituals have been borrowed from the text.

There is also the public appeal which Chairman Mao made to the 'Brothers of the Ko-Lao-Hui' (Elder Brothers Society) in 1936 in an attempt to bring about an united front of the Communists and the Society against the Japanese. He mentioned Hsieh Tzu-ch'ang and Liu Chih-tan as not only being leaders of the Red Army but also 'exemplary' leaders of the Elder Brothers Society. The last paragraph of this stirring appeal reads:

"Let the Elder Brothers' Society and the whole of the Chinese people unite to strike at Japan and to restore China! Long live the liberation of the Chinese people!"

What does all this mean?

Stuart Schram, the eminent biographer of Mao Tse-tung, opines that the secret societies may have been useful to the Chinese Communist Party before it came to power in 1949 but since that date they have been considered feudalistic and reactionary.

This may be so, but it is nevertheless intriguing to think that the Chi Kung Tang is still recognised as a political party in China.

For further details of the extraordinary story of secret societies in China and the part they played in China's political upheavals, I can do no better than to step aside and allow you to read Professor Chesneaux's book.

Leon Comber

Kowloon, Hong Kong
August, 1971

Publisher's Note

Perhaps a word of explanation about the romanisation of Chinese proper names would not be out of place as some comment has been made about this.

The book has been translated into English from French. Wherever possible, Chinese proper names mentioned in the French text have been transposed into the more familiar Wade romanised spelling. However, where original texts have been quoted, the names have been left in their original form although, wherever possible, the English version, if one exists, of the original material quoted has been consulted and this version followed.

It has not been possible to give the Chinese characters for all Chinese proper names as they are not always apparent, but wherever possible the Chinese characters have been sought out to make it easier to identify positively the names referred to.

L.C.

Contents

FOREWORD ....*Leon Comber*   v

INTRODUCTION: *From the Confucian Order to the People's China*   1
Documentary Material
The Confucian Order *c.* 1840
A Complete Conventional System
100 Years of Invasions and Revolutions

CHAPTER 1: *A Secret Society: The Triad*   13
An Initiation Ceremony (Singapore, 1824)
'Restore the Hung and Exterminate the Ch'ing'
The Five Legendary Founders
The Ritual of Initiation
The Oaths
Signs and Secret Language
Justiciary Brigands
The Lodges
A Scattering of Rival Factions
From Strikes to Gangsterism

CHAPTER 2: *A Few Other Societies*   36
The White Lotus *(Pai Lien Hui)*
The Eight Diagrams *(Pa-Kua)*
The Nien
The Big Sword Society *(Ta-tao-hui)*
The Boxers *(I Ho Ch'üan)*
The Observance Society *(Chai Li-hui)*
The Vegetarians *(Chai-chiao)*
The Red Beards *(Hung Hu-tzu)*
The Red Spears
The Association of Elder Brothers *(Ko-lao-hui)*
The Green Band *(Ch'ing-Pang)*
The Little Sword Society *(Hsiao-tao-hui)*
The Golden Coins Society *(Chin-ch'ien-hui)*
The Pure Tea Sect *(Ch'ing-ch'a-hui)*
The Golden Elixir Society *(Chin-tan-hui)*
The Way of Fundamental Unity *(Yi-kuan-tao)*

CHAPTER 3: *Secret Societies and Chinese Society*   55
Against the Established Order
Political Dissidence
A Quasi-Patriarchal Society
Official 'Commerce Tribunals'
The First Feminists
Social Banditry
A 'Code of Honour' of the Red Beards
'The Opposition to His Majesty'?
Religious Dissidence
The Image of Celestial Happiness
The Night and the Mountain
Recruitment
Sun Yat-sen's Analysis
Rural Outcasts
Disbanded Troops
The First Chinese Working Class
Doubtful Members
The Reaction of Imperial Power
A Less Rigid Practice

CHAPTER 4: *Against Imperial Power*   80
The Triad in Canton
The Small Sword in Shanghai
The Dismissal of the Emperor
The T'ai P'ing Rebellion
Were the T'ai P'ing a Secret Society?
The Origins of the T'ai P'ing
The Nien Uprising
The White Lotus in Nanking and Shanghai
The Observance Society in Inner Mongolia

CHAPTER 5: *Against Foreign Penetration*   108
The Carving-Up of China
Anti-Christian Agitation
The Reawakening of the Elder Brothers
The Big Sword against the Christian West
The Boxer Rising
The Boxers' Syncretism
The Social Framework of the Boxers
National Objectives

Against France in Indo-China
For Monarchic Restoration
The Attack on Saigon Prison
Against the Russians in Manchuria

CHAPTER 6: *In the Service of the Republican Cause*   135
Under the Republican Banner
The Kuomintang and the 'Three Principles of
   the People'
A Great Revolutionary Potential
Close Co-operation
Inter-Penetration: a Success
A Setback among the Émigrés
A Common Cause: the Example of Ma Fu-yi
Difficulties of a 'United Front'
Leaders in Exile; a little-changed Base
The Secret Societies' Influence on the Re-
   publican Movement
The 1911 Revolution

CHAPTER 7: *The Chinese Revolution (1919–1949)*   160
The Secret Societies at the Beginning of the
   Workers' Struggles
From Alliance with Reactionary Forces to
   Gangsterism
In the Country: The Red Spears
The Communists Become Interested in the Red
   Spears
The Communist Party and the Secret Societies
Guerrillas against the Japanese
Mao Tse-tung's Appeal to the Elder Brothers
Relations Sometimes Difficult
Some Pro-Japanese Secret Societies

CHAPTER 8: *An Interim Conclusion*   187

References   193
Bibliography   199
Chinese Character Index   201
Index   205
Illustrations   *Between* 98–99

From the Confucian Order to the People's China

In the early 1840s Queen Victoria's frigates and scarlet-coated infantry forced the gates of old China. It was the first Opium War.

At the moment when Westerners were about to strike at the framework underpinning the established order of the 'Middle Kingdom' there existed – alongside the imperial government and the traditional political, social, and religious systems – hundreds of picturesquely named secret societies: White Lotus, Green Band, Triad, Big Sword... These organisations, whose roots in the country were firm and often centuries-old, were powerfully active, and the imperial authorities knew them as forces to be reckoned with.

A century passed between this first shock and the great upheaval forced upon China by the Communist victory in 1949. Throughout that period the secret societies occupied an important place in Chinese political and social life, influenced the course of events, resisted Western penetration, and in general helped to determine the history of China.

At a time when so many works on modern China are put on sale with the sort of publicity better suited to the launching of the latest model of a washing machine, even though such books often do no more than repeat one another, it seems worthwhile to use this new approach to throw new light on the nineteenth and twentieth-century history of China. That is what the texts presented here are intended to do.

It was obviously impossible to transform this volume into a 'short history of modern China', though the absence of such a work is painfully evident today. Even so, the general historical outline which links together the texts included in the book may well appear too brief.

My concern – as I have said – is to illuminate certain aspects of the life of Chinese secret societies and of the part they played in China's political upheavals. For background information the reader is referred to the bibliography, where I have listed several general works on the history of modern China. General history will only be discussed insofar as it involves the secret societies and the really important stages in the transformation of China. Events such as the reform movement of 1898 or the modernist movement of 1919–20 (the 4th May Movement) are hardly mentioned, since the secret societies played little or no part in them. Conversely, far more space has been devoted to the Boxer Rising and the Sino-Japanese War.

Documentary Material

I have included in the book official documents obtained from the societies themselves: the Small Sword proclamation restoring the Ming dynasty (Shanghai, 1853), Boxer anti-Christian manifestos, part of a catechism of the Way of Fundamental Unity, and the oaths and ritual of the Triad. The relative rarity of these documents is natural in view of the nature of their origin and makes them all the more plausible.

More numerous are the recollections and eye-witness accounts of former members of the secret societies, or of people in close contact with them. Even in the People's Republic today such accounts and recollections are common. They often come from people with direct experience of the secret societies, which were so active in the final phase of the struggle against the old Manchu antagonists. Material of this type has been extensively used in Chapter 6, which deals with the rôle of the secret societies in the preparation and execution of the Republican Revolution of 1911.

The authorities responsible for maintaining order were naturally obliged to take a keen interest in the activities of these clandestine groups with their secret power. Mandarins of the old imperial bureaucracy as well as police forces of the colonial territories where there were large numbers of Chinese immigrants (Malaysia, Indo-China, Indonesia, etc.) built up a very important mass of documentation on the secret societies. It is from these sources that we know a good deal about the Triad, a society which was very influential among the Chinese of South-East Asia; they also throw light on many other aspects of the secret societies. Mandarin sources are of prime importance to our understanding of the nineteenth-century rebellions (see Chapter 4), while French police sources have the same importance for the study of the secret societies of Saigon in the period 1910–15.

Mention must be made of a fourth category of material – that produced by observers, men outside the societies who were nonetheless familiar with their activities. One of these was Munshi Abdullah, the Malay secretary to Sir Stamford Raffles, the founder of Singapore, who in 1824 attended a Triad initiation ceremony there. Other observers included the many Catholic and Protestant missionaries [see the texts of Fathers Leboucq (Chapter 2) and Palâtre (Chapter 4), and of the Rev. D.H. Porter (Chapter 2), etc.], who contribute valuable information, particularly on the numerous sects of North China in the nineteenth century. In the same category are Teichmann, the British consul who, in 1914, travelled through the regions troubled by the 'White Wolf' rebellion; and a Russian engineer from Manchuria who, about 1920, visited the wild Red Beards.

Journalists' reports fall into more or less the same category. They have been extensively used for the twentieth century, since they provide details of certain traditions and other information not otherwise available – for example, about the Red Spears of Honan, and the collusion between the Kuomintang and certain secret societies.

Lastly, a considerable number of important Chinese political figures have paid attention to the curious phenomenon of the secret societies and written on their place in the political and social life of China, and on the contact that they themselves have been able to maintain with the societies. Hung Hsiu-ch'üan, the T'ai P'ing emperor; T'an Ssu-t'ung, the unfortunate reformer of 1898; Sun Yat-sen, first President of the Chinese Republic in 1912; and Mao Tse-tung have all been anxious to consider these points. Mao is by no means the only Chinese Marxist to have made a painstaking analysis of the secret societies in modern China.

It will be seen that, if we are not dealing with impeccable 'archive material', (though all historians of modern China are in the same position), we have at our disposal richer and more varied documents than one might have expected.

About one-third of these sixty or so texts were specially translated from the Chinese; another third are Chinese documents of which a translation into English or French was already available; while the remainder are original texts written in English, French, or – in one case – Russian.

The Confucian Order c. 1840

At once spectators and actors in China's evolution towards modernity, the secret societies in the period 1840–1949 had deep roots in both the political and the traditional social system. It is worth pausing at this point to consider the latter.

It may be defined as a strongly centralised feudal bureaucracy.

Agriculture was the major activity. It involved the great mass of the population and provided the greater part of Chinese production in quantity and value. Rural crafts, fishing, and wood-collecting were also significant.

In the official social hierarchy of Confucianism, the peasants came immediately below the literate civil servants and above the artisans. The 'crafty tradesmen' came last of all.

Village communities still existed, often bound together by the tradition of being descended from one family and forming a sort of 'clan'. But ties of economic dependence had appeared a long time before with the private ownership of land, and many peasants worked the fields of rich landowners – the *ti chu* (land masters) – to whom they paid farm rent. The Chinese peasant, even if he worked his own land, was still subject to the power of the landowner by bonds of usury. The peasantry were poor, always at the mercy of a bad harvest, and always ready to rise up against the established order and feudal oppression.

The towns were large and prosperous, and included such huge cities as Peking, Nanking, and Canton. Essentially political and administrative centres where the upper classes and their clientele lived, they consumed the produce of the countryside without offering anything in return. The goods produced by the urban working class, though technically of high quality, scarcely went beyond the city walls, except for certain very specialised products which were exported far and wide.

Several centuries earlier the seeds of an industrial and commercial revolution had been sown in several fields such as luxury textiles, (in the lower Yangtze region), but the social system thwarted their possible development.

At the bottom of the social scale, as we have seen, were the tradesmen: it was the reaction of an agricultural society on the defensive, analagous to medieval Christianity's attribution of mortal sin to the money-lender. A wealthy merchant always preferred to enter the civil service, or to get his sons to enter it, rather than to carry on his trade and make his business prosper. Only in the civil service was it possible to find prestige as well as profit.

At the dawn of the modern period in imperial China the state machinery was an autonomous and all-powerful reality. It held functional power and in effect constituted a ruling class.

Its dominant position probably went back to the time when there was no private ownership of the means of production, to an 'Asiatic' society in which the leaders directed the work of village communities and lived off the proceeds. Certainly for two thousand years landowners had exercised a private system of control over agricultural production – the sort of ownership and control that were the main source of power and wealth in Western feudalism – and yet the civil service retained the real power, along with important economic responsibilities (building up rice stocks in the imperial granaries, control of irrigation, supervision of the mines) which were vestiges of its former rôle as organiser of production.

Civil servants were recruited mainly from upper-middle-class families and merchants – that is to say, from among those who had the time and money for education. Occasionally, however, sons of peasants were admitted.

The civil service constituted an immense and complex framework for all the regions and all the social activities of the empire (public works, defence, taxation, justice, economic affairs). Entry and promotion were by a series of imperial examinations dealing with knowledge of the Confucian classics and written culture – traditional scholarship, that is. The essential function of the civil service was to ensure that nothing should disrupt the stability of society, which ought to be a reflection of cosmic order. It was in fact fundamentally conservative, or – in Confucian terms – 'non-interventionist'. To govern was to maintain the status quo and in so doing to make sure that China continued to benefit from the 'Heavenly Mandate' (*T'ien Ming*).

As head of state, the emperor was the living symbol of the Heavenly Mandate.

In 1840 a foreign dynasty of Manchu origin, the Ch'ing, reigned in Peking. In the seventeenth century it had dethroned the last native Chinese dynasty, the Ming. It had had periods of glory in the eighteenth century, but as the nineteenth century advanced, faced with the incompetence and corruption of the civil servants, the peasants began to protest, the secret societies became active, and many Chinese came to question the validity of the Mandate of which the emperor was trustee.

Confucianism considered as legitimate rebellions which overthrew a weakened dynasty (as was the case with the Ming, whose last emperor·was reckoned to have 'lost the Heavenly Mandate'). The fortunate rival of the fallen sovereign benefited in turn from the Mandate and personally restored the social order. In Chinese, a re-volution is called *ke ming* – breaking of the mandate.

A Complete Conventional System

This bureaucratic and feudal society did not lack unity. On the contrary for thousands of years without a break China was characterised by a quite extraordinary cohesion.

The unity existed essentially at the level of the state organisation and its economic bases were minimal. Each province carried on its own social and economic life; its civil servants were allowed great administrative and financial freedom, even though they were often transferred from one province to another. The multiplicity of the secret societies and the local or regional character of their growth – traits of which we shall see numerous examples – were no more than a reflection of the geographical dispersal of Chinese society and the economy.

China's traditional social system was closed, complete, absolute. There was no distinction between soldier and civilian (the mandarins could take on duties in either sphere); between the religious and the secular (Confucianism was both a system of government and a view of man's place in the world); or between society and nature (man being regarded simply as one element among others in the cosmic order).

The system tolerated other popular religions beside itself:

Buddhism, brought from India in the Middle Ages, preaching renunciation, moral uplift, and the transmigration of souls;

Taoism, older and stranger: an agglomeration of magical practices and naturist techniques aimed at freeing the individual and helping him to transcend himself in searching for the 'Way' *(Tao).*

These two religions, however, did not embrace a complete system of thought and of political and social organisation, as Confucianism did.

Traditional Chinese society was extremely conventional. It was ordered by firm rules, by relations fixed for all time. The rules were expressed, for example, in the 'five relationships' (emperor-subject, father-children, husband-wife, elder brother-younger brother, friend-

friend), in family discipline, in the authority of the old, in the conventions of good manners, in the obligations of the apprentice towards his craft-master or the student towards the teacher, and in the 'rites' (*li*) governing relations with the emperor and his representatives.

The whole of Chinese life was highly socialised and conceptualised.

The secret societies were diametrically opposed to the Confucian order and its social conventions (we shall see, for example, that they were feminist in outlook). But at the same time they set out to create, at least symbolically, a system of rules and political conventions as complete as the one they opposed.

In short, they mirrored established society while constituting – for hundreds of years – the principal force of political opposition and religious dissent.

Most of the sects listed in Chapter 2 went back a long way – the White Lotus, for example, to the twelfth century.

In traditional China, where the political power of the ruling class (the civil servants) and its economic power (feudal exploitation of the peasants) were intermingled, discontent with the established order was directed against both the rich and the state. This was the cause of the peasant revolts which punctuated the history of the great Chinese dynasties.

In earlier centuries the secret societies often took the initiative in these revolts. They provided them with a framework, strengthened with their rituals and magic formulae the ideological mobilisation of the peasants against Confucian orthodoxy, and offered them a means of retreat after the rebellion had collapsed.

This association between secret societies and peasant agitation continued into the nineteenth and even into the twentieth century with the Red Spears movement.

Traditionally, too, the secret societies were associated with the struggle against the foreign invader. The leader of the revolt which in the fourteenth century hounded out the Mongols and founded the Ming dynasty was said to be a member of the White Lotus. In the same way, after the empire fell into the hands of the Manchus in the seventeenth century the secret societies – particularly the Triad – incessantly opposed these new barbarians and demanded their expulsion. In fact they contributed significantly to their downfall in 1911.

From 1840 to 1949 the modern and contemporary history of China[1] was marked chiefly by attempts at infiltration first by the West and then by Japan. These new foreign adversaries gave rise to a national opposition movement in which the secret societies sometimes played a leading part.

100 Years of Invasions and Revolutions

It seems sufficient here simply to indicate the broad outline of the evolution of China between 1840 and 1949 before returning in greater detail (in Chapters 4 – 7) to the activities of the secret societies.

In the mid-nineteenth century, the Opium Wars forcibly opened up China to trade dealings with foreigners, who gained a series of privileges as a result of 'unequal treaties', the most important being customs facilities and the occupation of certain parts of the towns (the 'concessions').

About 1895–1900 the Great Powers obtained new advantages, again by force: mining and railway concessions, zones of influence, etc. It was the break-up of China, a forced destruction. The Chinese state fell more and more under the joint control of the Powers, and was no longer, as Sun Yat-sen said, anything more than a 'sub-colony'.

In the twentieth century a new enemy appeared – Japan. Initially on the side of the West but soon its rival, it first sought only economic and diplomatic advantages. But in 1931 it annexed Manchuria and from 1937 to 1945

---

[1]Chinese historians normally call 'modern' (chin tai) the period from the Opium Wars to the 4th May patriotic movement (1840-1919), and 'contemporary' (hsien tai) the period from the 4th May to the Liberation in 1949. The two terms do not have the same chronological significance as they do in the West.

occupied all the big urban centres except those in the west.

But this century was also marked by Chinese resistance to foreign penetration; timid in the nineteenth century, in particular on the part of the imperial authorities, this resistance was much more determined in this century. Japan believed that it had the country at its mercy in 1937, but in fact it was militarily incapable of occupying China completely.

Time and time again the secret societies were to be found among the national resistance forces. The Boxer Rising was far from being an isolated instance of this.

During this same period, China found itself harshly confronted with the modern world, with Western science and technology. It had to undergo profound changes.

Enormous modern cities sprang up – like Shanghai, which only a century before had been little more than a village. These urban communities flourished on international trade, the steamship lines put in at them, and many factories were built. Daily life was completely transformed by public transport (trams and buses), electricity, the press, and Western-style universities.

From the end of the nineteenth century onwards many railways were built, especially in the north. Foreigners opened up and exploited the mines. A capitalist economy was developed in the first place by large-scale foreign financial interests; but a modern sector also appeared in the Chinese national economy–banking, wholesale trade, and light industry.

Naturally enough, this transformation of the economy brought about radical changes in the social system. The quadripartite traditional hierarchy – scholars, peasants, artisans, tradesmen – which still characterised Chinese society in 1840, was completely broken up. The number of artisans declined, as did the prestige of the Confucian scholars. In 1906 the imperial examinations were abolished. On the other hand, in spite of the fierce competition they had to contend with from numerous foreign businesses, the bourgeoisie made rapid progress. Other new social strata appeared: the modern intelligentsia, the young educated class, avidly interested in science and hostile to the old China. The industrial proletariat, drawn from the poor peasants and the unemployed of the cities, although wretched and lacking traditions, took its strength from its concentration in particular areas.

The secret societies drew their strength – even while they undermined them – from the sociological and ideological bases of the old society: economic stagnation, the local and narrow character of social relations, the weight of tradition and the respect for authority (even that of an outlaw), routine, and superstition. The changes in Chinese life in modern times meant that, sooner or later, the secret societies would disappear. But at the same time, these changes considerably widened the social basis of these archaic groups, particularly among the urban masses. The wretched peasants who flooded into Shanghai and the other big cities completely without means of support naturally clung to the secret societies. Until the beginning of the twentieth century, far from withering away in the cities, the societies regained their former influence.

In the hundred years or so which separated the Opium Wars from the Liberation, intense, modern-style revolutionary struggles were carried on, aimed at eliminating an *ancien régime* that was degenerate, corrupt, and incapable of standing up to foreigners or of leading the country in the path of progress. It was no longer a question of the traditional 'breaking of the Mandate' which simply brought a new dynasty to power.

The objectives of this Chinese revolution became apparent only gradually. Various social groups or political organisations took them up successively.

The T'ai P'ing peasant movement (1851-64) attacked the Manchus and tried to establish an unusual social system which resembled primitive agrarian communism and replaced Confucianism by a syncretism derived from traditional peasant cults and the teaching of Protestant missionaries from Canton. Victims both of their own weaknesses and of the help the West gave the Manchus, the T'ai P'ing inevitably failed.

The revolutionary wave ebbed for thirty years. It flowed again at the end of the nineteenth century when, with the new intelligentsia to give it impetus and with the support of the modern bourgeoisie, republican organisations were formed – in particular the Tung-meng-hui (Sworn League) of Sun Yat-sen, the precursor of the Kuomintang. In 1911, after many unsuccessful attempts, they finally succeeded in overthrowing the Ch'ing dynasty and in setting up a republic of which Sun Yat-sen became president. But this progressive republic quickly degenerated into military anarchy and social conservatism.

The 4th May Movement saw the intelligentsia and the bourgeoisie in protest against certain provisions of the Treaty of Versailles which were judged as unacceptable to Chinese patriotism. It was the point of departure for a more radical revolution which called in question the political régime and the social structure. From then on, the initiative was taken by the Chinese Communist Party, founded in 1921 by the 4th May organisers and closely linked to the the industrial proletariat, the radical intelligentsia, and the poor peasantry.

The communists allied themselves at first with the Kuomintang. They subsequently opposed it ruthlessly after its *volte-face* in 1927, concentrating their action in the industrial towns before moving the revolution's centre of gravity out into the country. Their objectives were radical agrarian reform and, from 1937 onwards, 'national salvation' in the face of the Japanese menace. Gradually the Party moved into the foreground, until in 1949 it seized power.

CHAPTER ONE

A Secret Society: The Triad

An Initiation Ceremony (Singapore, 1824)

About 7 o'clock they had all arrived and commenced to eat and drink spirits, which they did with a noise like a battle. In about an hour this finished, when they commenced to play on drums etc., the music of which was extremely loud. On this they all arranged themselves in order, sitting opposite the Datu (idol) but I observed their faces were red from drunkenness. Among them all there was one chief, who sat on a lofty chair, with 2 men standing at his right and 2 at his left. After them came 8 men, with drawn swords, who arranged themselves at the right and left; then came one man, who burned paper in front of the idol; after him came 8 men, with drawn swords, who guarded a man with dishevelled hair, and without any upper garment.... This man came in front of the chief and bowed down till his head touched the ground; the armed men on the right and left now advanced, shouting, and laid their swords on his neck. They remained silently in this position for a short time, when a man advanced to the candidate's side: the chief then spoke as follows in the Chinese language:— 'Who are you and from whence come you? Who are your father and mother? Are they still alive or are they dead?' These questions were explained to the candidate by the man who stood at his side, and were answered as follows:— 'I am such a one, of such a country, and my father and mother are both dead...' The chief then said: 'What have you come here for?' Answer: 'I wish to join the Heaven and Earth Society.'

The chief then said: 'You are deceiving, your thoughts are not as your speech.' Answer: 'I will swear that I am good in faith.' 'Then swear.' The candidate, then taking paper, burned it, while he repeated his assertion. The chief then said: 'Are you acquainted with the rules of the society?' Answer: 'Yes, I understand that I am required to take an oath by drinking blood.'

The chief then said something to which the following answer was made:—

'I promise not to divulge the secrets of this society to anyone, under penalty of death.' The chief said, 'Truly.'

Answer: 'Truly.' A vessel was then brought, containing arrack and a little blood from each of the members of the society, and, with a knife, was placed in front of the idol. The candidate then, taking up the knife, made a slight cut in his finger, from which he allowed some blood to fall into the cup. The chief then said: 'Drink in presence of Datok pekong.'[1] The candidate then drank a small cupful, on which the chief and all the confederates drank a little, each in his turn. The chief then said:'Tomorrow go to our secretary, and ask him for a book; in that book you will find all our rules and secret signs: you will pay one dollar for it'...

In this way four members were admitted... [Then] they brought a man with his hands tied with a cord. He was placed in front of the chief and ordered to prostrate himself, but he remained erect. A man then came and gave him 10 or 20 blows with a bamboo. He was then asked if he would join the society; he remained silent; the question was repeated 3 or 4 times without getting any answer. The chief made a sign to those who were armed with the drawn swords; they advanced and made a motion as if they were about to cut off his head, indeed, I thought he was killed, but the chief ordered them to desist, and again asked if he would become a member of the society; still he refused. The chief then ordered him to be stretched on the ground, and two men came and beat him on the back with bamboos. This beating frightened him greatly, but, on being questioned again, he still refused, when the chief said: 'Tomorrow morning let him be put to death.'

They confined him for that night, and the next morning he was killed, in consequence of his not wishing to join the society. (1)

'Restore the Hung and Exterminate the Ch'ing'

The Triad is today by far the best known of the Chinese secret societies. Its influence has been greatest among the southern Chinese. Many of these, seeking better living standards, emigrated at the end of the nineteenth century and the beginning of the twentieth to the ports, mines, and plantations of the European

---

[1]The English text (from the *Chinese Almanack*) has 'Datu Peking' an evidently false transliteration. The reference is to a patron deity (*topekong*).—*Translator.*

colonies of South-East Asia – Hong Kong, South Vietnam, Malaysia, and Indonesia.

The colonial administrators were bound to take an
interest in this powerful movement which might cause
them serious trouble. Their records and documentation
put at the disposal of sinologists material which is
unequalled so far as other Chinese secret societies are
concerned.

Thus, as far back as the mid-nineteenth century,
first-hand accounts and descriptions are available.
Particularly important is that of Schlegel, a pioneer in
the study of the Triad in the East, whose work appeared
in Batavia in 1866. About 1885 an English civil servant,
Pickering, actually managed to attend a Triad initiation
ceremony. Recently, the importance to the study of the
Triad of material originating from police records has
again been underlined by the work of W.P. Morgan,
published under the auspices of the British police of
Hong Kong.

The Triad was essentially a political organisation
directed against the Ch'ing dynasty – the Ch'ing being
Manchu usurpers who gained possession of the Chinese
imperial throne in the mid-seventeenth century. Its
slogan was: 'Restore the Hung and exterminate the
Ch'ing.'

The society had several names:

San Ho Hui: Society of the Three Elements in One
(Heaven, Earth, and Man).

San Tien Hui: Society of the Three Dots.

T'ien Ti Hui: Heaven and Earth Society.

Hung Men: Gate of Hung.

Hung Chia: Family of Hung.

Hung Pang: Hung Party or Red Party.

The last three names recall the society's connection with
the Ming dynasty.[1] In private the members of the society
called themselves 'sons of Hung'.

---

[1]Homophones are common in Chinese. *Hung* written as two different
ideograms can mean either the name under which the first Ming
emperor ruled *(Hung Wu)*, or 'red'.

The Five Legendary Founders

The hostility towards the Ch'ing and fidelity to the Ming are strongly evident in the semi-legendary tradition maintained by the society about its own origins.

According to this tradition, some seventeenth-century Buddhist monks of Shao Lin Monastery, in Fukien province, offered the Manchu emperor their support against a rebel tribe from Central Asia, the Eleuths. The emperor in question was the first of the usurping dynasty, that is, a Ch'ing. These war-like monks aroused the jealousy of a courtier, their monastery was destroyed by order of the emperor, and all but five of them were massacred. After a long series of adventures involving rebel generals, horse-dealers, and Buddhist deities, the five monks had a mystical experience in which the words of the legitimist slogan, *Fan Ch'ing Fu Ming*, were revealed to them. They took refuge in the town of Muh-yang, the City of Willows, and founded there within the Market of the Great Peace (T'ai P'ing) a secret society, the Triad.

There is no firm historical evidence to support this tradition. According to some experts, T'ao Ch'eng-chang for example, the Triad was involved in the struggle against the Manchus earlier than the war with the Eleuths, and the monks only took part in the war in the hope of infiltrating the imperial army. According to this hypothesis the burning of the monastery would have been the consequence of the discovery of their legitimist conspiracy.

It is at any rate certain that, from the end of the seventeenth century onwards, the Triad Society was very active in China and created considerable problems for the Manchu authorities. Together with the White Lotus, which will be referred to later, the Triad was the only secret society mentioned in the Ch'ing code, which imposed very severe penalties on its activities.

The Ritual of Initiation

The Triad did not limit its activities to politics. During the initiation ceremony, the new members completed a mystical journey recreating the 'passion' of the five founder-members of the fraternity, and then drank a mixture of wine and blood. These rituals clearly underline the religious character of the society.

At this same ceremony two officials of the lodge, the 'master' and the 'vanguard', recited a ritual dialogue[1] evoking the various stages in the mystical journey. Time and time again religious symbols are in evidence, whether Taoist (peach and plum trees, symbolising immortality; sacred numbers, 21, 36, 72, and 108 which equals 36 + 72), or Buddhist (various deities, and the City of Willows, which could represent the Buddhist paradise).

> Question: What business have you here?
> Answer: I am bringing you numberless fresh soldiers, iron-hearted and valiant, who wish to be admitted to the Heaven and Earth Society.
> Q: How can you prove that?
> A: I can prove it by a verse.
> Q: How does this verse run?
> A: The course of events is clear again, and sun and moon harmonious; the earth extends to the four seas, and receives the three rivers. We have sworn together to protect the throne of Chu.[2]
> And to help him with all the power of man.
> Q: Why do they wish to be admitted to the Heaven and Earth Society?
> A: Because they wish to overthrow the house of Ch'ing, and re-establish the house of Ming.
> Q: How can you prove that?
> A: I can prove it by a verse.
> Q: How does this verse run?
> A: We have restored the origin, searched the sources, and examined the ancient poetry;
> The people of Ch'ing usurped our patrimony;
> We'll restore now the empire, following the instructions of the leader,

---

[1] The ritual consists of 333 questions (symbolic number) put by the master of ceremonies to another official, the *hsien feng* or 'vanguard', whose task it was to introduce the postulants. It was the vanguard who answered, not the postulants themselves.

[2] Patronymic of the founder of the Ming dynasty, who ruled under the name Hung Wu.

We'll rise by this clear moon, and raise the banner of patriotism.

Q: How did you obtain your knowledge of military art?
A: I learned it at Shao Lin Monastery.[1]
Q: What did you learn firstly?
A: I firstly learned the art of boxing of the Hung brethren.
Q: How can you prove that?
A: I can prove it by a verse.
Q: How does this verse run?
A: The fists of the brave and valiant Hungs are known throughout the world;
Since the Shao Lin Monastery it has been transmitted.
Under the whole expanse of heaven we all are called Hung;
Afterwards we will assist the prince of the house of Ming.

Q: How many of you came hither?
A: Three men.
Q: Why then do you come alone?
A: The younger brethren were before me; the adopted brethren were behind me; I was in the middle.
Because I asked for valiant heroes, I arrived later.

Q: How can you prove that?
A: I can prove it by a verse.
Q: How does this verse run?
A: I held in my hand a red umbrella,
That I might have no fear on the road to the gates of the lodge.
The adopted brethren asked me whither I went—
The younger brethren went earlier, but I went later.

Q: Since you went away so early, how does it come, then, that you arrive so late?
A: I come so late because I asked for valiant heroes.
Q: Who accompanied you?
A: The Hung brethren accompanied me.
Q: Where are those Hung brethren now?
A: They are far off at the horizon; they are near before eyes. They roam about the world without a fixed residence. This is the reason why I came alone.
Q: Did you come by land or by water.

---

[1]As we have seen, the monastery from which the founders of the Triad came. According to the legend it was destroyed by the imperial armies.

A: I went first overland, and afterwards in a boat.

Q: How many roads were there along which you could come?

A: There were three roads..

Q: Along which road did you come?

A: Along the middle road.

Q: Which road was the broadest?

A: The middle road was the broadest.

Q: How can you prove that?

A: I can prove it by a verse.

Q: How does this verse run?

A: When I went out my door I saw three roads;
I went on the middle road and asked for valiant heroes.
I gathered the sons of Hung, by oath united,
To scheme the destruction of the Manchus, and return
to the allegiance of the house of Ming. (2)

The ritual goes on to evoke the postulants' overland journey, describing the temples at which they stop and their politico-religious inscriptions. Next the journey continues by sea, on the mystical ship with 21 holds and 21 decks, 72 seams and 108 nails, and with the goddess Kuan-yin on board. They put in to port for a botanical excursion to a mountain, to gather 108 sacred plants. The ship finally comes to land by the Market Place of the Great Peace (T'ai P'ing). Access to the market is by a bridge made of two planks, which the ritual connects with the one which the five founders crossed as they fled. Beside it stand a plum tree and a peach tree, one with 72 fruits and the other with 36. The postulants have to pass under the bridge out of respect for the five founders, who are above. Next they pass through the Hung Gate, which is guarded by generals faithful to the Ming emperors, go into the Temple of Loyalty and Fidelity, and enter the Circle of Heaven and Earth.

Question: Which place was within the Circle of Heaven and Earth?

Answer: The City of Willows, the seat of universal peace.

Q: Did you enter it?

A: Yes, I entered it.

Q: Who founded the City of Willows and who restored it?

A: A prince of T'ang has founded it; Wan Yun-lung has restored it.

Q: How high is the City of Willows?

A: As high as one's eyes can reach.

Q: How broad is it?

A: As broad as the two capitals and thirteen provinces.

Q: How many double walls are there round the Willow City?

A: There are five double walls.

Q: How can you prove that?

A: I can prove it by a verse.

Q: How does this verse run?

A: The Willow City has five double walls:
Within are the brethren who pledged fraternity.
Shields and spears are piled as high as sun and moon;
We have sworn before sun and moon to adopt all the name of Hung.

Q: What was on these walls?

A: On each wall were four large characters.

Q: Which characters were on the first wall?

A: Blending-Heaven's extensive conversion.[1]

Q: Which characters were on the second wall?

A: Obey Heaven, act righteously.

Q: Which characters were on the third wall?

A: Overturn the Ch'ing dynasty and restore the Ming.

Q: Which were the characters on the fourth wall?

A: Heaven's court be the pattern of the Empire.

Q: Which were the characters on the fifth wall?

A: The friendly cloud is widely beneficial.

Q: How can you prove that?

A: I can prove it by a verse.

Q: How does this verse run?

A: A friendly cloud rises pure and white as a happy omen:
The old seat of the house of Chu shall be restored.
The sons of Hung are, far and wide, warned to come and destroy the usurper,
To cross the river and to restore the prince of Ming in the empire.

Q: Who kept guard at the Willow City?

A: The four great faithful ones kept guard.

Q: How can you prove that?

---

[1] *i.e.* conversions to the society are so extensive that it blends with heaven.

A: I can prove it by a verse.

Q: How does this verse run?

A: Han-phang keeps watch at the East Gate;
Han-fu is immovable like a mountain at the West Gate;
At the South is Ching-tian like the ocean;
At the North Chang-kuo guards against the barbarian rulers.

Q: What else did you see?

A: Three large streets.

Q: Which street was the largest?

A: The middle street was the largest.

Q: How many shops were in it?

A: One hundred and eight shops.

Q: What are the names of all these shops?

A: The shop *Peace-united;* the shop *Patriotism-united;* the shop *Myriads-united;* etc. All these large shops are in countless quantity in the two capitals and 13 provinces.

Q: What is sold in these shops?

A: In the *Peace-united* shop is sold five-coloured stuffs for cotton jackets; in the *Patriotism-united* shop is sold all sorts of fruits and eatables; in the *Myriads-united* shop is sold five-coloured silk thread, floss, silk, satin, sarcenet, lustring, golden flowers, red silk handkerchiefs, white fans, large and small scissors, needles, buttons, foot-measures, mirrors, paper and pencils, ink and inkstones. Everything is on hand there, and all the shops are opened at broad daylight. (2)

The tour of the City of Willows continues with its temples, pools, peach and plum orchards, and 72 fields. In the next stage of the ritual questions are asked about the lamp, the five banners, and the wine mixed with blood. It ends with the last two stages of the mystical journey—the Volcano and, finally, the Red Pavilion, in which are gathered 'all the heroes of Hung within the four seas'.

The Master now says: 'I have examined you in everything, and there is no doubt about you being T'ien Yu-hung. Rise and prostrate yourself three times before our true lord. I have a precious sword and a warrant to give to you.

All the new members who are, in truth, faithful and loyal, you may bring hither to pledge themselves; but those who are unfaithful and disloyal, you ought to bring without the gates, cut off their heads, and expose them. (2)

The Oaths[1]

Whereas, on account of humanity, justice, propriety, wisdom, and faithfulness, of benignity, gentleness, respect, politeness, and condescension, of whatever is low, and whatever is great, in heaven or earth, we combine everywhere to recall the Ming and exterminate the barbarians, cut off the Ch'ing, and await the right prince. We humbly beseech Imperial heaven and Queenly earth, the *lares rustici* of the mountains and streams, the true spirit of the six rivers, the dragon god who rules the afflatus of our region in all its bounds and parts, the six spirits of fire and wood ruling over this day, the holy and honourable spirits who move to and fro through the expanse,—we beseech all these to descend together. Heaven and earth are spread out, and everything is happy and prosperous: what our founders have transmitted, we will teach to others, and now reassembled before our Incense Lord, we humbly pray to Imperial Heaven, and swear to live and die together.

We now bring the crowd of neophytes to join the association of Heaven and Earth; they take for their surname *Hung* (Great), for their country *Kin-lan* (Golden Orchid, brotherhood), and for their hall, *Hung-shun* (Obedient to Hung). As in ancient days, when Liu Pi, Kuan Yu, and Chang Fu[2] pledged each other in the peach garden, making loyalty and faithfulness the foundation, humanity and justice the head, and filial piety and obedience foremost; so now, the whole body of neophytes make these same six virtues the foundation of their oath. From the time of entering the Great Brotherhood, we will help and care for each other as brothers, we will defend and care for each other, and with full strength and firm purpose will support each other to the utmost, as would brothers by the same mother, never caring whether it is our private concern or not.

1. We reverence heaven as our father; 2. earth as our mother; 3. the sun as our brother; 4. and the moon as our

---

[1]Those formulated about 1840.

[2]Heroes of the famous Chinese epic of the Three Kingdoms, in which the exploits described are set in the period of the Han dynasty (1st cent. B.C.—2nd cent. A.D.).

sister-in-law; 5. we worship before the altar of the five ancestors; 6. we worship Wan Yung-lung as the founder of our
brotherhood; 7. the whole associated body as our righteous
brethren; 8. and the whole family of Hung as honoured relatives of the same blood. Kneeling before the white silver
tripod, with a pure heart we take the oath;—each one prick-
ing his finger and drinking the blood, we swear that we will
live and die together, and pledge ourselves for the good of the
Kin-lan country. We swear we will not disclose our connection with the brethren by any words. nor indicate our knowledge of the Triad by any motions of the hand...

Seeing that, in the revolution of heaven (or affairs), there
is now a prince in the court who is no prince, and ministers
who are no ministers,[1] there must be a determination to restore the Ming. Having received the special commands of our
'incense lord', we have set up the Red Flower Pavilion, raised
the bridge, opened the market, and performed plays at a
propitious hour. We who have the will, together enter the
Muh-yang city, and take an oath, like the seas and mountains
for unchangeableness, that we will act in obedience to heaven,
each one performing his own part; as the Ode says, 'He who
obeys heaven prospers, he who opposes it perishes.' In the
first place, we will restore the ancient dominion, and thus
revenge the wrongs received when of old they burned the
priests in the monastery of Shaolin; and in the second place,
we will avenge the defeat of our forefathers on the field of
battle, and in restoring the Ming dynasty, the whole country
will revert to the Great Brotherhood.

(The heads of the oath given to each member are as
follows.)

1.   After entering the Great Brotherhood, you swear not
to oppose the heavenly relations, nor alter your mind by
violating this oath, nor plan any injury against a brother:
if you do, may the god of Thunder utterly destroy and
exterminate you.

2.   After entering, you swear not to give clandestinely,
or initiate by, or sell the girdle, or coats of the Hung family:
if you do, may you vomit blood and die.

3.   After entering, you swear not to conduct a spy whereby
any brother will be apprehended, having in so doing a

[1]An allusion to Manchu domination.

covetous desire to obtain the reward offered (by government):
if you do, may you die by the wound of a snake, or the bite
of a tiger.

4. After entering, you swear not to debauch a brother's
wife, daughter, or sister: if you do, may you perish under
the knife.

5. After entering, you swear not to vilify the laws or acts
of the Association, nor introduce into the company of the
Brotherhood those who are not members, nor secretly
disclose its principles: if you do, may your body be cut in
pieces.

6. After entering, you swear, if you are a father, not to
reveal the laws of the Brotherhood to your son, if an elder
brother not to reveal them to your younger brother, nor to
disclose them to your relations or friends: if you do, may you
die under the sword.

7. After entering, you swear you will not oppress the
weak by employing the strong, nor the poor by means of the
rich, nor the few by the many: if you do, may you die by
myriads of knives.

8. After entering, you swear that wherever in the two
capitals (Peking and Nanking) and the thirteen provinces,
a brother, whom you know to be such, shall arrive, you will
lodge and feed him, receive him and see him on his journey:
if you do not, may you die under the sword.

9. After entering, you swear that whoever of your brethren meets with pressing difficulties, you will faithfully and
disinterestedly rescue him: if you do not, may you be cut
into myriads of pieces by thousands of swords.

10. After entering, you swear to regard the parents of a
brother as your own father or mother, and if a brother place
his wife, or deliver his son into your charge, you will regard
them as your own sister-in-law or your own nephew: if you
do not, may Heaven destroy you.

11. After entering, you swear to make no new enemies,
nor remember the old ones: if you do, may you vomit blood
and die.

12. After entering, you swear that whenever a brother
shall trust you with money or clothes to take to any place for
him, you will carry them for him, and not appropriate them
to yourself: if you do not, may the god of Thunder utterly
destroy and exterminate you.

13. After entering, you swear that whenever you commit

any transgression, your own body will endure its retribution, your own life will suffer its penalty, and you will not implicate a brother, not extort his money: if you do not, may you vomit blood and die.

14. After entering, you swear you will devise no scheme to injure a brother, or benefit yourself at his expense: if you do, may you be killed with the sword.

15. After entering, you swear that if you fill the situation of writer or policeman in the government offices, you will faithfully and diligently assist a brother in trouble: if you concoct any artful plans in this position, may the god of Thunder utterly destroy and exterminate you.

16. After entering, you swear not to compel a brother to sell you on credit, or force him to lend you, or rob him on the road: if you do, may you vomit blood and die.

17. After entering, you swear that if you become an officer of government, you will not injure a brother in order to obtain promotion: if you do, may you die by the wound of a snake or the bite of a tiger.

18. After entering, you swear that should a brother become prosperous, you will not stop him in his path to extort from him: if you do, may you die by the sword.

19. After entering, you swear you will not irregularly take a sister-in-law in the Brotherhood, to wife, contracting the marriage by a go-between, nor have any illicit intercourse: if you do, may you die under the sword.

20. After entering, you swear you will not, when the brethren become numerous, secretly get them into a gambling-house in order to cheat a brother out of his property: if you do, may the god of Thunder destroy you.

21. After entering, you swear that should you by mistake rob a brother of his property, you will restore it to him as soon as you find out that he is a brother: if you do not, may you vomit blood and die.

22. After entering, you swear that if you meet a brother fighting with another man, you shall enquire, and if he is in the right, you shall help him; but if he is not, you shall dissuade him; you will not assist another man and insult a brother: if you do, may the god of Thunder destroy you.

23. After entering, you swear not to avenge your private animosity under pretence of a public wrong, thus covertly scheming to injure a brother: if you do, may you be bitten

by a tiger when you ascend a hill, may you drown when you go into the water.

24.   After entering, you swear never to requite the favours you receive from a brother by evil acts, nor injure him in your lust of gain and pursuit of wealth: if you do may the thunder kill or fire destroy you.

25.   After entering, you swear that whenever a subscription is raised to relieve a brother who has met with distress, you will not appropriate that money to your own use: if you do, may you be cut in pieces.

26.   After entering, you swear that as each brother has his own share, whenever you borrow of a brother you will repay him, and not avail of a false pretext to cheat him: if you do, may you vomit blood and die.

27.   After entering, you swear that you will not give ear to slanderous reports tending to interrupt brotherly feeling: if you do, may you die by the sword.

28.   After entering, you swear that if your own brother be fighting with a brother of the Association, you will exhort them to stop, but will not secretly assist your own brother: if you do, may you vomit blood and die.

29.   After entering, you swear that whenever you see a brother oppressed or insulted by a person not a member, you will go forward to assist him, and not keep back from fear: if you do not, may the thunder kill or fire destroy you.

30.   After entering, you swear you will not conduct a diabolical man into a brother's house, or concoct his injury with persons not members: if you do, may you perish by the sword.

31.   After entering, you swear that whatever you receive in charge from a brother, you will faithfully and diligently attend to it, and not defraud or deceive him: if you do, may you perish by the sword.

32.   After entering, you swear that, in your intercourse with your brethren, you will not appear to agree with them while you are secretly opposing them: if you do, may you vomit blood and die.

33.   After entering, you swear you will not, on returning home, secretly discard your oath: if you thus privately release yourself from it, may you be struck down to Tartarus, and never undergo any transmigration.[1]

---

[1] An example of the influence of Buddhism, one of the fundamental tenets of which is the doctrine of the transmigration of souls.

34.   After entering, you swear to live in harmony with your brethren, mutually receiving and giving assistance: if you do not, may the god of Thunder strike you dead.

35.   After entering, you swear to wear mourning three years (for a brother); and if one is publicly nominated, and the documents and dresses are delivered to him, then you will acknowledge him as 'Incense Lord': if you deceive your brethren, may the god of Thunder destroy you.

36.   All you neophytes who have sworn this evening must remain united from first to last, and your faithful and righteous adherence to this oath without reservation will diffuse happiness among the brethren. (3)

Signs and Secret Language

The secrecy binding together all the members of the Triad again exemplifies the religious character of the society. In the oath of initiation (see articles 3, 5, and 33) the harshest punishment is laid down for those who do not respect it.

The members of the society communicated with one another by means of an accepted code of gestures and signs of recognition.[1]

How to offer a pipe:

There is a mode by which a pipe is to be offered; that is, when I hold a pipe between the thumb and forefinger of both hands, with both the thumbs upwards, and offer it to you, you will receive it in the same manner, but pressing my thumbs with yours, and if you are one of those who have joined the Society, in the flower garden, you will after taking the pipe from me, touch your teeth with the end of it, before lighting it.

How to offer tea:

Set aromatic Tea on the table, and when offering it, hold the edge of the cup, between the thumb and forefinger, with the middle finger touching the bottom of the cup.

---

[1]The signs of recognition which follow are those of an offshoot of the Triad established in Malaysia in the ninteeenth century—the Kian-Tek Society (Strengthen virtue).

The offering of Seeree:[1]

Hold the leaf of the *Seeree*, and offer the stalk end of it to the guest, in order to find out what he is, and if he takes the leaf, and turns the back up, and puts *chunam* (i.e. prepared lime) on it, from side to side, he is one of our members.

To find out a member by means of liquor at mealtime:

Three fingers are used in the offering of tea, so also in the offering of liquor; and if the guest be of the Society, he will offer the cup in return with his three fingers.

To offer rice to a stranger to find out what he is:

Stretch your fingers and place the chopsticks across them, and offer them to the stranger, who, if a member, will then push the cup away from him.

Signs used in times of fighting and disputing:

When two persons meet each other, and high words ensue, one, who is a member, will clench and raise his fist with his thumb pointing up, and the other, if also a sworn member, will smile and immediately apologise.

How to call men to resume fight:

If members are not satisfied, and wish to call men out to fight over again, clap your hands, twice or three times, and on hearing that noise, the members will go forward and fight without stopping.

Remedy against insulters:

When a member has been insulted and wishes to seek redress, he will appear before his fellow member, holding his nose between his fingers, and that fellow member, notwithstanding his engagement with strangers, shall immediately quit them, and go up to the insulted member, and inquire into the matter.

How to call out reinforcement in time of great need:

When you meet a member, raise both your hands above your head, and clap both palms together, in order to produce a sound. If the reason of your coming be asked, you shall say thus 'Seong' (Casuarina) and 'Pek' (Ara) send us to procure a reinforcement.

---

[1]Leaves to be crushed with lime; the *betel* of Indochina and Malaysia.

How to go to fight or to retreat:

No signs need by given, when we meet with our fighting men, only something to be tied round the crown of the head, as a mark of distinction. On beating a retreat, you shall use the words 'Soo Laing' (done) and to encourage the fighters to go forward and fight, use the words 'Tan Koh' (forward).

Meeting and touching in a dark night:

When you meet one another in a dark night, and pull (sic) one another, you shall use two kinds of voices, one, when you pull him towards you, and one, when you let him go. You shall pay particular attention to the voices.

Means of escape after commission of murder:

A person who has committed a murder, shall conceal himself, cut off some of his hair, and tie the same round his right arm; and when he goes to seek refuge among his brethren, he shall wipe his left eye, and the brotherhood shall provide him with expenses and means of escape.

How to recognise one by the features:

Pass the fingers of your right hand over your eyebrows, as if you are wiping them; such recognition will cause merriment. Tong (summer), Cheng (green), Seong (Casuarina), and Pek (Ara) are our people. Pass your forefinger between your lips, touching them at the same time. (4)

In addition to these conventional gestures the members of the Triad used a secret code. For them, a magistrate was an 'enemy'; the police, 'current of air'; the imperial troops, 'storm'. The society's resources were 'the brother of the night'; its statutes, 'the clothes'. To belong to a lodge was 'to be born'. 'Shooting partridges' was the term for highway robbery; 'eating ducks' for looting a boat; 'taking a long walk' for holding a village to ransom. A two-handed sword was 'the planks of the bridge', and killing was 'washing one's ears'.

The ideographic nature of Chinese writing lends itself particularly well to cryptograms understood only by the

initiated. Thus the expression 'lodge of faithfulness to Hung' is normally written: 洪 順 堂
and as a cryptogram: 浉

Justiciary Brigands

The Triad did not only oppose the Manchu dynasty: it made a clean break with the entire established order, as much in China as in the colonial territories where it flourished among the Chinese emigrants. The two inseparable aspects of its activities were political opposition to imperial rule and disregard for law and order. Members knew, for example, what special passwords they had to use if attacked by bandits or involved in a scuffle, which suggests that they were very likely to come across other members in such circumstances.

As early as 1838, a Mandarin complained to the emperor that members of the Triad kidnapped the rich, held tradesmen to ransom, attacked convoys on land and sea, disguised themselves as policemen, and started fires. Their victims were forced to become members and never dared to set themselves free.

Throughout the nineteenth century, according to the historian Leon Comber, the British authorities in Singapore attributed the colony's recurrent crime waves to the Triad. They finally outlawed the society altogether in 1890.

As a rule this criminal activity hit the rich more than the poor. Article 7 of the oath was very explicit on this point: 'You will not oppress the weak by employing the strong, nor the poor by means of the rich.'

If members of the Triad sometimes became brigands, they nevertheless had their own sense of justice. This is well illustrated by an incident which occurred in Singapore in 1831, when members of the Triad attacked and freed a chain of convicts being driven to a hard-labour prison.

The Triad had its own internal order, as rigorous as the one it opposed. In Malaysia, for example, in the nineteenth century, it had what amounted to its own police force, and imposed its clandestine jurisdiction not only upon its own members but on outsiders too. It forged extremely strong bonds of solidarity between members which are emphasised by numerous articles of the oath: solidarity against the police (article 3), mutual assistance (article 8), respect for the property of other members (articles 12, 16, 18, 19, 21), the promise not to use one's position in the state to the detriment of another member (articles 15, 17), etc.

The Lodges

The Triad does not seem to have had any sort of centralised organisation. Tradition has it that its local lodges were grouped into five 'major lodges' and five 'minor lodges', an arrangement which would perpetuate the memory of the five founder monks and the five horse-dealers who helped them. It appears, however, that these intermediate groupings never in fact functioned.

Each of the local lodges was autonomous. It had its own officers: the lodge master (*shan-chu,* master of the mountain) and his deputy *(fu-shan-chu)*, the 'master of the incense' *(hsiang-chu)*, and the 'vanguard' *(hsien-feng)*. The last two, as we have seen, were responsible for the initiation ceremonies.

The lower grades were called 'red staff' (who had to assist the officers), 'white fan' (counsellor), 'straw sandals' (messenger), and 'forty-nine' (ordinary member).

Each lodge had its own name too—or rather four names: a 'mountain name' *(shan)*, a 'lodge name' *(tang)*, a 'river name' *(shui)*, and a 'perfume name' *(hsiang)*.

As for the major and minor lodges, they each corresponded to a province: Fukien, Kansu, Yunnan, Szechuan, Hupeh, Chekiang, Kiangsi. All these provinces, with the exception of Kansu, are in South China (the Yangtze Basin and beyond), a region which—until the uneven expansion of a modern economy pushed the centre of gravity of Chinese life northwards—was the most advanced both economically and culturally.

These are some of the reasons why the Triad Society flourished in South China.

PLAN OF THE TRIAD LODGE

It is the City of Willows on a small scale. It contains the different elements which mark out the stages in the symbolic journey taken by the candidates: bridge, fiery pit, circle of Heaven and Earth, etc. Like traditional Chinese towns, the plan is rectangular in form. The doors correspond to the four points of the compass.

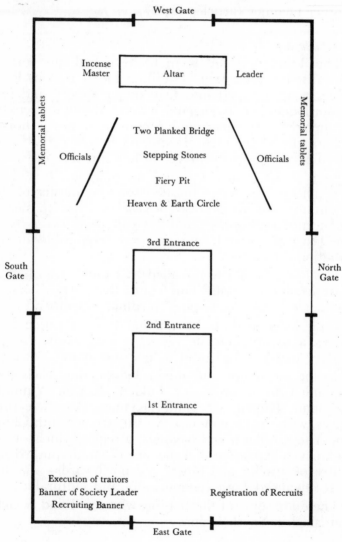

A Scattering of Rival Factions

In the nineteenth and twentieth centuries the Triad has been associated with the great Chinese exodus to the south. Lodges multiplied among the emigrants in Indochina, Indonesia, and especially Malaysia; they were even to be found as far away as California and Hawaii.

This diffusion only served to accentuate the disintegration and centrifugal character of the society. From this period onwards, as the writers who have studied it in Hong Kong (Morgan) or Singapore (Comber) have rightly suggested, it is more accurate to speak of 'the Triads' than 'the Triad'. A scattering of factions, often opposed to one another, grouped together Chinese emigrants from different provinces, speaking different dialects. Rivalry was often bitter.

This factionalism contributed greatly to the Triad's degeneration into purely criminal gangs, as will be seen later. But this phenomenon is not new. In 1854, in Singapore, two offshoots of the Triad, the Ghee Hin Society (formed of Cantonese) and the Ghee Hok (made up of emigrants from Fukien) met in a series of bloody street battles which claimed several dozen victims.

From Strikes to Gangsterism

The Triad will appear time and time again in the following chapters, which deal with the role of the secret societies in Chinese politics since the Opium Wars. Quite often it occupies the foreground.

After it had opposed the Manchu dynasty for two and a half centuries, participating actively in first the mass struggles against the Ch'ing and then the resistance to foreign imperialist domination, the Triad associated itself with the Republican movement which achieved its objectives in 1911 with the fall of the Chinese empire.

The men who in the mid-nineteenth century started the great T'ai P'ing revolutionary movement were closely connected with it. Sun Yat-sen himself came into contact with it in his youth and may have done so again later, indirectly, through the lodges in Honolulu and Hong Kong; the same applies to several of his associates.

Always very influential among the peasants and the urban poor, the Triad was also behind two of the earliest appearances of the modern proletariat on the Chinese political scene: the Hong Kong dock strike, triggered off by the presence of a French boat which had taken part in the Tonking campaign against the Vietnamese and Chinese armies; and the 1906 insurrection of the P'ing-hsiang miners, directed against Manchu imperial power.

From 1911 onwards, however, the Triad entered a new phase and its activities became more and more gangster-like.

It is too simple to explain this degeneration, as W.P. Morgan now does, by saying that the historical mission of the Triad had been accomplished with the fall of the Manchus in 1911, and that from then on the society found itself in a political vacuum.

The fact is that, from the nineteenth century onwards, the criminal and political aspects of its activities were inextricably linked. They represented two facets of the same sociological reality, provoked by the sheer severity of imperial order. But in modern times, and especially since the Republican revolution, the political function has been assumed by other organisations: political parties, trade unions, and various professional and cultural bodies. The Triad was therefore forced to fall back on its criminal activities. From then on it became much more than before an instrument in the hands of politicians and intriguers.

The spread of its criminal activities, especially in the great ports—Shanghai, Singapore, Hong Kong—grew with modern developments. Capitalist activity, in particular by concentrating in these ports immigrant communities of both Chinese and other nationalities, helped to speed up the process.

The Red Band *(Hung-pang)*, like its numerous off-shoots, controlled the opium-smoking dens, gaming houses, and brothels. It practised kidnapping and racketeering at the expense of rich tradesmen. It exploited the working class: it more or less monopolised the market system for the recruitment of dockers and sailors (many of whom were employed by the Eastern companies), and in the process it appropriated a generous percentage of their wages.

Such was the situation in Shanghai in the Kuomintang period.[1] It is still found today in Singapore and Hong Kong, since the gangster chiefs withdrew to these cities after the Communist victory in 1949.

In his preface to Morgan's study, the Hong Kong Police Commissioner, wrote in 1960:

> In earlier centuries the Triad Society might well have been a massive and fearful organisation, but it cannot be too strongly emphasised that in present day Hong Kong the Triad member is nothing more than a run-of-the-mill hoodlum masquerading in the name of a long-dead giant. Today, the word 'Triad' should not engender fear, but contempt; should not command subservience, but determination to assist the authorities in ridding Hong Kong of its presence.

Conservative political forces have tried to make capital out of the potential for stirring up trouble that the Triad still represents, now that its own political dynamism is exhausted. This was the case in Shanghai between 1927 and 1937, and in Hong Kong since 1949. The Hong Kong police seem to have been very concerned about recent attempts by the Formosan authorities to launch operations—unsuccessfully, as it has turned out—against Communist China with the support of gangs from the Hong Kong Triad.

During the period of the Japanese occupation of China (1937-45), the society split into three different movements—or at least divided its activities in three directions. One continued to be associated with the Kuomintang, then taking refuge in Chungking in the southwest; another was opportunistic and double-dealing; while the third collaborated with the Japanese and the pro-Japanese government in Nanking.

[1]See Harold Isaac's report quoted in Chapter 7.

CHAPTER TWO

A Few Other Societies

At the conference of Protestant missions in China held in Shanghai in 1890 the Rev. F.H. James estimated that in his mission's province alone—Shantung—there were more than a hundred secret societies.

In the empire as a whole they must have been countless, and it appears that in the nineteenth and twentieth centuries their numbers, far from declining, actually increased.

Basically, these secret societies belonged to two major systems, two big 'families': the White Lotus, established mainly in North China, and the Triad, influential in the South. Chinese writers call the first *chiao-men* (sects) because they were predominantly religious in character, and the second *hui-t'ang* (political organisations).

The following chapters will enable the reader to recognize the rôle that both have played in the political transformations of China and the position they held in Chinese society. In this chapter we shall briefly consider the leading societies.

The White Lotus (Pai Lien Hui)
It was also called, as in the text below, the White Water-Lily. In any case, the Chinese ideographs are identical. It was one of the oldest societies. It went back to at least the twelfth century and played an important part in the mass struggles against Mongol occupation in the thirteenth and fourteenth centuries. The founder of the Ming dynasty, who drove out the Mongols in 1368 with popular support, was probably a member of the White Lotus.

Time and time again, after the Manchu conquest, supporters of the White Lotus organised insurrections in the hope of restoring the Ming—in particular those of 1774 and 1794-1803.

Like the Triad, the White Lotus combined in its beliefs

and rites both Buddhist elements (such as *Maitreya,* the Buddhist Messiah) and Taoist ones (sacred numbers, and the correspondence between colours, the points of the compass, and virtues). Some scholars have detected Manichean influences—in the rules of abstinence and dietary restrictions, for example. It is true that Manicheanism, from Persia, had a certain currency in China in the Middle Ages.

After the failure of the two great insurrections of the late eighteenth century, the White Lotus was the victim of violent persecution. During the nineteenth century it continued its activities under cover of other names. Thus the 'Five Banners' (red, white, black, yellow, and green) into which the members of the White Lotus were divided were each active in their own right. From 1861 to 1863 in the provinces of Shantung and Honan, the Black Banner was behind a big peasant rising.

Western missionaries were very interested in the White Lotus:

> Until the eighteenth year of the reign of Chia Ch'ing[1] the members of the White Lotus had hoped that dedicated and ardent propaganda spread about by the *hao-shih* and the *fa-shih*[2] would be sufficient to win hearts and gain devoted followers. Experience showed that in a time of crisis, just when valour was needed, faithful and courageous support was hard to find and there were only deserters and cowards all around. Among members above all, for the most part farm labourers trying to eke out a living from their land, only half-hearted sympathy was expressed... In the grand council they decided that it was necessary to endow political matters with religious significance in order to enrapture the discouraged supporters and turn them into fanatics.

> It remained to choose a divinity. To take one from among the gods who were already well known and revered would have removed all the glory and charm from the new dogma.

---

[1] *i.e.* until 1813, when the White Lotus and the Eight Diagrams tried to seize the Imperial Palace in Peking.
[2] Officials of the White Lotus.

An entirely new divinity was needed.[1]... One was found and was named *Wu-cheng Lao-mu* (Ancient Mother without Origin or Mother-creater of Heaven and Earth).

Here follows in outline and in detail, the entire religion given by the Ancient Mother without Origin to her followers. I have translated it from a little Chinese manuscript, the only one to have been composed, or at least distributed up to this time to the simple country brethren.

Dogma: We recognise no other god than the Ancient Mother without Origin. It is she who gave us our body which we use for working, our intelligence which raises above all other created beings, and our soul whose beauty is so great that it resembles the gods.

Cult and practices: Although we worship none but Wu-cheng Lao-mu, we must appear to venerate all the divinities honoured in the villages where we live; this is a way of living on good terms with everyone, creating no suspicions as to the superiority of our beliefs. Every member of the society must revere gold, silver, precious stones, and the valuable boxes designed to contain precious objects, locks, keys, and generally all that the divinity without origin has created for our use. (1)

The Eight Diagrams (Pa-Kua)

This was one of the most important branches of the White Lotus. Taoist influence was clearly evident. The diagrams or trigrams were geometrical figures used by Taoists for divination.

The members of the Eight Diagrams quoted as their authority the 'Ancient Mother who was never created'. A medium *(ming-yen,* clairvoyant eye) played a major part in their ceremonies, which always took place at night. At these religious services the faithful brought to the sect's dignitaries sums of money proportional to their means—usually 100 to 200 sapekes, but as much as 1500

---

[1]The missionary who wrote this letter sees in the White Lotus's religion nothing more than a simple expedient hastily resorted to in order to 'boost the members' morale'. In fact, this religion was very old.

on the four feast days (solstices and equinoxes).

This sect was strictly vegetarian, and it forbade the use of alcohol, tobacco, and opium.

In 1813, the Eight Diagrams attempted a bold coup against the Imperial Palace in Peking, coinciding with a rising in the provinces. The emperor was travelling in the west of the country at the time. The attempt just failed, thanks to the presence of mind of the Crown Prince, the future emperor Tao Kuang.

Anyone desirous of joining the sect may do so. He must give evidence of his sincerity and must have a sponsor. The ceremony of admission is simple; as are all their rites. A table is placed in the centre of the room, upon which are placed three cups of tea, and an incense pot, with three sticks of incense. Besides the candidate and his sponsor, there must be the Fa Shih,[1] or the Hao Shih.[2] Before the vow is taken a bowl of water is used to wash the face, and rinse the mouth, a symbol of purification. They all then kneel, and the candidate makes the vow never to break the law, reveal the secret sign, or change the customs of the sect. The leader repeats a vow often containing several hundred lines. The vow is sealed by the threat, that if broken within a hundred days the body of the individual will turn into pus and blood. If the candidate be a man he is received by a man, if a woman or girl, she is admitted by a female member. After admission to the sect the upward progress is determined by the amount of accumulated merit in the upper world. Merit is obtained by faithful observance of the rules, by sincerity in worship, and by purity in life. This merit is made known by the 'Ming-Yen', who watches their ascent through the 'nine heavens', until they enter the 'nine palaces' (Chiu Kung) of the blessed.[3] All the Fa Shih and Hao Shih must have passed the lower and middle grades of progress before aspiring to the rank of a leader. All aspirants to the position must be known by their fellows as virtuous, and the 'Ming-Yen' must inquire of the

[1] Priests.

[2] Masters.

[3] Taoist beliefs which became part of the currency of popular religion. The world is made up of nine successive heavens. The nine palaces (or mansions) of the cosmic order correspond to the eight magic diagrams grouped around a ninth which is in the centre.

spirit as to his fitness for office. Believing in the transmigration of souls as they do, it is laid down as a rule that the aspirant for office must have been so virtuous as to have escaped transmigration through seven or eight successive generations. This happy condition of special merit can of course only be made known through the 'Ming-Yeng'. Ascent from one grade of office to another is also the reward of merit and is pronounced upon by the inevitable 'Ming-Yeng'. The members all wear their common dress, but the officers are bidden to wear felt hats in winter at the meetings, and cool hats in summer. In winter they are also to wear a long robe, and in summer a long loose gown without a girdle, after the supposed garb of the Ming dynasty. The shoes must be of a peculiar shape and trimming. Should the officer wear shoes for mourning such shoes must be exchanged for others when officiating. (2)

The Nien

This peasant organisation was very powerful in North China in the years 1850-68. The precise significance of its name is not clear—*nien* possibly refers to sacred scrolls, or perhaps to the basic military units of the society. The Nien resisted the imperial armies in North China for a long time (see Chapter 4). Mandarin sources mention it from the early-nineteenth century onwards, connecting it with the White Lotus and the Eight Diagrams.

The Big Sword Society (Ta-tao-hui)

This society, too, was a branch of the White Lotus.

Its activities were attested throughout the nineteenth century in the provinces of Shantung and Honan. It must also have had connections with the Triad, which its founders wanted to combine with the White Lotus.

At the end of the nineteenth century its activities were very close to those of the Boxers. Like them, it attacked Western infiltration of China and particularly the preaching of the missionaries (see Chapter 5).

The Boxers (I Ho Ch'üan)

For a very short time (1897-1900) they played a leading role in Chinese politics and were even in the international limelight (see Chapter 5). But they too had been known from the early-nineteenth century onwards as an offshoot of the White Lotus. Their official name was *I Ho Ch'üan* (Righteous harmony fists). The name recalls the importance of their practice of sacred gymnastics. It indicates, too, their concern to quote as their authority the traditional principles of Chinese ethics.

The Observance Society (Chai Li-hui)

The Chinese ideograph for "Li" can be written in two different ways with different meanings. According to which of the two ideograms is used, *Chai Li-hui* can mean 'abiding by rites and morals' or 'abiding by reason'.

The Protestant missionaries called the members of the Observance Society 'rationalists', and the Catholic missionaries called them 'Brothers of Truth and Beauty'.[1]

When you ask the members of the Society of Truth what is the real character, the real aim of their association, they reply that, if their purpose cannot strictly be described as being exclusively religious, it is certainly not political: the aim it sets itself is to practise and teach the moral virtues which make man good. According to the Brothers of Truth, the other societies, whether political or religious, are like feathers dropped into a muddy ditch, while the Observance Society is clear as the morning dew that rests on the pure, fresh leaves of mountain trees.

The Brothers of Truth and Beauty have for external insignia a long, wide, white leather belt, intended, according to some, to be worn in mourning for the founder, but according to most to be a perpetual protest against the destruction of his tomb. If the Brothers are ill when away from their families, they never lack medicines; if they are penniless, their fellows provide them with money or lend them some without charging interest. If they are insulted, if they are pestered, whether deservedly or not, by a neighbour, the members of the Chai Li take up their cause as if it were their own. In China, where the poor and the weak are helpless and without support, the fraternity of the Chai Li wins many

---

[1] In modern China, *Chai Li* is used of the observance of every individual rule about food and drink. It is for that reason that the name is here translated as 'The Observance Society'.

followers... This also means that the leaders have a pretext for levying contributions and making them less resented.

To mark itself out from the common run of humanity, the Chai Li Association has established rules and mysterious practices unique to itself, the sense or reason for the existence of which no one can understand. For example, its members are forbidden to smoke pipes or drink wine, and only four kinds of meat are allowed—beef, mutton, duck, and chicken.

Unlike the White Water-Lily, this society does not usually recruit its members from among the countryfolk. These simple and industrious people, unaccustomed to the tumult of crowds, do not seem to suit it. A number of poor men of letters, a few military Mandarins out of employment, form its general staff and grand administrative council. Ordinary members are drawn from the watermen, thimble-riggers, fortune-tellers, firemen, pedlars, etc. The society's main concern is to admit only men who are bold and pugnacious. (3)

This sect, established in North China and in Manchuria, derived from the White Lotus and the Eight Diagrams. According to some, it may have been founded in 1866 by a wealthy young man from a good family who had been led astray and had taken up magic (after deep study of Confucianism). It preached abstinence and observed numerous dietary restrictions—some of its members were in fact complete vegetarians.

In 1891, it fomented a big insurrection in Manchuria against the imperial government (see Chapter 4).

The Vegetarians (Chai-chiao)
A sect of abstainers. It was made up of a large number of different groups, all strictly opposed to meat eating.

The Red Beards (Hung Hu-tzu)
T'ao Ch'eng-chang, a well-informed writer, thinks that they were affiliated to the White Lotus, but this is less certain than in the case of the societies previously mentioned.

The Red Beards appeared in Manchuria at the end of the nineteenth century. They were also known as the

'Horse Thieves'. Brigandry was their main activity.[1] They were organised in bands called 'mountains' and their leader was designated by the title 'Living Tiger' (huo-hu). We shall see later how at the time of the Tsarist invasion of Manchuria, they created serious difficulties for the Russian troops, especially as regards railway communications.

They remained very active even in the twentieth century, and in 1931, during the period of Japanese aggression against Manchuria, encouraged bands of peasant guerrillas, who continued to fight for several years.

The Red Spears

About 1920, in the region of the Great Plain of North China (Honan, West Shantung, South Hopei), where the Nien and the Boxers had operated earlier, there appeared the Association of the Red Spears, with its numerous variants—White Spears, Yellow Spears, etc.

Li Ta-chao, one of the founders of Chinese Marxism, who was at the time very interested in the Spears, regarded them as direct heirs of the Boxers and the White Lotus.

The members of this association practised sacred boxing and wore amulets of invulnerability.

Under their direction, the peasants organised themselves in village self-defence groups which often held bandits and 'warlords' in check. In this way, the Red Spears made an important contribution to the strategy which the Chinese Communists and the Comintern applied to the Chinese peasant movement (see Chapter 7).

The Association of Elder Brothers (Ko-lao-hui)

Once more, T'ao Ch'eng-chang gives details of the founding of this society—details which are all the more

---

[1]See Chapter 3 for the text of their Code of Honour regulating their depredatory conduct. It should be noted that 'hu' may mean either 'beard' or 'tiger' in spoken Mandarin, depending on the tone used.

interesting for his having been a militant of the revolutionary party, co-operating with the secret societies
against the Manchus: he wanted to find out about them
in the very interests of this co-operation (see Chapter 7).

This is what he tells us. As it became evident (about
1860) that the T'ai P'ing revolution would be unsuccessful, the leaders of the Triad, who were directing the
movement, decided to plan for the future by infiltrating
the ranks of the victorious imperial armies. It was on
their initiative that the Association of Elder Brothers was
founded with the aim of attracting government troops
to the anti-Manchu secret societies.

It was in the Middle Yangtze, at the very time when
the insurrectional power of the T'ai P'ing was fading,
that the Association of Elder Brothers appeared.

As Sun Yat-sen recalled in a famous passage quoted in
Chapter 3, this society was in fact extremely influential
in the army. Its structure of autonomous lodges and its
ranks showed many affinities with the Triad. Indeed, the
ritual and religious practices were relatively unimport-
ant, certainly less so than in the societies of the Lotus
group – the Boxers, for example. It was essentially a
political organisation opposed to the Manchus.

The Association of Elder Brothers distributed to its
members amulets and charms in the form of small pieces
of material with ritualistic significance on which anti-
Manchu slogans were written. It was considered essential
that these pieces of material should never under any circumstances fall into the hands of the police, and when a
member of the society was arrested, he swallowed them at
once.

The Elder Brothers played a leading rôle in the preparation of the 1911 Revolution. Many militant Republicans joined the association. Several of them—Chu Teh,
Wu Yu-chang, Ho Long—were to become leading figures
in the Communist Party and later, indeed, its respected
doyens. Mao Tse-tung's appeal to the Elder Brothers (in
1936) to co-operate in the effort against Japan, bears
witness to the influence of the society in rural areas up to

that date. From then on, it tended rather to lose its uniqueness and to mingle with other archaic groups of the same kind, such as the 'San-fan brigands'.

At the confines of the three provinces of Shantung, Honan, and Hopei, in the region of Guanping, Chengan, Jouzhou, and Weixian, gangs of bandits circulate, notably the San Fan. This is another name for the *Ch'ing Hung Pang* (Green Band and Red Band). They claim the *san tai* (i.e. the three ancient dynasties Hsia, Shang, and Chou,[1] which are respectively the great-grandfather, grandfather, and father of subsequent dynasties) as their ancestors, whence the name San Fan, the three successions. They have meeting-places *(kung suo)* and resemble the Chai Li, 'Followers of Reason', except that they do not abstain from smoking or from drinking alcohol. For this reason they are still called *Chia Li*, the false *Li*. Those who abstain from smoking and drinking are the *Shuang Li*, the two *Li*, the two rules, or *Shuang Li p'eng-yu*, the friends of the two *Li*. These are the most important.

It is said that after the fall of the Ming, from the time of the revolts aimed at overthrowing the Ch'ing and restoring the Ming, the secret societies gathered together the vagrants and organised to this end the Society of Elder Brothers. So that the Ch'ing should not become suspicious, the purpose was kept strictly secret; the vagrants who made up the society became bandits.

Another tradition suggests that the foundation of the Elder Brothers goes back to the time of the emperor Ch'ien Lung (1736–96). Later, under the emperor T'ung Chih (1862–74) the army of Huai, a province of Honan, was disbanded. Without food or clothing, reduced to extreme misery and not knowing where to seek refuge, the soldiers joined the Ko-lao Society in great numbers, and it became very strong. It was able to divide into two branches, Hung-Pang and Ch'ing pang.[2] The latter gave rise to the *An-ch'ing pang*,

---

[1] The oldest dynasties known (albeit sketchily) in Chinese history. They stretched through the entire 2nd millenium and early part of the 1st millenium B.C.).

[2] All the chronological details included by the author of this 1930 report are somewhat confused. It is likely that at this time the members of the secret societies had only a vague notion of the history of their sect. In fact, as has already been stated, it is the Triad

Society of Peace and Happiness, or *An-ch'ing-tao-yu*, friends of peace, happiness, and Tao. The Ko-lao Society is still called the Society of Elder and Younger Brothers in Kuan-ping. Many *Hung-ch'iang* ('Red Spears') belong to it. Many of them are well to do.

Most junk and sampan owners are in league with the bandits. For that reason, the most important section of their rules is the one dealing with 'communications by water', *T'ung-chiao-ta-ch'uan*, together with the 'revised and augmented section on communications by water', *Hsin-cheng-t'ung-chiao-pu*. Members must be closely united, observe Justice *(i)*, and submit to strict discipline; those who break the rules are to be dealt with severely. From the moral point of view, they must be persevering, not be quarrelsome, so as to avoid unpleasant incidents, not mock at others, and maintain their self-respect: then they will be of a good spirit. All are equal and none must keep anything hidden from the rest.

They have to honour the Three Refuges, *San Kuei* (Buddha, Dharma Sangha,[1] Fo Fa Seng), observe the five restrictions,[2] not give themselves up to debauchery or theft; they must take poor, but not wicked people as passengers. Due respect is to be observed between masters and disciples, *shih* and *t'u*.[3] Masters and disciples are like father and son, they are like the feet and hands of the same body.

The master of the incense is called *lao-ta*, old elder brother. When attending a ceremony, members must be bareheaded, properly attired, and sober in speech. They pay homage to the ancestors of the dynasties.

Before the Tablet of Heaven and Earth, they pray for the happiness of the sovereign and his family, his ancestors and

---

(*Hung-pang*, Band of Hung or Red Band) which appears to be the older. The Association of Elder Brothers seems to be only an offshoot dating from the nineteenth century. However, certain traditions outlined in the above text give it anteriority.

[1] The *Dharma* is the Buddhist law; the *Sangha*, the community of the faithful.

[2] The 'five restrictions' of Buddhism: not to kill, not to steal, not to fornicate, not to speak rashly, and not to eat meat or drink alcohol.

[3] The master-disciple relationship is not officially part of the Confucian 'five relations', but it obeys the same rules, made for the sake of both humility and solidarity.

his leaders; they revere the wise men and the saints, the favourable spirits. They make the nine genuflections, invoke Heaven and Earth, the sovereign, the parents, the Masters, and the light (*kuang-ming*); they beseech the five great spirits to come to them; etc.

When they get home, they must venerate Heaven and Earth, the Sun, the Moon, and the stars, the saints and the Masters of the three doctrines (*san-chiao*),[1] the five elements,[2] etc.

A secret code is used in conversations between watermen: to recognise each other on meeting they ask questions which have to be answered in a set fashion... (4)

The Green Band (Ch'ing-Pang)

The *Ch'ing-pang* was founded in the third or fourth year of the reign of the emperor Yung Cheng[3]. At that time, the cereals levied as duty in the Yangtze Basin were transported to Peking by way of the Grand Canal. Many boats and many people were employed in this transportation, which was often accompanied by unrest and scuffles. The regulations and severe punishments applied by Yu-Ch'eng-lung and Shih Shih-lun, general supervisors of grain transport, starting and stopping the flow, had had no effect. Three men—Wen Yen, Chian Jian, and Pan Ching—put up to the sovereign a communal project for organising convoys.

They started a society called *An-ch'ing-hui*, 'Society for Peace and Happiness', and all who worked in grain transport were to be members, though new employees were only admitted after rigorous training.

As a result of this initiative, order was restored on the Grand Canal.

After the creation of the An-ch'ing Society, the number of boats was restricted to 10,254. The employees came from eight provinces and were divided into 128 *pang* (groups), as follows:

[1]The three doctrines are Confucianism, Buddhism, and Taoism.

[2]Water, earth, wood, metal, and fire, which are linked by magical correspondances to the five principal colours, the five cardinal points (the centre being regarded as a cardinal point), the five main virtues, etc.

[3]*i.e.* in 1725 or 1726.

21   pang for Soochow;
21   pang for Chekiang;
18   pang for Ch'angchow;
 9   pang for Sunkiang;
10   pang for Huguang and Kiangsi;
16   pang for Anhui;
11   pang for Honan;
10   pang for Shantung;
 1   pang for Chihli;
 2   pang for Tongchuan and Mabao.[1]

The number of transporters is not known; the number of boats had been greatly reduced and the number of employees was about two hundred thousand.

The members of the An-ch'ing Society honoured their distant ancestors through Buddha, Sakyamuni, and the Da-mo from the East. They considered Wo-tou-shan-shi, the religious master of the head and the goose, to be the ancestor of their sect, and they venerated Wen, Chian, and Pan, the founders of the society.

During the twenty-seventh year of the reign of the emperor Kuang Hsu,[2] when cereals began to be carried by sea, the members of the Green Band saw their society and its historic past threatened with extinction. They therefore reorientated themselves and enlarged the organisation of the *pang*, while maintaining the name, the flags, the insignia of the boats, and all the rules. Admission was no longer restricted to cereal transporters and the association's influence spread throughout the North and South, while the number of members suddenly increased. Its activities changed, too, and gradually lost their social character, taking on a political colour instead.

At the time of the Revolution of 1911, the Green Band gave valuable service to the underground struggle and its position strengthened daily. It is one of the two great secret societies of social organisation in our country, the other being the Red Band, from which it must be distinguished. Their power grows imperceptibly and their strength is impressive. They are in close touch with the working classes and all those who have had contact with the labour force know that in the

[1]Each of these *pang* corresponds to an area or province crossed by the Grand Canal.
[2]1901.

ports—on the water as well as on land—it controls the workers. The *yi-shi* and the *bei-shi*[1], who have complete power to help or punish the workers, are all members of the Green Band or the Red Band.

The ritual of the Green Band conforms to Buddhist ritual for the most part. The general spirit of the ceremonies is quite different from that of the Red Band. Anyone wanting to be admitted must be guided by a master called the *Ying-jing-shi*, and a master of studies or Master of original life the *Ben-ming-chi*, and a master of preaching, the *Chan-dao-shi*. These three masters must not belong to the same *pang*[2], hence the term *san-pang*, the three *pang*. Within each *pang* there is an ancestor-master, the *shi-tai*; a grandfather-master, the *shi-ye*; and a father-master, the *shi-fu*. It is from these that the name of the nine generations stems. The sign of recognition between members who have never seen each other before is the faultless recitation of the 'three pang' and the 'nine generations', the laws and rituals, etc.

Members of the same generation call each other brothers and observe the recognised code of good manners. Those of the preceding generation are known as *shi-shu* (maternal master-uncle) or *shi-bo* (paternal master-uncle). Members separated by two generations are called 'master-grandfather' and have the right to the *kou-li*, a greeting accompanied by a genuflexion and the placing of the head on the ground. This is all a fact. New members come first into the small incense hall, the *Hsiao-hsiang-t'ang*, which corresponds to the *wai-ba-tang* (outer palace) into which new members of the Red Band are admitted. When they have studied the rules, which the Master of original life expounds, the members are admitted into the Grand Incense Hall, *Ta-hsiang-t'ang*, ard finally they enter the sanctuary and may introduce novitiates according to the rank granted to them in the hierarchy of the generations by the ideogram of their name. To conform to the *pang* system, they must be under the orders of a Master of original life, whose name bears witness to his great antiquity. The ideograms of the hierarchy of the generations are as follows:

---

[1] Foremen and contractors of the labour-force.
[2] *Pang* means here the sections originally established within this society according to the boatmen's work, not the whole society.

Ch'ing:	Clarity.	Ch'eng:	Accomplishment.
Ching:	Tranquillity.	Fo:	Buddha.
Tao:	Truth.	Fa:	Law.
Te:	Virtue.	Lun:	Relationship.
Wen:	Literature.	Chih:	Knowledge.
Wei:	Shrewdness.	Tien:	Literary allusion.
Pen:	Origin.	Li:	Rites.
Lai:	Arrival.	Ta:	Grandeur.
Tzu:	Oneself.	T'ung:	Connections.
Hsing-	Character.	Wu:	Illumination.
Yüan:	Circle.	Hsüeh:	Study.
Ming:	Radiance.	Jen:	Charity.

These ideograms were the twenty-four used at first, but twenty-four had to be added, and then another twenty-four, making 72. The order of the ideograms is definitively fixed, and no one dares to transgress it.

During the early years, women were not admitted to the Green Band; this rule disappeared after the twenty-seventh year of the reign of the emperor Kuang Hsü, but women can only be admitted by women, men cannot admit them and they are not allowed to admit men. In the Red Band, women have never had access to the *Nei-ba-tang* (inner palace), whereas in the Green Band they have been granted their own system of organisation. In both societies there are different statutes for the two sexes. (5)

The historian Ma Chao-jun reveals in this text traditional beliefs which he gathered together, according to which the Green Band was doubtless a boatmen's organisation. Little by little it reorientated itself towards political opposition to the Manchus.

According, however, to another tradition, described by T'ao Ch'eng-chang, the society was founded by a man named Pan Ching, who belonged to the Association of Elder Brothers and who sought to extend the influence of the movement to the boatmen of the North, whence the name 'Band of Ch'ing'. By a graphic slip of which we have already met other examples, the simple character *ch'ing* which figured in the founder's name was replaced by another pronounced in the same way but meaning 'green'. In the twentieth century this impressed itself even more easily than it would otherwise have done by virtue of the fact that by a similar slip the Triad or *Hung-bang* was more and more often called the 'Red Band'.

According to this second tradition, the Green Band was derived from the Triad by way of the Elder Brothers. This derivation, a very convincing one, is confirmed by other sources. Nevertheless there are a certain number of differences between the rituals of the two organisations which support Ma Chao-jun's theory.

In the twentieth century, it became more and more common to confuse the two societies in a single name: ch'ing-hung-bang', Green and Red Band. The Green Band was drawn into the same process of degeneration as the Triad. In Chapter 7 we shall see that, as a result of the indifference of the Kuomintang, they both took to criminal activities about 1930.

The Little Sword Society (Hsiao-tao-hui)

About 1850, the Triad lodges in Shanghai and Amoy bore this name, which should not be confused with the 'Big Sword', a branch of the White Lotus in North China. At this time in the above-mentioned cities the Little Sword Society tried to restore the Ming (see Chapter 4).

The Golden Coins Society (Chin-ch'ien-hui)

This group carried out its activities in Chekiang province between 1850 and 1860. In 1861 it organised a rebellion to coincide with the T'ai P'ing revolution.

It is not easy to link the Golden Coins either with the Triad or with the White Lotus system. We possess an account of the circumstances of its foundation (see Chapter 3) which suggests that it was organised along the lines of the Eight Diagrams. It was thus close to the Northern societies; but on the other hand the term 'big brother', which it used, makes it seem closer to the more democratic societies of the South.

The Pure Tea Sect (Ch'ing-ch'a-hui)

At the beginning of the nineteenth century the founder of this sect proclaimed that the Buddhist Messiah, Maitreya, would be reincarnated in his family and would lead all the members of the Pure Tea Sect to the land of immortality. He was executed in 1816.

Twice a month, his followers continued to make sacrifices to heaven, to the five elements, and to the ancestors.

The Golden Elixir Society (Chin-tan-hui)

This went back to the Sung dynasty (twelfth century). In Shan-tung at the end of the nineteenth century, according to the Rev. James, it was still highly influential. Magic practices formed an important part of its activities.

The Way of Fundamental Unity (Yi-kuan-tao)

The 'Way of Fundamental Unity', Taoist in affinity, but with significant Buddhist elements, appeared in Shantung at the end of the nineteenth century.

It revered an 'Ancient Mother without end' (Wu-chih-lao-mu) and its religious practices were based on the 'three jewels': special invocations to the Buddhist Messiah, Maitreya; techniques allowing 'the opening of a way towards the forehead and the soul'; and a special position of the hands during obeisance.

I, Deng Guang-jiao,[1] come here to speak by order of the Mother, See! Laying down my brush on the sandtray,[2] I, who am dead, appear. I come here today so that intimate things may be revealed. When I was sick in this world, I hoped for cure, morning and night; once cured, I fell back into my erring ways. I then received the order to return to the world beyond, the world of infernal spirits; in truth I was tortured. Hearing my cries, my mother came to me, but

---

[1] This text, which occurs in one of the sect's own publications, reproduces the spiritualist revelations of a dead man who returns to earth to describe the tortures suffered by those who have rejected the Way of Fundamental Unity.

[2] Used for predicting the future.

in the world beyond, mother and son cannot be united. When I groaned, cried out, and called aloud for help, the god of hell set me free at my first cry. A single glance from his eyes made me tremble with fright. In my heart I began to ponder the causes of this punishment; I reflected on the evil committed on this earth; what I have done over the years is truly abominable. In my youth, it was opium, covetousness, and impurity; it was wine, gambling, and lust, too. I myself was guilty of all these things; I was lax in observing abstinence, I did not follow the Way, I smoked and drank.

Now, descended into hell, I am full of sorrow. In spite of my repentance, my faults cannot be pardoned. From hell I send up a sorrowful cry and beseech the Sovereign Mother. Who would have believed it? She seems not to hear me.

This night, I have come to this hall to meet you. You my brother-in-law who is before me, hasten to my aid! We shall offer recompense for a long time with great kindnesses. My brother-in-law says nothing on hearing my cry of grief. I charge him to appeal to my son to be converted to the Way. May he hasten to practise virtue in order to save me from the abyss. My sins are well known—it is useless to repeat them. If I wanted to say more about the things that are in my heart, I should never finish. I speak of my family affairs to you as to my representative: convert my family, forsake your evil ways and make a brave effort to go forward. I intend to lay everything bare once more during this meeting. But as I have sinned against the law, I cannot follow my will. Cruel demons wait at the door to take me away again. With a cry of supplication to my mother, I return to hell. (6)

The catechism of the Way of Fundamental Unity defines the ritual obligations of the members: incense morning, noon, and night, with the member holding the sticks in particular positions dictated by the circumstances and by the rank of the participant; and offerings of fruit and vegetables (never meat).

In 1920, when a severe famine affected North China, especially the countryside of Hopei around Tientsin and Peking, the Way of Fundamental Unity preached the imminence of the end of the world and a sort of apocalypse.

During the war, some of its supporters collaborated actively with the Japanese. We shall see how, immediately after the Communists came to power. the Way of Fundamental Unity made a great show of active liaison with the Kuomintang agents in Formosa.

Secret Societies and Chinese Society

Against the Established Order

Vicious sects (*Hsieh-chiao*), obscene sects *(yin-chiao)*, pseudo-religions (*wei-chiao*), perverse sects *(yao-chiao)*, brigand members of sects *(chiao-fei)*—such were the sort of names which the Mandarins used to denote the secret societies and their members. These designations reveal the double character which has already been stressed: these politico-social organisations of opposition were at the same time dissident religious groups.

About 1850 a Mandarin wrote an account of the foundation of the Golden Coins Society. His text reflects the same derogatory opinion and confirms the double aspect of this organisation. Following a dream with a religious interpretation, an athletic restaurant proprietor who seems to step straight out of a medieval Chinese picaresque romance gathers round himself and his acolytes, vagabonds and law-breakers seeking to escape from justice, as well as 'men who possess great wealth but are cut off from power'. Such are the *chin-fei*, the 'brigands who quote gold as their authority'.

The bandits of the Golden Coins Society began their activities in the early years of the reign of the emperor Hsien Feng. A man of about thirty named Zhao Chi had a restaurant in his native village of Chiancang, a district of Pingyi. He was thoroughly acquainted with the techniques of wrestling and boxing, and all his friends were boxers or athletes.

When his friends were in need, Zhao Chi gave them money or helped them with presents. On account of this, his name was known in North and South, as far as the boundaries of Fukien province. Many common criminals had come to him to take advantage of his protection. People called him *Zhao-da-ge* (big brother Zhao).

In the eighth year of the emperor Hsien Feng's reign, 1858, a man named Mu Yuan, who was proficient at writing ideograms, liked reading biographies of former heroes, and was vigorous and brave, dreamed on the night of 15th August that there were two moons in the sky. The next day he went to see Zhao Chi and asked him about the dream. Zhao replied: 'The two moons make the word *p'eng* (friend);[1] friend means of the same category.' He then quoted the *I Ching*,[2] and declared: 'You have great ambitions; in the future your dream will be fulfilled.'

The two men became more and more intimate friends.

Later, men named Hsie Gong-da, Zhu Hsiu-hsian, Chen Shi-yi, Zhou Hsiong (this last a paint-brush seller from Huzhou), together with a man from the province of Shantung who was condemned to serve in the army at Mengzhou, and a coppersmith called Huang Hsiu-jin, joined Zhao Chi and Mu Yuan. The eight men became united by the bond of holy brotherhood.[3] They allocated the eight sacred diagrams among themselves.

Later, Zhao Chi declared: 'We are united for life and death; we hope that our bond will be long-lasting. Today the long-haired revolutionaries[4] are spread throughout Kiangsu and Chekiang. It is likely that we shall be separated again. When that happens, what shall we be able to use as a rallying cry?'

In the course of the meeting, one of those present declared: 'I have an idea. Let us ask the divinity if it is best for us.'

At that time, an opera was being performed in the temple of Chian-cang, and it was that that gave rise to the suggestion of the term *Chin-ch'ien* (Golden Coins). Everyone replied, 'Excellent', and the response of the divinity was equally satisfactory.

They took sixteen coins of the emperor K'ang Hsi,[5] tied them together in pairs, with the side bearing the word 'hand'

---

[1] The ideogram for the word *p'eng* is formed by drawing the ideogram for *yüeh* (moon) twice.

[2] One of the most esoteric Chinese classics.

[3] i.e. they took an oath and drank wine mixed with blood drawn from each person's arm.

[4] A reference to the T'ai P'ing, who for fourteen years were to keep the whole of central China up in arms against the Manchus. They let their hair grow long, in spite of Manchu regulations that the Chinese should wear pigtails (see Chapter 4).

[5] One of the great Manchu emperors of the seventeenth century.

inside, and fastened them inside their clothes with ribbons.[1]

Every year on the same date they organised a great feast and put on plays. This was much appreciated by the people.

More and more vagabonds came to join them, but among those who joined were a few men who were very rich but not in the hierarchy or power. They raided the villages and no one dared to oppose them. Thus the power of the Golden Coins Society became greater and greater. (1)

Political Dissidence

The secret societies claimed a rival order to that of emperor and Mandarins. Vis-à-vis established society they constituted an 'anti-society' in the sense in which modern physicists talk of an anti-matter or an anti-universe. One might say – borrowing an apt expression used by Françoise Aubin about the Chinese peasant revolts of the Middle Ages — that the secret societies had a juridical system '*sui generis*'.

Their rites, secrets, oaths of initiation, conventional ideograms — features of which the Triad has provided very typical examples but which are found also in all similar associations — made a powerful contribution towards the consolidation of this autonomous order. The discipline was extremely strict, and any violation, betrayal, or collusion with the authorities were punished by death.

A Quasi-Patriarchal Society

The leaders had limitless authority which was never contested. They possessed quasi-patriarchal powers, symbolised by the fact that the members were often classified by fictitious 'generations'. The leaders were maintained by the contributions, often very heavy, imposed on the ordinary members. One such was the White Lotus (White Water-Lily) leader described by a Catholic missionary in Chihli at the end of the nineteenth century:

The White Water-Lily Society has its royal palace in every province; one might say that it preserves the former division

---

[1]Chinese coins at this time had a hole in the middle.

of China[1] and regards as not having occurred the unification of the principalities and conquests of the emperors who, to the White Water-Lily, are nothing short of tyrants.

I know the little Water-Lily king of Chihli province; I used to visit his village and dwelling and I always received a kindly welcome. The prince of Chihli is now an old man of 68, in remarkably good health. His revenue has increased considerably in recent years. When he was made 'Great Orient'[2] about twenty years ago, he had only a few acres of poor land lying fallow; today he owns more than 1200 acres of arable land which bring him an annual income of eight or ten thousand francs. They say that his wealth in real estate is immense; but caution keeps him out of the public eye, besides which he is obliged to hold in trust large sums of money for the day when his subjects have once more to take up arms and try their hand at revolt. (2)

The patriarchal character of the secret societies was intensified by the fact that recruits were often members of the same family, and the sect's secrets were passed on from father to son. The authors who have studied the Nien movement in North China around 1860, for example, have stressed the frequency of their coming across group membership of a whole family and often of a whole clan. The same phenomenon occurred in the anti-French secret societies in the Saigon area about 1910.

Official 'Commerce Tribunals'

The secret societies wanted their own order to become dominant, and this is apparent in their claim to exercise jurisdiction over not only their own members but also outsiders. In Malaysia and Saigon under colonial rule

[1]Until the unification of the country under the Ch'in dynasty (3rd century B.C.) China was divided into rival principalities—the 'Warring Kingdoms'.

[2]Father Leboucq mistakes the meaning of the Chinese here. The actual title is *ta-tung*, great leader. But *tung*, written with another ideogram, can also mean 'orient', and Leboucq probably wanted to discover in China the equivalent of the terminology of French Freemasonry.

they set up genuinely juridical systems, parallel to the official ones, which passed sentences and had them carried out, which played the part, as G. Coulet has said, of formal 'commerce tribunals'.

The biographers of Ma Fu-yi, a Triad leader who was executed by the Manchus in 1905 for having conspired with supporters of the Chinese Republic in Honan, like to stress the fact that he frequently intervened to restore good relations between neighbours. In doing so he acted as a benevolent substitute for the weakened Mandarin officialdom.

Besides this, the secret societies gave evidence of a very strong sense of mutual solidarity between members. We have seen, in the statutes of the Triad, the obligations in case of unemployment, illness, or accident. In Saigon in the early twentieth century, one of the leading societies was called *Phat-Te* ('distribution of assistance'). Here again, in fulfilling functions for which the state machine took no responsibility, the secret societies substituted for the official order.

The First Feminists

Confucian tradition reduced women to a state of docile obedience towards their fathers and husbands. It declared them incapable of carrying on the ancestor cult, and saw something impure and despicable in the female element *(yin)* as opposed to the male *(yang)*. The secret societies, on the other hand, by treating men and women on an equal footing, appeared as the earliest champions of the rights of Chinese women, well before the feminists of 1920.

Women, just as much as men, could be initiated and succeed to responsible positions. We shall see when we come to the Boxers how important women were in that organisation.

In his previously quoted letter, Father Leboucq, a missionary in Chihli, opposes the secret societies' coolness towards Confucian scholars and their liberal attitude towards women. The *bon Père* is alarmed by them. He has visions of a China beset by dangerous communes and

fire-raising women, not altogether surprisingly considering that the France of the time was dominated by
'Moral Order':

> The recruitment chiefs in general mistrust scholars, es-
> pecially those with inherited wealth and a reputation for
> honesty. Moreover, since their aim is to overthrow authority,
> honorary titles bestowed by the emperor, whether in literary
> examinations or military contests, are not of a kind to inspire
> them with confidence in those that bear them. They do not
> openly refuse them admission but they despise and mistrust
> them. I know a bachelor full of talent and ambition who,
> having succeeded in gaining the certificate of membership,
> could not attain even the lowest official rank—not even that
> of decurion.

> I do not know whether European secret societies admit
> women in their midst, but in China it is the harpies of the
> Water-Lily who hold sway in the society. It is they who inspire
> and encourage the faint-hearted. Should the Water-Lily
> Society ever come to set up a Committee of Public Safety or
> a Commune... it is certain that it would not lack women
> fire-raisers. China has wished to give women, even matri-
> archs, only a slave's rôle, or at least a rank well beneath that
> of the man. This is one reason why the masons[1] of the Water-
> Lily offer women a degree of consideration which, by ap-
> pealing to her vanity and *amour-propre*, keeps her loyal to the
> common cause. When a married woman is a member of the
> Water-Lily, she must promise under oath never to admit
> as much to her husband or her parents, unless she knows for
> certain that they too belong; in that case, the couple have
> the right to argue about who should have precedence and
> authority in the household as in the society to which they
> belong. If the wife's admission is earlier than the husband's,
> she is from then on mistress of the house in everything con-
> cerning domestic management. (3)

Social Banditry

The secret societies' refusal to recognise the established
order was total: it was directed at both the social and
political structures. Their lawless activities were never

---

[1] The writer is again concerned to link Chinese secret societies with
Freemasonry so as to tar them with the same brush.

clearly differentiated from the politico-social struggle. To borrow a phrase which the historian Eric Hobsbawn uses of the 'primitive rebels' of the West, it was 'social banditry'.

The secret societies practised armed robbery, the kidnapping of children for ransom, and piracy on exactly the same principle as that on which they attacked prisons, government convoys, or administrative buildings *(yamen)*.

However, the banditry was aimed mainly at the rich, the merchants, the landowners, and the Mandarins. It claimed to be based on a higher justice than that of the imperial state.

The slogan under which it operated: *ta-fu-chih-p'in* 'strike at the rich and help the poor' was as popular in the ranks of the secret societies as the slogan of the anti-dynasty campaign: *Fan Ch'ing fu Ming,* 'overthrow the Ch'ing support the Ming'.

Behind all this was a vital tradition nourished by, and expressed through, folk literature. For example, the famous popular romance of the late Middle Ages, *Shui-hu-ch'uan* (The Water's Margin), which is extremely well known in China, presents 108 brigand-heroes from the Liang-shang-po Forest and exalts their prowess. The members of the secret societies were steeped in the *Shui-hu-ch'uan* and often borrowed titles and slogans from it.

A 'Code of Honour' of the Red Beards

Valuable evidence of the vitality of the popular tradition is provided by these rules of the Red Beards of Manchuria *(Hung Hu-tzu)* which constitute a sort of 'code of honour'.

The power of this almost indestructible Chinese organisation of horse thieves resulted partly from their chivalrous character and, more important, partly from the strict discipline in their ranks. It is for that reason that we quote the thirteen articles of the rule drawn up by their chief Chang Pai-ma (Chang of the White Horse), who is very famous in

Manchuria. These articles reveal something of the life of the Bearded Thieves, and also help to confirm that their power grows constantly even today [1927].

1.   It is forbidden to attack single travellers, old people, or children. Those who do not obey this order will be punished.

2.   If civil servants or official persons trespass on the ground which is subject to our authority, whether they be good or corrupt, they must be attacked boldly. If it is someone with a good reputation, we shall leave him half of his possessions; if it is someone who is corrupt, we shall take everything he has, and all his baggage. If one of our members allows such travellers to pass, let them be exiled to Siberia.

3.   If any of our members travel abroad or in other parts of China, the Master of the Mountain will give him cigarettes with a label bearing a flying horse, in case they meet without recognising one another. If one sees another smoking these cigarettes he knows for certain that is a distinguishing sign of our Mountain. In that case, they must help one another. If anyone fails to do so, he must submit to capital punishment.

4.   If members of our Mountain act according to the principles of justice, it is not necessary to give publicity to their actions. But if anyone gathers people together in China for the sake of stirring up trouble, he must be severely punished.

5.   Manchuria touches on the frontiers of foreign countries. If we meet foreigners, however rich they are, we must not rob them; rather, we should offer them discreet protection, so as to avoid diplomatic complications.[1]

6.   Those who wish to enter as subaltern members (*Mou*, i.e. So and So) must be proposed by at least twenty members of the Mountain. They must humbly accept the suzerainty of a master and go through an investiture ceremony performed by this master. After these ceremonies they must still undertake a testing expedition before being admitted to the Mountain.

7.   If our comrades, wherever they may be, are the victims of attacks (from bandits of other associations) we must

---

[1]This article hardly tallies with what we know of the Red Beards' struggles first with Tsarist Russia and then with Japan.

help them with all our might in so far as it is possible. Those who do not obey this order will be severely punished.

8. Comrades of our Mountain who betray our secrets must be killed without mercy.

9. Those who have been chosen by lot to carry out an execution, even if they are close relatives, will not be exempted. If any bad executioner fails at the moment of execution, or lets the victim go, he must be killed without mercy.

10. On expeditions, if anyone violates women or plunders for his own personal gain, without putting what he has taken into the cash-box, he must be killed without mercy.

11. If anyone shows evidence of negligence or laziness with regard to the society's affairs, or causes a delay, he deserves death without mercy.

12. The spoils of an expedition, however little or great, will be divided into nine parts: two for the communal cash-box, one to whoever provided the information which made the raid possible, four to be distributed among the members, one to encourage those who took part, and one to be given to the families of those wounded or killed in the service of the Mountain in previous years.

13. Those who have entered the Mountain as 'So and So' members (subalterns), if they practise suitable professions, may continue to do so after joining; but those whose professions are parasitic, such as soothsayers, bonesetters, astrologers, etc., cannot continue in them after joining, for this sort of profession runs directly counter to the things we undertake. Those who attach a great deal of importance to such activities cannot hold positions of responsibility in the Mountain. If they have entered the Mountain and have managed to get themselves positions of responsibility, they must be killed without mercy. (4)

'The Opposition to His Majesty'?

Certainly, then, secret societies were forces of social and political opposition. In 1853, in an article in the *Chinese Almanak* of Shanghai, the Scottish missionary A. Wylie wrote that the secret societies were the equivalent of an 'opposition to His Majesty' in a despotic empire. The historian Teng Ssu-Yu himself describes them as 'the nerve centres' of anti-government action, 'which profit from favourable circumstances to start insurrections and rebellions'.

More significant still is this confession by a White Lotus leader taken prisoner by the imperial authorities in the mid-nineteenth century:

> In peace time, we preached that by reciting sutras and phrases one can escape the dangers of swords and arms, water and fire... In time of confusion and rebellion we planned for greater enterprises. (5)

Religious Dissidence

In traditional China, family life was strengthened by ancestor worship; trade guilds had their patron saint whom they honoured every year in a Taoist temple; and every spring the emperor, Son of Heaven, celebrated the rite of the first furrow, along which he himself guided the plough. Man was regarded as a tiny part of a vast cosmic system whose movement he must adjust to and whose hidden forces he must reconcile to himself. Every human activity had a religious dimension.

It is not therefore surprising that the activities of the secret societies reflect this tendency; that their political dissidence was matched by religious dissidence; that the beliefs and rites of these organisations ran directly counter to official Confucianism. And if the degree of religious organisation stretched from the all-embracing, elaborate systems of the White Lotus, the Triad, or the Boxers to the embryonically simple ones illustrated by the potion the Red Spears put in their water before drinking, religious elements were never completely absent.

With extremely rare exceptions, these elements were not unique to the secret societies as such, but were drawn from the common source of the great religions of the Far East and from popular Chinese religiosity. Hence their great variety: initiation rites (the Red Beards of Manchuria had to perform various exploits during a probationary period); sacred numbers (as in the Triad ritual); recourse to mediums and fortune-tellers (in the case of the Boxers and sects around Saigon); the use of charms, potions, and amulets of invulnerability; the practice of naturist techniques (sexual taboos, sacred boxing, special diets, usually vegetarian and Taoist in inspiration); and Buddhist ethics.

Nearly all the secret societies relied on the support of heavenly forces, and invoked all the characters of a composite pantheon in which historical heroes like those of the Three Kingdoms, legendary figures, and Taoist or Buddhist divinities such as the Buddhist Messiah Maitreya or the Goddess of Mercy, Kuan-yin, all had their place.

One of the few myths which does not seem to derive from the popular 'open' religions, and which is unique to the secret organisations, is that of a mysterious female deity—*Wu ch'eng Lao-mu,* the 'Ancient Mother who was never created'.[1]

The great historian of Chinese popular cults, Fan Wen-lan, has even discerned Manichean influences in the White Lotus's religious system.

The Image of Celestial Happiness

Among the members and the faithful constant reference was made to the hope of immortality and the search for consolations which would help them to forget the miseries of life on earth. Here, for example, is the picture of celestial happiness which, according to a Protestant missionary, the members of the Eight Diagrams painted for themselves:

> The summit of reward, the goal of aspiration, worship and effort is entrance into the 'Palace of the King'. This is a reward of merit and growth, and maintains its material elements. It reminds us of the Mohammedan Heaven. It is merely an expansion of the picture of wealth, ease and re-

---

[1] Also called *Wu-chih-lao-mu* (the Ancient Mother without end) and *Wu-sh'eng-fu-mu* (the Father-Mother never created), this divinity was neither masculine nor feminine. It belonged to the 'Previous Heaven' of Taoism which preceded primitive chaos and knew neither male *(yang)* nor female *(yin)*.

finement of Chinese mandarins of high rank. Each now per-
fected spirit is to live in a princely mansion, with courts and
gardens untold. A thousand gates enter these courts, each
guarded by stone lions crouching, with stone steps for
mounting horse, or for descending from chariots. The court
entrance is adorned with tablets in myriads. Within the courts
are gardens and flowers, myriads of birds of rare plumage and
wonderful songsters flit from tree to tree. Fish ponds and
fountains adorn the view.

The appointments within all correspond. Fine houses with
quaint roofs, adorned with dogs and chickens in stone, and
elephants upon the ridges. Scrolls and couplets adorn all the
rooms, while many towers, retreats for scholars and students
are seen, containing books without limit. Again mirrors of
great size and beauty, and household utensils of jade and
pearl, golden bowls and silver cups, larders too filled in like
abundance.

Mien Shan, Mi Shan, 'Mountains of flour and mountains
of rice', the rice all of gold and the beans of jade and of pearl.
Added to these are the wonderful Houris, 'golden boys and
pearly maidens', in great abundance, waiting to render every
service.

To such a summit of material joy, the votaries of these sects
are urged. By such incentive ease and pleasure, they are
urged to a moral life and discipline. We saw a girl in Shantung, whose husband was small and insignificant, made more
uncomely by a scald-head. 'Never mind,' said she, 'In my
dreams at night, I have a celestial husband, I eat the food of
angels at night, and am consoled.' Into the common half-
wakened mind of a Shantung peasant, living his dull life
upon that sandy plain, there come such gleams of immortality
and joy. We cannot wonder at its attractive power. (6)

The Night and the Mountain

The night and the mountain were equally important.
They underline the antithetical character of the secret
societies, their tendency to dissociate themselves from
the normal structure of social life and the established
order.

Meetings and ceremonies often took place at night, the
day, in contrast, being reserved for normal public activities.

On account of their peasant population and output, the irrigated rice-fields of the plain were both the basis of state power and the area in which it normally carried out its activities, to such an extent that the ideograms designating juridical ideas usually start with the 'radical' of water (three dots on the left). The mountain regions, underpopulated and poorly administered, were by contrast the natural place for illegal activities and retreats far from policed society.

The mountain theme, Taoist in origin, recurred frequently in the rituals and nomenclature of the secret societies, even if its value was often no more than symbolic, because many of them could not possibly have set themselves up far from the plains. A Triad leader was a *shan-chu*, a 'master of the mountain', and we have already seen how the Red Beards of Manchuria referred to their organisation as 'the mountain'.

The fact that nearly all these religious elements were borrowed from popular cults and beliefs is worth repeating. But what is specifically original about the secret societies is that they were organised into a complex mass of rites and beliefs which were considered pernicious by Confucian scholars. They associated them with a politico-social dissidence either real or likely to become so, and which did in fact regard itself as the antithesis of the official system of thought and social organisation.

The dissidence of the secret societies was not unique to the nineteenth and twentieth centuries. From the Chinese Middle Ages onwards, as we have seen, they had appeared as the vigorous expression of a latent social banditry and religious opposition. Their anti-dynasty activities were also the expression of a very ancient tradition. A study of their social basis in the contemporary period brings new characteristics to light. Although still dependent for support on the poor peasantry, their traditional source of membership, they adapted themselves to the modern developments of the Chinese economy, especially in the cities and in the long-distance transport sector. Paradoxically, they found in this modernisation of Chinese society an opportunity to extend their influence: what remained at bottom an archaic movement actually strengthened itself.

Recruitment

Here is a list of the occupations of 39 Triad leaders of Canton, captured by the Manchu authorities about 1855:[1]

Salaried workers:	10
Small tradesmen:	8
Farmers:	6
Fishermen & boatmen:	5
Craftsmen:	5
Beggars:	2
Smugglers:	1
Low-grade state employees:	1
Gentry:	1

Sun Yat-sen's Analysis

The plebian character of recruits is apparent in this list. It is equally underlined in a famous passage of Sun Yat-sen which praises the fidelity of the working classes to the national ideal through the secret societies, while vilifying the ruling classes for having, since the seventeenth century, betrayed this ideal by allying themselves with the Manchus:

> While speaking about these secret revolutionary societies, we ought to know something of their origin. They were most powerful during the reign of the Manchu emperor K'ang Hsi.[2] After Shun Chi[3] had overthown the Mings and had become master of China, the loyal ministers and scholars of the Ming dynasty rose everywhere to oppose him. Even up to the first years of K'ang Hsi there was still resistance and China was not yet completely subjugated by the Man-

---

[1]Statistics kindly supplied by Mr Charles Curwen. These figures, it is worth noting, are those for a large maritime city. Also, the term 'salaried workers' is vague, and probably covers both town and country workers.

[2]1662-1723.

[3]Founder of the Manchu Ch'ing dynasty in the seventeenth century; K'ang Hsi's predecessor.

chus. In the latter years of K'ang Hsi, when the veterans of the Ming dynasty were slowly passing off the stage, a group of intense nationalists, who realised that their day was over and that not enough power was left to fight the Manchus, looked out upon society and conceived a plan to organise secret revolutionary societies. They were men of farseeing vision and profound judgement and keen observers of society. Just at the time when they were organising the various societies, K'ang Hsi inaugurated the *Po-hsueh Hung-t'zu* examinations which caught almost all the old Ming scholars in the net of the Manchu government service. The thoughtful group among them saw that they could not depend upon the *literati* to keep alive the national spirit, so they turned to the lower strata of society, to the homeless class upon the rivers and lakes. They gathered these people together, organised them into groups, and gave to them the spirit of nationalism to preserve and perpetuate. Because these people came from the lowest class of society, because of the rude behaviour which made them despised, and because they used a language not spoken by the educated to spread their doctrines,[1] their part (in the antidynastic movement) attracted little attention. Those Ming veterans showed true knowledge and discernment in their plan for saving the nationalistic ideal. Just as wealthy men, whose treasures have in time of peace naturally been kept in expensive iron chests, when they see looters breaking into their homes, are afraid that the costly chests will be the first things opened, and therefore bury their treasures in places that will not be noticed, and possibly, during times of extreme danger, in the midst of the worst filth, so the Ming veterans, seeking to preserve China's treasure, sought to hide it in the roughest and lowest class of society. Thus, no matter how despotic the Manchu government became in the last two centuries, the national spirit was kept alive in the verbal codes transmitted by these secret societies. When the Hung-men Society[2] wanted to overthrow the Manchus and restore the Mings, why did they not plant their nationalist ideas among the intellectuals and transmit them to posterity through literature, in the phrase of the well-known historiographer, Ssu Ma Chien, 'store

---

[1]Confucian scholars, who for the most part came to support the Manchus, used literary Chinese *(wen-yen),* as opposed to the popular tongue *(pai-hua).*
[2]One of the names of the Triad.

them in famous mountains and bequeath them to worthy men'? Because, when the Ming veterans saw the Manchus inaugurating their examination system and almost all the men of wisdom and learning enticed by it, they perceived that the intellectual class was not dependable, that 'treasure could not be stored in mountains and bequeathed to worthy men', and must therefore be hidden in the lower class of society. So they rallied the secret societies, whose organisation and initiations were simple and adaptable, and entrusted to them the preservation of nationalism, not through literature but through oral language. Even if the societies had had a literature, it would have been destroyed in the reign of Ch'ien Lung.[1] (7)

Rural Outcasts

In rural areas the secret societies exercised a very strong influence over the peasantry (see below, the Nien and Boxer episodes, and the evidence of a very important Mandarin about 1845). They were capable—as is shown by the case of the Golden Coins Society in 1861-62 in Chekiang province—of organising revolts directly against the landowners. But rural outcasts, poverty-stricken peasants, and vagrants of every kind seem to have played a particularly important part.

In 1926, Mao Tse-tung, analysing the class structure of Chinese society, saw in these very elements the specific social basis of the secret societies:

> The *yu-min* [rural vagrants] consist of peasants who have lost all opportunity of employment as a result of oppression and exploitation by the imperialists, the militarists and the landlords, or as a result of floods and droughts. They can be divided into soldiers, bandits, robbers, beggars and prostitutes. These five categories of people have different names, and they enjoy a somewhat different status in society. But they are all human beings, and they all have five senses and four limbs, and are therefore one. They each have a different way of making a living: the soldier fights, the bandit robs, the thief steals, the beggar begs and the prostitute seduces. But

---

[1] The greatest of the Manchu emperors (1736-96). He submitted a number of ancient works to the censure of his officials and destroyed them.

to the extent that they must all earn their livelihood and cook rice to eat, they are all one. They lead the most precarious existence of any human being. They have secret organisations in various places: for instance, the Triad Society in Fukien and Kuantung; the Ko-lao-hui [Association of Elder Brothers] in Hunan, Hupei, Kweichow and Szechuan; the Big Sword Society in Anhui, Hunan and Shantung; the Society of Morality [Observance Society] in Chihli and the three northeastern provinces; the Green Gang in Shanghai and elsewhere. These serve as mutual aid societies in the political and economic struggle. To find a place for this group of people is the greatest and most difficult problem faced by China. China has two problems: poverty and unemployment. Hence, if the problem of unemployment can be solved, half of China's problems will be solved. The number of *yu-min* in China is fearfully large; it is roughly more than twenty millions. These people are capable of fighting very bravely, and if properly led can become a revolutionary force. (8)

Craftsmen (often itinerant), smugglers (who provided the majority of the Nien's general staff), sorcerers and geomancers, porters, watermen (in the case of the Boxers the ones from the Grand Canal ruined by the competition of steamboat transport between North and South China), victims of disasters, floods, and droughts, semi-literate men who had failed the Confucian examinations, often for lack of 'connections'—the importance of all these marginal elements of rural society becomes even clearer when the officials of the secret societies, rather than the rank-and-file members, are under consideration.

Disbanded Troops

From the early nineteenth century onwards, disbanded troops must be added to the list. The onset of civil and foreign wars—the Opium War, the T'ai P'ing War, the Franco-Chinese War of 1884-85, etc.—caused the authorities to increase their manpower abruptly during crises. Unable to pay the soldiers, they subsequently dismissed most of them and sent them home to their families.

T'an Ssu-t'ung, a militant revolutionary whose participation in a reform movement thwarted by the Court's ultra-conservatives cost him his life in September 1898, stressed the rôle of 'deserters' in the secret societies:

> In the imperial army, men are enlisted for temporary operations and they receive no regular training. When the enemy attacks a region the peasants first use their tools as weapons. These are eventually replaced by guns, of which the peasants have little or no experience. But if the guns fail to repulse the enemy and the enemy captures the weapons, what happens to the peasants? If they are killed in battle, their bodies are abandoned, it being considered a merited punishment. As for posthumous awards, these are meaningless words. No one listens to the women and children's grief and anger. Sometimes peasants may be more fortunate and survive with their weapons to perform valuable service. In this case, once the troubles are over, they are sent home to tend their wounds, and they then have no means of support whatsoever. But often they may find themselves hundreds of miles from home. They cannot get home even if they want to, and they are inevitably forced to beg. The laws prescribing the execution of vagrant soldiers are extremely severe.
>
> At first I thought that these soldiers turned vagrants were deserters become brigands, but I had no proof of that. Now I know that I was wrong. They were demobilised troops with no means of getting home.
>
> When vagrants are arrested, before anything else, they are asked if they have been soldiers. If they answer 'yes' they are at once executed. The report states: 'So many vagrant soldiers were executed.' The superior officer will consider this a just action.
>
> As if the putting to death of vagrant soldiers were not enough, the 'rebels of the secret societies' are killed as well. These are men who belong to military mutual-aid societies. We ought to be satisfied with that: the secret societies are an important product of the laws of human society. But officially they have no right to exist. Therefore—and this results also from the societies' laws—they must keep their affairs private. Now they have received the label of 'rebel' and their members are constantly pursued and killed. Tens of thousands die every year. (9)

The First Chinese Working Class

With the Opium Wars and the coming of Western business to the 'open ports' of Shanghai, Canton, and Amoy, an entire working-class population was attracted to these cities, mainly from the country. There were dockers, seamen, porters, workers in the first modern-style industries (both Chinese and foreign), and labourers of every kind. These men, cut off from the traditional social structure, organised themselves into the only system they knew—that of the secret societies. The societies had already influenced the urban lower classes for many years, but the capitalist development of the big coastal cities considerably enlarged their area of recruitment.

The detailed work of G. Coulet allows one, for example, to make a list by occupations of a large number of rank-and-file members of the secret societies arrested by the French authorities in and around Saigon in the years 1913-16. (These societies were direct offshoots of those existing in China, or to say the least showed many affinities to them.) These men belonged to the small urban trades (hairdressers, cafe-proprietors, bicycle-menders); to the stable artisan class and to that of the skilled industrial workers (firecracker makers, munitions workers, carpenters, jewellers, smelters); to the small itinerant professions (boatmen and pedlars); and to the lower and auxiliary ranks of the colonial establishment (employees of shipping lines, policemen, Annamite ex-travailleurs, cooks in private households).

According to Coulet, these urban elements were at least as substantial as the rank-and-file members of the secret societies from rural Cochin-Chinese society—farmers, day-labourers, journeymen, soothsayers, Buddhist priests, hermits, bonesetters, village scholars, or members of the upper classes who had been in trouble with the French authorities.

Doubtful Members

The secret societies did not, however, lack connections

with the ruling classes—which raises the difficult question of the ambiguity of their political and social position. In the country, the societies were often controlled by rich landowners who, anxious to build up a clientele for themselves, had to depend upon unscrupulous adventurers.

A nineteenth-century Chinese document quoted by the Marxist historian Wang Tian-chiang declares that a great many secret society members belonged to one of the following five categories:

those who wish to promote concord between social classes and to assure themselves a political clientele;

those who are anxious for personal vainglory, who seek a guarantee of mutual aid against adversity and are looking for personal advantage;

those without fixed profession, who speak only of amusement, who smoke opium and gamble;

those who want to be the strongest, who brandish their cutlasses from morning till night and provoke disorders, the village 'strong-arm men';

finally, those whose profession is stealing. (10)

That is why, declares Wang Tian-chiang, 'such associations are easily manœuvred by exploiters and men of ambition.'

In the cities, as the Nien historians such as Teng Ssu-yu have observed, wealthy merchants seem to have seen in the activities of the secret societies an opportunity to make a lot of money easily—if illegally—by taking part in brigandry, raids, etc., or by agreeing to dispose of merchandise gained in this way. The secret societies' connection with smugglers—that curious substratum of the growing bourgeoisie in proto-capitalist societies—is very significant in this context.

Even within the secret societies (see the Triad statutes in Chapter 1 and the text about the White Lotus leader in Chihli province in Chapter 2), financial problems predominated, and wealth was accumulated from the imposition of subscriptions—often very heavy—on the members. These points doubtless justify the raising, if not the answering, of the question of what part the secret societies took in the process of the early accumulation of capital in modern China. The lucrative nature of participation in the secret societies' activities (looting, racketeering, armed robbery,etc.) seems hitherto to have been insufficiently stressed by historians.

The Reaction of Imperial Power

In general, any activity connected with the secret societies, any membership of these associations, any complicity, even indirect, was punished with extreme severity.

The penal code of the Manchu dynasty made this very clear:

An Uncompromising Code

All persons who, without being related or connected by intermarriage, establish a brotherhood or association among themselves, by the ceremonial of tasting blood, and burning incense, shall be held guilty of an intent to commit the crime of rebellion; and the principal or chief leader of such an association shall, accordingly, suffer death by strangulation, after remaining for the usual period in confinement. The punishment of the accessories shall be less by one degree...

Whenever vagrant and disorderly persons form themselves into a brotherhood by the initiation of blood, as aforesaid, and endeavour to excite factious or leading men to join them, or tamper with the soldiers and servants of public tribunals, with the same intent, having for their ultimate object, to injure the people, and disturb the peace of the country; and further, when such criminal practices have been duly reported by the country-people and heads of villages, to the magistrates and governors of the division of district; if the said magistrates and governors refuse or neglect to take measures for suppressing such proceedings; or in any other manner countenance or connive at them, so that in the end an open sedition breaks out, and rapine and devastation ensue, such culpable officers of government shall be forthwith deprived of their dignities and employments, and prosecuted for their misconduct, by accusation laid before the supreme court of judicature...

All associations connected together by secret signals, whatever be their extent, are obviously instituted with the design of oppressing the weak, and injuring the solitary and unprotected. Wherefore the leaders or principals of all such societies shall be held to be vagabonds and outlaws, and accordingly be banished perpetually to the most remote provinces: the other members of such associations shall be considered as accessories, and punished less severely by one degree.

Those persons who, though not regularly belonging to, had suffered themselves to be seduced to accompany such associated persons, shall not be banished, but shall suffer the punishment of 100 blows, and wear the cangue for three months. All persons who, after having been employed as soldiers or civil servants of government, enter into any of the said unlawful associations, shall be punished as principals.

Any inhabitants of the neighbourhood, or heads of villages, who may be convicted of being privy to, and not reporting these practices to government, shall be punished more or less severely, according to the nature of the case. Magistrates neglecting to investigate and take cognisance of the like offences; or from corrupt and sinister motives, liberating and pardoning offenders after examination, shall be punished as the law applicable to similar cases directs...

All those vagabond and disorderly persons who have been known to assemble together, and to commit robberies, and other acts of violence, under the particular designation of 'Tien-tee-whee' or 'The Association of Heaven and Earth' shall, immediately after seizure and conviction, suffer death by being beheaded; and all those who have been induced to accompany them, and to aid and abet their said practices, shall suffer death by being strangled.

This law shall be put in force whenever this sect or association may be revived. (11)

A Less Rigid Practice

The reality, however, was more complex. Thousands of acts of complicity occurred at all levels of the administration. Many *ya-men* (state agents) were in fact spies in the service of the secret societies. There are also known cases of Mandarins showing them a degree of tolerance, either for fear of reprisals or—by more subtle reasoning —to keep these troublesome elements permanently at a moderate and controllable level of agitation. By so doing, civil servants could justify requests to Peking for supplies (on which they themselves made a middle-man's profit) for more-or-less fictitious 'repressive operations'—see the Canton Mandarin's report in Chapter 4.

Instances also occurred of leaders of secret societies becoming temporarily reconciled with the imperial authorities and even collaborating with them against their former comrades, only to resume their outlaw existence a few years later. Such were the cases of several Nien leaders and of Sung Ching-shi, leader of the Black Banner rising in North China about 1860.

Finally, important state officials tried to penetrate the secret societies so as to control them more successfully from the inside. One such, according to Sun Yat-sen, was the high-born Mandarin Tso Tsung-t'ang, at the end of the nineteenth century:

When Tso Tsung-t'ang[1] was leading troops to suppress Sinkiang, he started from Hankow across the Yangtze River in the direction of Sian, with a large number of Hunan and Huai valley troops.[2] At that time the revolutionary societies in the Pearl River valley[3] were called the San-ho-hui (Triad Order) and the societies in the Yangtze valley the Ko-lao-hui (Order of Brothers and Elders). The leader of the latter order had the title of 'Great Dragon Head'. A certain Great Dragon Head committed a lawless deed in the lower Yangtze and fled to Hankow. The Manchu post-couriers carried news very fast, but the Ko-lao-hui horsemen were still faster. When Gen-

---

[1]In 1867 the Viceroy Tso Tsung-t'ang, one of the victors in the T'ai P'ing war, was sent by the imperial government to put down the Moslem rebels in Chinese Turkestan, who had set up an independent sultanate under Yakub-beg.

[2]Armies of Central China. They had played an important part in the repression of the T'ai P'ing movement.

[3]District of Canton. The Pearl River passes through the city.

eral Tso Tsung-t'ang was on his way, he one day noticed his army falling in of its own accord and forming a long line of several miles. He was much puzzled. Before long, he received a communication from the viceroy of the two Kiangs (Kiangsu and Kiangsi), saying that a notorious bandit chief was fleeing from Hankow to Sian and asking him to arrest the fugitive. General Tso had no way to carry out the order immediately, so he considered it as so much official paper and put the matter aside. Then he observed a serious commotion in the long army line and heard all the soldiers saying that they were going to welcome the 'Great Dragon Head', which nonplussed him all the more. But when he found out that the Great Dragon Head whom the soldiers were getting ready to welcome was none other than the bandit chief that the viceroy wanted him to arrest, he became extremely agitated and at once asked his secretary:

'What is this Ko-lao-hui I hear about? And what is the relation of its Great Dragon Head with the bandit chief?'

The secretary answered:

'In our army, from private soldier up to highest officer, every man is a member of the Ko-lao-hui. And this Great Dragon Head whose arrest is sought is the leader of our Ko-lao-hui.'

General Tso asked,

'Then how can I keep my army together?'

His secretary replied:

'The only way to keep the army intact is for you to become the Great Dragon Head. If you refuse, there is no hope of our marching on Sinkiang.'

General Tso could think of no better method; moreover, he wanted to get the most out of his army, so he called an outdoor council and became the Great Dragon Head, bringing all the secret society under his command. From this it is evident that General Tso's subsequent pacification of Sinkiang was not by means of the redoubtable Manchu authority but rather through the ideas and spirit of the old Ming veterans. Nationalism had been conserved since the beginning of the Manchu dynasty; but when Tso Tsung-t'ang became the Great Dragon Head and learned the inner workings of the revolutionary society, he broke up their warrior leadership and destroyed their organisation, so that at the time of the recent Revolution we had no organised body to get hold of. The Hung-men Society had been made a tool[1] and China's national spirit had long since been lost. (12)

We can see that the barrier between the establishment and the secret societies was far from insurmountable; that their opposition was not inevitably unyielding. When one has made these important qualifications, it remains true that the secret societies were essentially forces drawn up in opposition to imperial power and established order.

---

[1]Sun Yat-sen's assertion here hardly fits the historical facts. On the contrary, the Triad played a very important part in the anti-Manchu movement which led to the Republican Revolution of 1911 (see Chapter 6). Sun Yat-sen constantly sought to minimise the secret societies' part in the Chinese political struggles of his time.

CHAPTER FOUR

Against Imperial Power

The years 1839-42 marked the beginning of a period of major importance in China's history. The British Empire imposed on the Middle Kingdom not only opium, grown in Bengal by the East India Company, but also the cession of Hong Kong, the opening of five ports to international trade, and other economic obligations.

For more than 200 years the Manchus had ruled China. Manchu garrisons still occupied the major cities. Every Manchu received an allowance for life in memory of the help given by his ancestors to the Ch'ing dynasty in the mid-seventeenth century. The Manchus imposed on the Chinese the wearing of the pigtail. These 'barbarians', occupying an imperial throne to which they had no right, with their privileges and their insolent bearing, aroused bitter resentment among the people, as is proved beyond doubt by the struggle to which the secret societies committed themselves. The Triad in the South, the White Lotus and its branches in the North—all venerated the old Ming dynasty and kept alive the hope that it would be restored.

This pro-Ming legitimism was never entirely separate from a profound questioning of the established order, the complex character of which has already been discussed.

Religious syncretism opposed to the official Confucianism; 'social banditry' which was directed against the rich as much as against the state representatives and frequently had sympathisers among the mass of the population; primitive egalitarianism which attacked the rich and aided the poor—all these traits were characteristic of the secret societies at the time when the Opium Wars were opening up China to the outside world.

The rebellion fomented by the White Lotus at the end of the eighteenth century in the provinces of Hopei, Hunan, and Szechuan had not been stamped out. The troubles provoked by the Eight Diagrams were still continuing in the North. The Triad, too, was fully active.

The Triad in Canton

A high-up Mandarin of the Canton region described in an official report the activities of the Triad about 1845. What is striking about his text is not only the accuracy of his information on the rites and organisation of the Triad, but the anxiety aroused by the enormous prestige of the secret society. The writer stresses the fact that in cases where proceedings were held against Triad members who had fallen into their hands, local Mandarins were so frightened that they avoided invoking the very severe articles of the Code relating to the secret societies and pretended to believe that they were dealing with ordinary brigands.

> In the autumn of the 24th year [of the reign of Tao Kuang] (1844) certain of these vagabonds, belonging to other provinces, came to the villages of Kiang-k'au and Lung-tu, in your servant's native district, Hiang-shan, to entice people into the society. At first but a few scores would assemble for the purpose, and by night; but, in course of time, bodies of several hundreds held their meetings publically and in broad day. The place of these assemblies was always a cross-road, and here those assembled would post themselves with guns and small arms, to keep off the troops, should any attempt be made to surround or seize them. Every new member, on entering, subscribed 300 cash, and members were allotted 20 cash for every recruit they induced to join. Members already sworn attending at subsequent meetings, which was termed 'going to the play', were allotted each man ten cash. When members were sworn, a paper tent was set up; on the wall hung a large horizontal label, which the memorialist is unable to describe. By the side of it sat a man in white clothes and cap, who was called the Ama. The new members passed in by a sword gate (i.e. under two swords crossed), and kneeling down, were instructed in the mystic language of the society. Each one pricked the tip of his finger with a needle till blood was drawn, and then took a sup from a bowl in which this blood was mixed with water. The Ama then with a loud voice read certain words of rebellious

import, responses to which were repeated by the whole of the initiated together. They then rose.

The chief in degree at each place of meeting was styled the Red Staff; the second, the Paper Fan; the third, Straw Shoes. The Red Staff might preside over some score, some hundreds, or some thousands of members. The prefecture of the provincial city, the outer prefectures, the districts, and the village, were all recognised as the lodges of such and such a president; the lodge being considered a great or small one according to the number presided over. The Red Staff pretended to the title of *yuen-shuai*, generalissimo, as he was styled in the secret language of the society; the Paper Fan, to that of *kiun-shuai*, general of the grand division; and the Straw Shoes to that of *tsau-pau-t'ung-sin*, intelligencer-general. The military and runners attached to the official establishments were all members, and while the poor, who knew no better, were seduced to become so by their eagerness for a trifle of gain, some even of the orderly agricultural population as well, and respectable people in trade, were forced to enlist themselves in self-defence against the persecution to which they were exposed. They found, however, that even then they were liable to exactions as before; on every occasion they were called on to supply the funds; and as their treatment grew more and more vexatious, bringing with it repentance, which was now too late, they would have been disposed, one and all, to face the authorities and denounce themselves. None of the official establishment, alas! would have cognizance of the matter. On the contrary, one ignored it in the other's interest, and the other in his.

In the winter of the same year, some houses in the great South Street of the city of Hiang-shan, your servant's native district, were entered in broad day by a hundred and more Triads armed with swords, who threatened the dwellers, and kept them in until they had extorted money of them. It happened fortunately that Lin Kien, a magistrate, having temporarily vacated his post to mourn for a parent, was at home in his district; he put himself at the head of the gentry of Sz'-ta, Tehnang, and other places, and with them drew up a code of regulations, in which it was strictly provided that any Triad coming from any other part of the country and attempting to induce men to join, as also any son or younger brother of any family in the aforesaid places, who should enlist in the Triad Society, should be seized and delivered up to the authorities for trial and punishment. A proclamation was likewise obtained from the Imperial Commissioner, Ki Ying, authorising the people to kill any persons committing robbery with arms, without fear to prosecution. But, though Hung Ming-hiang, brigadier of Chinese troops in Hiang-shan, and Luh Sun-ting, magistrate of that district, did on different occasions seize Kau Wang-yuen, Chan Pei-kii, and Li Atwan, Triad leaders, who were so severely dealt with, that for a time little more was seen of Triads in Hiang-shan, yet they were punished only as if they had been robbers in the ordinary acceptance of the term. The authorities dared not utter the word *hui*, [secret society], and the consequence was, that not only throughout the major and minor districts of the province were other confederacies formed, and Triads enlisted in untold numbers, but even on the White Cloud Mountains, close to the provincial city, meetings for enlistment were held at all times and seasons; and from this period not only were merchants, travelling by land and sea, carried off and plundered, but walled cities and villages were entered, the pawnbrokers' and other shops, as well as private houses, ransacked, and their proprietors held to ransom...

In 27th and 28th years of Tao Kuang (1847–48) members of unlawful societies in hundreds and thousands, carrying tents and armed, took up whatever positions they pleased, first at one place and then at another, throughout districts of Ung-yuen, Ju-yuen, Ying-teh, and Tsing-yuen, barred the ways, made prisoners, and committed robbery. The authorities feigned ignorance of this. In the 29th year (1849) they did proceed against some parties in Ying-teh and Tsing-yuen, but they still described them as outlaws of particular gangs, or as roving outlaws. On no account would they utter the word *hui*. It was in view of this demeanour on the part of the authorities that these villains became more reckless than ever. They proceeded accordingly with their secret enlistments, and in the spring of the present year they commenced disturbances in the prefecture of Chan-chau. The districts of Lien-chan and Ying-teh were overrun by large bodies of them committing robbery in all directions. In the fifth moon the city of Tung-kuan was lost, but subsequently retaken.

The village of Ta-shih in Puan-yu was harassed by these people, and before they could be exterminated, Fuh-shan in Nan-hai was regularly occupied by outlaws, while Lian-lung and Chin-tsun in Shunteh, Kiang-mun and Lo-ti in Sin-hui, and Shaping-yu and other places in Hoh-shan, joined in the cry. In the seventh moon the cities of the prefecture of Shau-king, and the districts of Shun-teh, Ho-shan, Tsang, Tsung-hwa, Hua, and Ying-teh, were all taken, and those of the prefectures of Huwichan and of Shau-chau, and the major districts of Lien-ping, invested; the government couriers and official communications being stopped along every line of road. Now, the outlaws from other provinces were not more than a hundred or a few hundred men, while those of Kuang Tung, turbaned in red and with banners of red, as a signal to their friends, were in bands of such force as to occupy positions. How could it have come to pass, unless enlistment had been going on for several tens of years before, that a rising in one place should have been responded to in so many others?—that those partaking in it should have had the audacity to attack provincial cities and seize district towns?—should have, flood-like, inundated the land as at present? All that he narrates has been witnessed in his own country by your servant himself; he is nowise indebted to rumour for his information.   (1)

Thus the Manchu government, far from being able to count on its own people to stand up to the West, had to fight on two fronts. Its rearguard position was by no means safe: the secret societies exerted constant pressure on it. They played a far from negligible part in the government's final decision to take the easy way out and yield to foreign demands. By the Nanking Treaty of 1842, Hong Kong was ceded to Great Britain, and Shanghai, Ningpo, Amoy, Foochow, and Canton, the 'five ports', were opened to international trade.

This policy of appeasement gave the secret societies a new field of action. Impoverished peasants, outcasts of every kind, and adventurers ready to turn brigands flooded into the five ports, whose level of activity was stimulated by Western trade and the impetus provided by capitalism. It was not by chance that in the period separating the First Opium War (1842) from the Second

(1856), Triad insurrections burst out in Canton, or that the Small Sword Society stirred up trouble in Amoy in 1853. Of the latter, the Scottish missionary A. Wylie reported that 3,000 of its members, who had been in possession of the city for several months, 'met with far more sympathy than opposition, as much from the inhabitants as from the soldiers.' (2)

The-Small Sword in Shanghai

It was again the Small Sword Society that seized Shanghai in 1853, if we are to believe this report which appeared in the *North China Herald,* an English weekly paper published there:

> *Wednesday, September 7:* The Small Sword Society men attacked the city early this morning, and about six o'clock the district magistrate Yuen, and one of his attendants were killed. The 40 militia men on guard all fled, supposed to be in league with the rioters. The magistrate's office was gutted, and the prisoners liberated. A man at the north gate was also killed; his body is still lying there. The S.S. men wear a badge of red cloth on their jackets and caps; they walk about without the least fear; no one molests them, and they abstain from plunder. They are now said to be at the Taou-tae's[1] office which they have surrounded, having taken possession of the guns in front. Some say the Taou-tae is inside; a further report says that he has submitted to the rebels, who have in consequence spared his life, others that he has escaped. The shops are all closed, but the people seem quiet and there is no disposition to remove or flee. We suspect it will end in the S.S. men taking possession of the city, as they have already done of Kading,[2] and organising a government of their own, which will soon be in correspondence with' the insurgents at Nanking.[3] Foreigners need be under no apprehension. They had better, however, be on their guard.

---

[1] Circuit administrator for Shanghai, the first Chinese magistrate of the city.

[2] District in the Shanghai region, previously occupied by the Small Sword.

[3] The T'ai P'ing were occupying Nanking at the time and had made it their capital.

Thursday, September 8: Yesterday afternoon, the Taou-tae made his escape out of his office. Some say that he was escorted out of the city in the evening by a number of his former adherents, who wore the red badge, thereby proving that they had already joined the cause of the rebels. He was taken, it is said, to the Canton guild,[1] outside the east gate, where, affected by seeing his former most confidential servants among the rioters, he attempted several times to destroy himself. It seems that all along his supporters have had connections with the secret societies, and when the attack was made on the office of the Taou-tae, on the morning of the 7th, these made a show of resistance by firing into the air, and then opening the gates to the rabble.There were two proclamations issued by the insurgents, on the 7th, one by the noted Le, the head of the secret society from Fukien; and the other by one Lew, said to be a sugar-broker, the head of the secret society from Canton. Neither of these men have any presence or dignity; they appear to inspire little awe among their followers and are evidently not endowed by nature with such gifts, as would be likely to render them permanently successful in the management of affairs. They are surrounded by a number of young men from Singapore, who speak remarkably good English; one of whom stood up boldly before some foreign visitors, saying, 'I am a British subject.'

They said that they were in correspondence with T'hae-ping-wang, the chief of the insurrection at Nanking; and the general belief among the influential natives is, not only that these are thus in league with the Kuangsi men,[2] but that an organised plan is in existence for a simultaneous rise in Sungkiang, Soochow, Tae-tsang, and other places. The natives say, that Shanghai was the soul of Kiangnan, and that being lost, the whole province may be considered as gone.

The Custom-house on the bund[3] was plundered this morning of its doors, windows, planks, beams, and everything movable, which was all being carried off by coolies and countrymen, no man forbidding them. (3)

The Dismissal of the Emperor

In Shanghai, the Small Sword Society was run by newcomers to the city—Liu Li-ch'uan, native of Canton,

---

[1]Traders' association started in Canton and with a Shanghai branch.
[2]i.e. the T'ai P'ing; the movement had started in Kuangsi province.
[3]Business and commercial quarter of Shanghai.

former interpreter for the West, part-doctor, part-sor-
cerer who treated people for nothing; and one Le, native
of Fukien province and a sugar-broker. They were supported by small craftsmen, porters, boatmen especially,
and seamen from the junk crews which happened to be
in port at the time.

Contraband — particularly that coming from the
French concession — was their source of arms. On all
the city gates they posted proclamations announcing the
restoration of the Ming, and their leaders assumed
honorary titles in the name of the dynasty. The official
Ming line of descent had in reality died out long before,
and, for want of an effective pretender, they contented
themselves with announcing the coming of a legitimate
emperor, and recommending patience during the wait
for a new bearer of the 'Mandate of Heaven'.

This is how the fall of the Manchus was announced:

> Lew, the great generalissimo, having command of the
> cavalry and infantry throughout the empire, under the great
> Ming dynasty, issues this proclamation in order to tran-
> quillise the people, that they may all peaceably follow their
> several avocations. Whereas we have undertaken to abolish
> tyranny and pacify the people, and this being on behalf of
> the public we do not intend [*sic*] to make it the means of
> injuring the public: we have also undertaken to root out
> villainy and banish flatterers, and this being our method of
> putting down confusions, we do not mean to make this a
> pretext for creating confusion: therefore let none either inside
> or outside of the city feel alarmed or run away; let scholars,
> husbandmen, mechanics, and traders,[1] all quietly follow their
> occupations. At present the young prince on the throne is
> dark and stupid,[2] covetous mandarins and filthy officials are
> occupying both the court and the market; the Tartar bar-
> barians must therefore be exterminated, and the Ming dyn-
> asty again revived. I, the generalissimo, have assembled my
> righteous and benevolent soldiers, in order to obey heaven
> and comply with the wishes of mankind. On this account

---

[1] i.e., according to the traditional quadripartite classification of
Confucianism, all classes of society.

[2] The Manchu emperor Hsien Feng, who came to the throne in 1851
at the age of 20.

I now issue this proclamation prohibiting the people from disorderly removing from their dwellings; I have strictly forbidden my troops taking one thing belonging to the people or injuring one of their females; those who disobey shall be severely punished. Let all be obedient. A special proclamation.

Struck up at the north-gate, 7th September 1853.   (4)

Another proclamation dealt with the organisation of supplies for the city:

Lin, assistant generalissimo, charged with the conduct of military affairs, and provisional magistrate of Shanghai under the great Ming dynasty, issues this proclamation, with the view of declaring the overthrow of the Tartar and the restoration of the Ming dynasty. Above, we regard the will of heaven in what we do, and below we consider the feelings of the people assembled around us, in order to exterminate the Manchu barbarian. Reflecting upon the Chinese emperors of the Ming dynasty, we cannot help thinking that their apparel and adornments were sufficiently grand and imposing, so as to hand down the fame of the same to a thousand generations: but these Tartars, as ignorant of courtly affairs as they were of right principles, have caused the people in their clothes to resemble horses,[1] from which it is evident that they themselves are not men. These stubborn barbarians have thus entailed on our nation a disgrace, that will last for a thousand years; we have now however raised the righteous standard, to exterminate them, but we must wait until our emperor issues his decree, before we can direct the people how they are to change the fashion of their dress. From of old, in undertaking a war, the most important thing is the commissariat, when the troops are well trained, and provisions abundant, we can then joyfully set about the accomplishment of an object, of which history furnishes us with a hundred examples. Now Shanghai is but a small city,[2] and that which it produces is inconsiderable —it is therefore necessary to see, not only that the provisions for the troops

[1] The imperial government forced the Chinese to wear pigtails, to distinguish them from the Manchus.

[2] When Westerners moved into Shanghai, it was still only a small city. It grew under their influence at the end of the nineteenth century.

are sufficient, but that the wants of the people are supplied. Previous to this, when boats happily came from Shangsha to trade at Shanghai,[1] there was no anxiety regarding rice. I, the generalissimo, having now become the magistrate of Shanghai, am afraid lest rice should become as scarce as pearls, and fire-wood as dear as cinnamon, and although we may have enough for the troops, the people may be ill-supplied: I therefore issue this proclamation, directing you gentry and people to bring as much as possible to Shanghai, inviting merchants of every place, to come hither to trade; which on the one hand will be good for the government, and on the other will allay the anxieties of the people. Do not purposely oppose. A special communication.

The 1st year of the great Ming dynasty, 8th moon, 11th day, (13th Sept.)

For two years the Small Sword managed to hold on to Shanghai. Finally, the Westerners abandoned their wait-and-see attitude and decided to come in on the imperial side. Together they blockaded the city and took part in military operations against the rebels. Lin, the general in charge of the Ming infantry and cavalry, was killed while trying to resist the final assault on 17th February 1855.

The T'ai P'ing Rebellion

The Shanghai rising only lasted as long as it did, in spite of the poor resources at the disposal of the Small Sword, because the imperial government was occupied elsewhere. Since 1850, in fact, a far more powerful rebel force had established itself in Central China and was defying the Manchu dynasty—the T'ai P'ing and their 'Heavenly Kingdom of Great Peace' *(T'ai-p'ing Tien-kuo)*.

Starting from a remote south-western region, Kwangsi province, the movement rapidly won over the whole of the lower basin of the Middle Yangtze. In 1851 the T'ai

---

[1]The river route, which went from Shangsha (capital of Honan) to Shanghai, via the River Hsian, Lake Tongtin, and the Yangtze, was one of the major rice-trade routes.

P'ing took the city of Nanking and there proclaimed the coming of a new dynasty. Their projected expedition against Peking came to nothing, but they resisted the imperial forces until 1864, the year in which Nanking was won back.

The T'ai P'ing movement was characterised by its triple content: national, religious, and social.

It was an anti-Manchu movement, which attacked the reigning dynasty as foreign and barbarous. As a sign of defiance its members refused to wear pigtails, and let their hair flow loose.

It was at the same time a religious movement, which combined in a curious fashion archaic Chinese popular cults and borrowings from Christianity, while breaking completely from Confucianism. Hung Hsiu-ch'üan, the T'ai P'ing leader who was proclaimed emperor under the name of *T'ien-wang* (Heavenly King), declared himself Jesus Christ's younger brother, and the sacred books of the new dynasty drew extensively on the Bible.

Finally, it was a social protest movement which tried to free the peasants from the feudal yoke of the Mandarins and landowners. The T'ai P'ing promulgated an agrarian law which was perhaps never applied by anyone else, and which instituted a sort of primitive communism with regard to land, agricultural labour, and harvests. The harvests were gathered into 'heavenly granaries', to be distributed later to everybody in equal parts.

Were the T'ai P'ing a Secret Society?

The exact nature of the connections between the T'ai P'ing and the secret societies has long been a very controversial question among both Chinese historians and sinologists. The T'ai P'ing themselves always denied having any connection whatever with the *hui*. The most they would admit to was having co-operated for a time —particularly with the Triad—against the common enemy, the Manchus. Even in that case they claimed to have quickly taken an independent line. They insisted that their political aims (to establish a new dynasty and not to restore the Ming), as well as their very original

religious system, radically differentiated them from the
old secret societies. Such, for example, is the version
reported by a Protestant missionary in Canton, the Rev.
Theodore Hamberg, who talked to a representative of
the rebel emperor of Nanking in that city.

During the time that Hung Tsiu-chuen was encamped at
the above village [Tai-tsun], two female rebel chiefs of great
valour, named Kew-uhr and Szu-san, each bringing about
two thousand followers, joined the army of the God-worship-
pers,[1] and were received upon submitting to the authority
of Hung and the rules of the congregation. Tsiu-chuen placed
these two female chiefs with their followers at a distance from
the main body of his army, serving as outposts one on each
side. About the same period eight different rebel chiefs belonging to the San Ho-hui or Triad Society, intimated to
Tsiu-chuen their wish to join his army with their respective
bands. Tsiu-chuen granted their request, but under the
condition that they would conform to the worship of the
true God. The eight chiefs declared themselves willing to do
so, and sent their tribute of oxen, pigs, and rice, etc. Tsiu-
chuen now despatched sixteen of the brethren belonging to
the congregation, two to each chief, in order to impart to
them and their followers some knowledge of the true religion,
before they had taken the definite step of joining him. When
this preparatory instruction had been received, the chiefs
dismissed their tutors with a liberal sum of money, as a
reward for their trouble, and soon after they and all their
followers joined the army of Hung Tsiu-chuen. It now occurred that fifteen of the teachers who had been sent out to
the chiefs, in accordance with the laws of the congregation,
gave their money which they had received into the common
treasury, but one of them kept the money for himself, without
saying a word. This same individual had several times before
by his misconduct made himself amenable to punishment,
and had only been spared in consideration of his eloquence
and talent for preaching. He had in the first instance not
fully abstained from the use of opium, but to procure the
drug, he had sold some rattan-bucklers belonging to the

---

[1]From their foundation in 1845 in Kwangsi, under the name 'God-
worshippers', the T'ai P'ing were subject to the influence of
Christian monotheism, which they knew of through Canton
missionaries.

army; another time he got excited with wine, and had injured some of the brethren. As soon as his concealment of the money was proved, Tsiu-chuen and the man's own relatives, who were present in the army, decided to have him punished according to the full rigour of the law, and ordered him to be decapitated as a warning to all. When the chiefs of the Triad Society saw that one of those who had just been despatched as a teacher to them was now killed for a comparatively small offence, they felt very uncomfortable, and said:

'Your laws seem to be rather too strict; we shall perhaps find it difficult to keep them, and upon any small transgression you would perhaps kill us also.'

Thereupon 'Fall large head', 'Great carp fish', and five other chiefs, with their men, departed, and afterwards surrendered to the Imperialists, turning their arms against the insurgents. Lo Tai-kang alone remained with Tsiu-chuen, because he liked the discipline of his army, and the doctrine which they had adopted as a rule of their conduct. It is said that six of the above chiefs of the Triad Society ultimately fell into the hands of the insurgents while fighting against them, and were killed. Tsiu-chuen had formerly expressed his opinion of the Triad Society in about the following language:

'Though I never entered the Triad Society, I have often heard it said that their object is to subvert the Ch'ing and restore the Ming dynasty. Such an expression was very proper in the time of K'ang Hsi,[1] when this society was at first formed, but now after the lapse of two hundred years, we may still speak of subverting the Ch'ing, but we cannot properly speak of restoring the Ming. At all events, when our native mountains and rivers are recovered, a new dynasty must be established. How could we at present arouse the energies of men by speaking of restoring the Ming dynasty? There are several evil practices connected with the Triad Society, which I detest; if any member enter the society, he must worship the devil and utter thirty-six oaths; a sword is placed upon his neck, and he is forced to contribute money for the use of the society. Their real object has now turned

[1] Second Manchu emperor. His reign (1662-1723) was one of the most illustrious of the Ch'ing dynasty.

very mean and unworthy. If we preach the true doctrine, and rely upon the powerful help of God, a few of us will equal a multitude of others. I do not even think that Sun Pin, Wu Khi, Kung Ming,[1] and other famous in history for their military skill and tactics, are deserving much estimation, how much less these bands of the Triad Society.'

Tsiu-chuen afterwards ordered his followers not to receive any Triad men among their number, but such as were willing to abandon their former practices, and to receive instruction in the true doctrine. (6)

The Origins of the T'ai P'ing

The Rev. Hamberg's informant saw the matter in simple terms, but it appears in fact that the situation was far more complex.

An old tradition going right back to the origins of the T'ai P'ing uprising claimed that the movement had, in the first place, not one but two leaders: Hung Hsiu-ch'üan, who later proclaimed himself emperor in Nanking under the name of T'ien-wang; and a Triad leader who passed himself off as a descendant of the Ming and called himself T'ien (Heavenly virtue). According to this tradition it was the latter who was the real leader of the movement, and it was only after his death in 1850, in the course of a battle against imperial troops, that the T'ai P'ing separated off from the Triad and renounced pro-Ming legitimism.

Innumerable discussions have divided Chinese historians on this point. This is not the place to weigh up the arguments. It is sufficient to point out that, even if they later denied it, the T'ai P'ing leaders may well have had initial dealings with the Triad, just as the anti-Manchu nationalists of the late-nineteenth century and early twentieth century made a similar admission (Sun Yat-sen first did so) in claiming ties with both the Triad and the T'ai P'ing.

Rather than try to establish between the two organisa-

---

[1] Generals famous for their tactical skill in the period of the Three Kingdoms. During that period (A. D. 220-264), three rival principalities fought for control of China.

tions either a dissociation or a direct line of descent, it is perhaps more worthwhile to observe that the T'ai P'ing originated from the same common source as the great secret societies of their time. Like them, they were strongly anti-Manchu; their favourite colour was red; the very term *T'ai P'ing* (Great Peace) occurred time and time again in the course of Chinese history, in the slogans of the peasant revolts led by the secret societies, for example under the Han in the early centuries A.D. The marked feminism of the T'ai P'ing again related them to the tradition of the secret societies.

But if their origins lay in this common source, their originality lay in the way in which the T'ai P'ing very definitely developed along their own lines. Their interest in Christianity reflected a desire not only to hark back to the distant past, but also to turn towards the West, whose superior strength had just triumphed over the imperial armies. Their overwhelming success among the masses led them to found a *new* state, a *new* dynasty, and not to be content with claiming to want to restore the Ming.

Although following these different paths, the T'ai P'ing never completely broke with the secret societies. It is true that they did not support the Small Sword's insurrections in Shanghai and Amoy in 1853, and seem to have shown no interest whatsoever in these. But in other cases their policy was one of genuine co-operation. Thus, in 1861-62, they provided assistance to the Golden Coins' uprising in Chekiang province, and after the failure of this movement they absorbed the society's troops. Most notably, they were in close co-operation with the Nien, whose great movement held the imperial forces at bay for more than fifteen years in the very heart of the Great Plain of north China.

The Nien Uprising

The Nien movement certainly had links with the White Lotus, and its name, as we have seen, appeared in the late-eighteenth century, its significance being uncertain. Its territory was a low-lying region, mainly open country (which lent itself to raids and horseback guerrilla tactics), on the borders of Shantung, Kiangsu, Anhui, and Honan—a poorly administered zone, far removed from the Mandarin authorities whose establishments were in the capitals of the provinces concerned.

In the years 1850-60, the activities of the Nien, which had already been carried on sporadically over a long period, suddenly broadened in scope with the help of two events—the T'ai P'ing rebellion, which kept the imperial troops far away, and the economic crisis which struck hard at the northern Chinese (catastrophic floods in Huang-ho in 1853, poor harvests, and increased taxes to pay for the war against the T'ai P'ing and also that against the West from 1856 to 1860).

The Nien provide a good example of a phenomenon in the history of modern China—the way in which the activities of the secret societies were marked by continuity and the peasant revolts by the lack of it.

The account which follows was written by a Mandarin charged with putting down the Nien. It is a good analysis, setting into relief the boldness of the society's members, their 'justiciary brigands' character, and also their popularity.

1. *The Nien's Beginnings*[1]

The Nien began in 1797 (second year of the reign of the emperor Chia Ch'ing). The rebel members of the sects created disturbances in the provinces of Szechuan and Hupei-Hunan. They enrolled men in the villages.

In that period there were several years of bad harvests in the basins of the River Ying and the River Yu (Honan), and great numbers of men enrolled. After several years, these bandits became peaceful. The administration disbanded the troops and sent them back to their homes. But these men, having been in the army, had grown bold and arrogant; they had become used to looting, and when they returned home, they practised no regular profession that would enable them to earn their living. They drank and gambled, and the local vagrants followed their example: by day they laid down the law in the market and by night they stole in the villages.

---

[1]These sub-headings derive from the original Chinese.

The local population, mortified by this state of affairs, instituted a strict curfew. One night, however, about ten of these brigands banded together and one of them, going up to a house, removed the bars from the door. The rest then rushed in to loot it.

An appeal was made to the authorities. Young Mandarins and old soldiers then declared: 'These men entered without being seen, but they left without hiding; their crime is less than bandits' or thieves .

This was the attitude at first adopted by the authorities. It constituted an encouragement for the bandits; no one realised that it was going to produce immense damage, misfortunes for the people, and difficulties for the authorities themselves.

2.   *The Red Beards*

By this judgement, based on the fact that they 'had entered without being seen but left without hiding', the bandits had escaped capital punishment. Even when they had wounded their victims, they claimed that it was by accident. They grew daily more fierce and tyrannical. They even scized torches and arms quite brazenly to attack the villages and set fire to them. There was no crime that they did not commit. But they always showed themselves by night. They painted their faces black, with a red beard, to disguise themselves, as if they still had some fear of justice. That is why they were called the Red Beards.

3.   *The Masters of the Table*

For every ten men, there was a captain called *chang*; for every hundred men, a leader, *hsiong*. Bandits who were rich and powerful led the expeditions: they gathered their men together to commit atrocities; they banded together in the market-place and gambled; they formed groups specialising in the manipulation of knives, spears, and hatchets, calling these groups *cheng-peng*. They were generally referred to as *chao-chu*, 'the master of the table'. It was the same in all the markets. When taking advantage of public meetings to see each other, some ten leaders would come along, and people would say: 'There's a Nien here, a Nien there. . .' (A Nien is a bundle of indissolubly linked elements.) From then on, they began to be called *Nien-zi*. Thus, from the name *Chao-chu*, they passed to that of *Nien-sho* (Nien leaders), and the power of the bandits grew greater and greater.

4. *Instigators of Trouble*

The Nien leaders, excellently dressed, went out riding on horseback, and their entourage carried arms to protect them. When they went into a market-place, they first had the trumpet sounded, so that the local notables and the director of the market would come to greet them. They dressed correctly, wearing hats, and sometimes the rich landowners invited them to their homes and gave banquets in their honour. The leaders were called 'Old so-and-so'. Thus, Chang Tuan-yang was called Lao Tuan (Old Tuan). They also said 'Old Brother so-and-so', 'Old Uncle so-and-so', 'Old Grandfather so-and-so'. Those who had the opportunity to pass the time of day with Nien leaders boasted about it, saying: 'We are great friends with Old So-and-so!' and that was a great honour for them. All the vagrants, riff-raff, and good-for-nothings longed to be able to boast in the same way. The Nien leaders themselves were very proud of it. People said to one another: 'That man looks like a *Hun-chia-zi* (trouble-maker)', because that was the term used by the Nien when talking about themselves.

5. *Nien Enrolment*

If there was a Nien in a village, that village's peace was assured. If there was a Nien in a clan, its happiness was guaranteed. If there was a Nien in a village, Nien from outside would not enter it; they would say: 'Both they and we are all *Hun-chia-zi*.' If a Nien was in a clan, they said: 'Even if Uncle So-and-so had succeeded in passing the civil-service examinations he wouldn't be as famous as he is today.'

On the other hand, if there was no Nien in a village, it was called 'the village of tortoises'. The Nien took prisoner the village chiefs and their sons and hung them up and beat them. That was known as 'capturing tortoises'. When the village attacked by the Nien arranged a parley to get the prisoners released, the Nien asked 300,000 or 500,000 sapekes or up to a thousand ligatures[1] for the wealthiest ones. The result was that if in a clan there was someone very courageous, he was urged to join the Nien, he was helped by subsidies and gifts of grain, they gathered men together to help him win his way into the Nien; that was how the Nien's members were recruited.

---

[1]The ligature is 1000 sapekes.

6. Enemy Families

If disputes occurred between the Nien, they were attributed to *Shou-chia-tsi* (enemy families). They would gather men together to fight; that was called *fa* (attack). Those who were attacked resisted with all their might, provided that they were strong enough. The losses in each camp would amount to tens or even hundreds of people. After the battle, they assembled to burn the houses down. If the attackers were repulsed or dispersed, they took their revenge later. If those attacked were too weak to defend themselves, their houses were burned and they were allowed to take refuge elsewhere; the notables, village and market chiefs, and landowners had to dress correctly and put on fine hats to welcome the enemies. They had to ask for peace three times, and then three times more. Sometimes they even had to remain on their knees before the horses for a long time. If peace was granted, they had to prepare a great banquet and offer a large sum of money, to be used to buy guns and powder. If they did not do this, the houses were burned. All these expenses were borne by the inhabitants of the village. They even fel relief at having to pay.

7. Invitations to the Nien

Those who invited the Nien were unworthy village leaders, scoundrels, who used the Nien to amass riches at the expense of the people for their own profit. When they invited the Nien, they made themselves responsible for welcoming them, organised great banquets, and forced people to provide food and wine. No one dared disobey. Afterwards people had to pay out vast sums of money for the buying of guns and ammunition. The village chiefs kept half the money paid for themselves. If the wine and food provided did not suit the taste of these scoundrels, the tables and crockery were broken and sometimes people were even injured.

Since the losses sustained were much greater than the amount originally demanded, the large tradesmen and money-lenders went away, leaving their merchandise. The markets were devastated and there was a dearth of everything. From then on, the Nien used this method everywhere. They came even if they had not been invited, and the people were left with no means of subsistence.

1. Triad seal in 1841. The ten lines of ideograms above the seal indicate the five main lodges of the Chinese provinces. The nine central ideograms are drawn in their archaic form, and those round them are mainly symbolic compounds of the Society

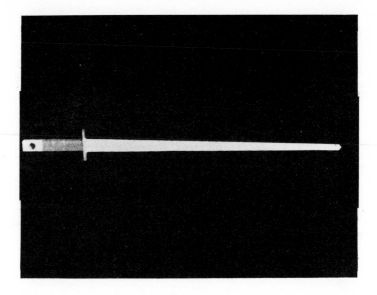

2. Sword in peach and plum wood

3. Triad fighting chain

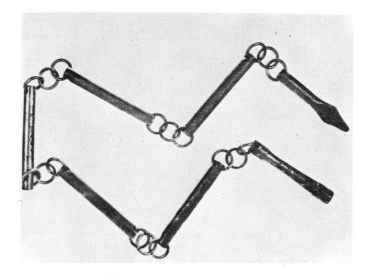

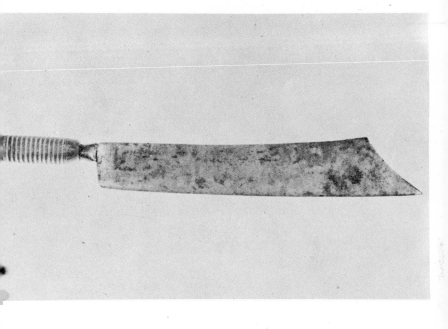

4. Triad fighting sword

5. Straw sandal which comprised part of the costume of certain Triad officials (straw sandal is also one of the names given to the members of the Society)

6. Triad official's costume (photo taken in the Hong Kong police studios)

7.   Boxer standard: the ideograms mean: "Support the Ch'ing and eliminate the Ming"

青万炉胡拐李鉄子仙盆日扇離鍾

萬金止德都坐如来定坐在坐時裡國象

才万千
家后
洪
洪洪和合
結万為記
龍開不洪
閃不正便
洪飄
介五嬴来認圓

8. Small Sword Society seal, captured in Amoy in 1853. The ideograms in the four corners are designed to be read diagonally and mean Faithful *(Chung hsin)* and Just *(I chi)*. The ideogram in the central trapezium is Hung, the name of the Triad. The other ideograms represent the society's symbolic values and retrace part of its history

9. Emblem of a secret society

10. Chinese engraving showing
1853 against Nanking, which ha

al troops' unsuccessful assault in
e rebel capital of the T'ai P'ing

11. Pictures distributed to the people in 1891, at the time of the campaign of agitation against the foreign missionaries. Buddhist priests ward off pigs which represent the Christians

12. Tigers, representing Chinese patriots, attack goats which symbolize the foreigners

13. Church burned down by the Boxers.

14. Europeans fleeing from the Boxers. Illustrations from the Shanghai newspaper *Tung-men How-pao*

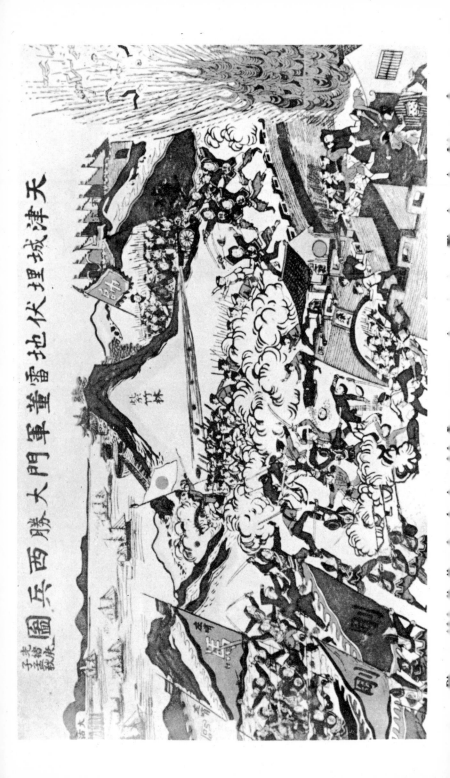

天津城埋地雷轟軍門大勝西兵圖

16. Chinese engraving showing the start of a peasant rising in the village of Tingtou in 1895

17. **Ma Fu-yi, head of a Triad lodge, after his arrest in 1905**

18. Sun Yat-sen, the great figure of the 1911 Revolution

19. Popular participation in the 1911 Revolution: enrolling recruits

20. The Sino-Japanese War in 1938: supporters of the Red Army carrying tree-trunks stuffed with explosive

8. *The Information Service of the Nien*

Those who provided the Nien with their information were employees of the administration who allowed themselves to be corrupted. The Nien had looted a great deal, but they were afraid of the imperial army which came to attack them and might crush them. They therefore sent to the cities the boldest and most intelligent of their numbers, and these obtained positions in the state offices, and corrupted the influential captains into serving them. These captains even went secretly into the villages themselves to provide information.

When the mandarins wanted to take the Nien by surprise, they had first to assemble troops, but before that could be done, the captain had already sent his report to the Nien by express messenger. Thus, when the mandarins, delayed by other business or simply through fear, finally arrived, the Nien had already dispersed to their hiding places. The mandarins' excursion was then a completely wasted journey.

The Nien even went into the cities and lived with their accomplices, the captains, sometimes for months, sometimes for a few days. They gambled and frequented prostitutes. People knew who they were but dared say nothing. They visited tea-houses and restaurants as they pleased. Inevitably, when they observed the prosperity of the big cities they wanted to enjoy it.

9. *Membership of the Nien*

It was not by intimidation that men entered the Nien. They were glad to enter. When the Nien had carried out a looting expedition, they came back with carts, men, and animals laden with plunder—with whole flocks even. Half of the plunder went to their leaders, half to the men. The Nien had administrators whose task was to arrange this distribution. The animals were killed and cooked, and everyone could eat them. Neighbours too desired their share of the spoils; they armed themselves and followed the Nien bands. The Nien plundered, burned, ate well, raped, and shared their spoils when they returned; ordinary men were filled with enthusiasm at the thought of helping them. Where then were virtuous men to be found? If any chanced to exist, they had to move house almost every day to avoid the Nien.
(7)

Documents issuing from the Nien themselves are extremely rare; many of the Nien, including their leaders, were no more than illiterate peasants. But even from sources that are Mandarin in origin, it is possible to see that the movement was anti-governmental and not mere banditry. Their leader had taken the name of 'Lord of the Great Han Alliance' (i.e. of the true Chinese, as opposed to the Manchus). They also used legitimist slogans, such as 'let us sweep away the Ch'ing and restore the Ming', or 'let us restore the Han and get rid of the barbarians'. They attacked not only the rich merchants and the big landowners, but also the state machine—the public granaries, the offices (*yamen*) of the Mandarin administration, and the prisons. Their custom of allowing their hair to flow loose was also a clear indication of their hostility to the Manchus and related them to the T'ai P'ing.

The Nien movement was essentially peasant in character. Entire villages and clans joined it. It profited, as we saw in the preceding text, from having large numbers of sympathisers in the country areas. Evidence of its popularity was given by a French missionary who in 1861-62 accompanied troops in action against the Nien (whom he calls the White Water-Lily, thus expressly linking them with the White Lotus group).

> Having had the opportunity, in 1861 and 1862, of living among the imperial troops engaged in combating the Water-Lily rising, it was easy for me to observe the sympathy of the masses for the rebels. Almost everywhere, when we were not strong enough to intimidate the villages we had to go through, we were refused even water for our horses; if we asked if we could buy a measure of millet or a feed of corn, we were invariably told that there was none. It seemed as if we were in a wilderness, whilst, when the rebels approached, everyone rushed to entertain them and to procure everything they needed. (8)

If the Nien benefited from reliable popular support, their leaders were recruited not from the peasants but from other rural classes which, as we have seen, provided most of the secret societies' leaders—vagrants, flood victims, disbanded soldiers or deserters, survivers of the T'ai P'ing movement, salt smugglers, small village scholars, 'black sheep' of good families, and even money-ed men who co-operated secretly with them by acting as receivers for their stolen goods. One of their chief leaders, Chang Luo-hsing, was the black sheep of a wealthy family who had carried on salt smuggling (very widespread in these areas) and had once co-operated with the T'ai P'ing. Another of their leaders, Lai Wen-kuang, had been on the general staff of the T'ai P'ing and had taken refuge among the Nien after the collapse of the 'Heavenly Kingdom of the Great Peace' in 1864.

The Nien's organisation was strong. It was made up of three different types of unit, though it is not clear how they fitted together: fortified villages, supporting the movement en bloc under the direction of their 'eld-ers'; mobile cavalry units, the basis of the Nien's offen-sive force against imperial power since they could make very effective raids; and lodges called 'mountains' *(shan-t'ang),* whose characteristics were those of the common tradition of the secret societies—eight diagrams, five colours corresponding to the five points of the com-pass, an oath (the text of which has not been preserved), an initiation ceremony in the course of which a finger-print was taken and a mixture of wine and blood drunk, and expressions with secret meanings.

In 1864, the imperial forces put an end to the T'ai P'ing rebellion; in 1868, they did the same to the Nien rising. In both cases, the West had provided military advisers, equipment, and munitions. But both movements had mainly fallen victim to their own incapacity to promote a genuine new social order or to break out of their narrow limits.

For thirty years, however, it was the continued, per-sistent, sporadic activity of the secret societies which maintained a link between the two great surges of the 1850s and the modern nationalist organisations—re-publican in character — which, with Sun Yat-sen, brought about the 1911 revolution.

The Chinese historian, Wang Tian-chiang, recently listed the risings attempted by the secret societies of North and South China during this period of transition, and in the years 1860-85 alone he counted 65. None, it is true, was particularly spectacular, but their continuity is worth stressing.

The White Lotus in Nanking and Shanghai
In Nanking and Shanghai, in 1876, the members of the White Lotus launched an agitation movement which caused the authorities much anxiety. A Catholic missionary left this interesting account of it:

> The Viceroy of the two Kiang[1] and the mandarins under his jurisdiction have affirmed and even published in their proclamations that the disturbers of the public peace[2] are and always have been members of the White Lotus. The people are far from denying the magistrates' word. The White Lotus has indeed been plotting for a long time; it has recourse to magic to make its cause triumph, and the Chinese are in agreement that it is the Empire's most formidable enemy. Today it has headquarters where it prepares its weapons and arranges its plans of attack. As in the time of Hung Hsiu-ch'üan,[3] it is under the command of a leader, a veritable emperor who reigns at least over his own subjects, if it is granted to him to replace the last sovereign of the fallen dynasty...

> Towards the end of 1876, two agents of the secret police seized a man who was acting suspiciously near the Bridge of the Eight Immortals in Shanghai. He was called Wang

---

[1] The provinces of the Lower Yangtze, Kiangsi and Kiangnan (the latter having been later divided into two, Kiangsu and Anhui), were formerly thus named.

[2] The writer has just related that in 1876, in Shanghai and Nanking, there had been rumours that many Chinese were cutting their pigtails as a sign of defiance against the Manchus, that posters had proclaimed the return of the son of the rebel T'ai P'ing emperor, that human silhouettes in red paper were being left in public places. Many witnesses confirmed the rumours, to the great anxiety of the authorities.

[3] Leader of the T'ai P'ing rebellion.

Wen-fo, was a soldier, and said he was a native of Ch'ang-chow, but he spoke the Hunan dialect. He wore a piece of white linen, eight fingers long and six fingers wide, on which there were characters printed in blue ink with dragons round them...

Some of the characters of the above message have meaning which only the initiated can understand, but the significance of the others is clear, and besides, the presence of the imperial dragons is an indication of rebellion[1] of which there can be no doubt. Compared with the bills posted in Nanking, this note appears both as a means of propaganda, since it sets out the White Lotus's views, and as a sign of allegiance to the custom of the society which again seeks ways of causing trouble in the Empire...

A member of the sect who was arrested in Posi in August 1866, summoned before the court of that city, then sent back to Ouyun Ping, governor of the province of Kiangsu, sent the emperor an account of the whole affair, and made the following confessions. When a sworn member wishes to ascertain whether a man belongs to the White Lotus, he greets him with the words *Hung-fu*, which means 'I wish you great happiness'. If the man answers with the same polite formula, the member asks him: 'What country are you from?' The other must answer: 'I am from Yung-ni-hsiang-bao'. These words do not designate any place and are pure convention. When the answer does not contain them, the member stops his questioning, for he knows that he is definitely not dealing with a White Lotus brother. But if the stranger replies that he is from Yung-ni-hsiang-bao, the member asks him: 'Where do you come from?' The stranger must say: 'I come from Tsung-chiang-si-ke,' conventional words like the preceding ones. When the answer has thus been formulated, the two members are deemed to have met. They then enter into a relationship according to the instructions they have received and work for the realisation of the White Lotus's plans. The sworn member captured in Posi was decapitated in Soochow. (9)

This incident was far from being an isolated one; throughout this period the activity of the secret societies

---

[1]Dragons were the emblem of imperial majesty; it was a criminal offence to use them. Moreover, the Chinese characters for 'dragon' prefixes many ideographs used in secret society documents.

was diffused among any number of small fights and small risings directed at once against the Manchu dynasty, the rich landowners, the state machine, and so on. The slogans then used by the secret societies show clearly that at that time, as before, their struggle against the Manchus could not be dissociated from their social struggle: 'Let us overthrow the Ch'ing and restore the Ming', but also 'Let us strike at the rich and help the poor', 'Let us act in the name of heaven to practise virtue', and 'Let us plunder the noble houses and invade the *ya-men*'. Disbanded soldiers, always influential in the secret societies, were particularly numerous in this period, now that the wars against the T'ai P'ing, the Moslems, the West, and the Nien were over. All these campaigns had more or less coincided between 1850 and 1870. But as before it was the poor peasants who were the mainstay of the secret societies; it is significant that their activities were carried on every year during the difficult period of the 'welding'.

If this unflagging activity was nonetheless very scattered, that was because in the years 1860-90 imperial power and the dynasty somehow recovered as best they could from the terrible shocks of the middle of the century. In the reign of the emperor T'ung Chih (1860-75) and at the beginning of that of Kuang Hsü (1875-1908) the traditional order was more or less restored.

The Observance Society in Inner Mongolia

After the lost wars against France, in 1884-85, and Japan, in 1894-95, however, the weakening of the central government was immediately revealed by action from the secret societies, this time on a much larger scale. There was, for example, the Boxer movement which will be discussed in the next chapter, and, before that, the great insurrection of the Observance Society in Jehol (Inner Mongolia). The account that follows is again that of a Mandarin concerned with quelling the movement. The force of the rising is to be noted, as is the fact that the leaders of the sect had taken princely titles, thus clearly expressing their opposition to the imperial authorities.

We have received a memorial from Yeh Chih-ch'ao in which he reports that the Imperial troops have gained successes over the rebels at Maochiawop'u and have dislodged the rebel encampment in the neighbourhood of Kaoerhteng. On the 2nd and 3rd of the present month the rebels of Hsish'iaot'ou fell back and joined their forces with those of Maochiawop'u, the aggregate force amounting to over two thousand men prepared to stake their lives in the defence of their stronghold. On the 4th they were attacked from different sides by the troops under Colonel P'an Wan-ts'ai and another officer named Chiang Kuang-tung, with the result that they were defeated with great loss and obliged to seek shelter in a village. Here they were again assailed on three sides and completely routed. Over ten prominent leaders were killed, amongst them the so-called Princes Chao Chin-kuei and Hsu Hsiao-chih, and the *soi-disant* Marquis Ch'en Chang. The number of the killed comprised three hundred mounted brigands and over one thousand of the rebels belonging to the rationalist sect.[1] The quantity of arms and flags that fell into the hands of the Imperialists was past all computation, and one so-called Prince, Liu Hsien-t'ang, who was captured alive, was instantly decapitated. On the 6th of December the three originators of the movement, Wang T'ing-hsu, Sung Hsuo-chih, and Sung Lo-ta were captured at a place called Erhshihchiatzu and immediately decapitated. Another detachment of the rebels, which had encamped at a place called Kaoerhteng in the Chien-ch'ang district, was attacked by the troops under the command of Brigadier General Tseng T'eng-fang who gained a series of victories over them, capturing the books of their membership, killing a great number of them, and taking alive eight of their prominent leaders, all of whom were decapitated on the spot. Another band, led by a Taoist priest named Wu Kuang-sheng, was completely exterminated. Brigadier General Lin-Fu-shan reported having captured in the neighbourhood of Chien ch'ang the *soi-disant* Prince entitled 'Subduer of the West', T'ung Chih, who was handed over to the magistrate for trial and punishment. All the country in the vicinity of

---

[1]As noted earlier, this was the name given by the Protestant missionaries to the Observance Society *(Chai Li-hui)*.

Kaoerhteng is now tranquil, and the campaign against the rebels has been conducted with marked success. Let Yeh Chih-ch'ao take advantage of his present success to make a concentrated assault upon the enemy and leave not a remnant of them to cause further disturbance.

We have received a memorial from Ting An and his colleagues reporting further successes against the rebels in the Ch'aoyang district. Ting An despatched troops to make a concerted attack upon them and gained repeated victories. The rebels retreated and took up a position in the neighbourhood of Ch'aopeiyingtsu. Here they were attacked on the 3rd and 7th of December by the troops under General Chang Yung-Ch'ing. Over 1000 of the enemy were captured or killed. Following up this success, the Imperialists assailed the rebel encampment at Chaoshukow and captured a noted ringleader named Li Chiao-ming, who was decapitated on the spot. General Feng Sheng-a advanced against the rebels in the direction of Tamiao and the Palace of the Mongolian *Pei-tsu*, killing over 100 of them in the engagement which ensued and capturing twenty prisoners, amongst whom were a leader known as Ch'en Lo-ming and a Taoist priest called Sheng Hsin-ts'ang, all of whom were summararily decapitated. General Nieh Keui-lin pursued the rebels to a place called Hsinglungwa where he slaughtered about 150 of them. In a subsequent engagement the enemy lost over 600 of their men, one of their leaders, Hou K'o-chun, being captured and beheaded. The operations have so far been conducted with great success, and we command Ting An and Yu Lu to lose no time in joining their forces with those from Chihli and employing their concentrated strength in bringing about the total extermination of the various rebel bands. (10)

The secret societies were probably incapable of overthrowing the imperial authorities, and we shall come back to this point, yet by the part they took in the wave of popular uprisings between 1850 and 1870, on their own account, and in the support they gave to the Shanghai, Canton, and Amoy revolts and to the Nien movement, their co-operation with the T'ai P'ing and the influence they eventually had on the latter, they caused the establishment constant anxiety. During the thirty years which preceded the Republican movement, they constituted the only real opposition to the régime.

In the late-nineteenth century, it was estimated that 70 per cent of the population of Tientsin belonged to the Observance Society, and that 70-80 per cent of the workers of Szechuan and Kwangsi were members of the Association of Elder Brothers. The senior Mandarin Liu Kun-i, viceroy of the Lower Yangtze, declared in 1893 that the secret societies were 'a disease hidden away in every province'. (11)

CHAPTER FIVE

Against Foreign Penetration

The privileges obtained by the West in China from 1840 to 1860 were concerned only with the facilitation of commercial activities. In the late-nineteenth century, foreign penetration became more insistent, more direct. From then on its aim was to control much more closely the Chinese economy and even the Chinese state itself, to satisfy the demands of financial expansion.

At the time of the Opium Wars, France, Britain, and Russia had obtained the restriction of customs duty to 5 per cent, the direction of the customs service by foreigners, diplomatic extraterritoriality, and the right to administer entire quarters in certain ports (the famous 'concessions'). These advantages were no longer enough. About 1880, the economy of the West entered into a phase of capitalist concentration and expansion. The great financial interests born of the fusion of industrial and banking capital sought, from then on, stable, reliable overseas investment, and no longer simply the buying and selling of goods.

New rivals—Germany, the U.S.A., and in particular Japan—came to compete with the three powers which had benefited from the Opium Wars.

In 1894 Japan, which had recently modernised itself on Western lines, attacked China. After a few months it gained an easy victory, and exacted considerable concessions from China: very heavy war compensation, the annexation of Taiwan (Formosa), and the right to exploit the railways and mines of Manchuria and to establish factories in China.

The Carving-Up of China

Thus, as much to limit the expansion of their rivals as to assure themselves of new advantages, the Great Powers began to practise a policy of assertive outbidding with regard to China. Within a few years each of them, with the exception of the U.S.A., which tried in vain to get the 'open door' principle accepted, imposed on the Chinese government politico-economic agreements very advantageous to the West. It was the 'break-up' of China, the 'forced entry' of the foreigners.

Japan and Russia disputed the North-East of the Empire, then divided it between themselves in 1905. Germany moved into Shantung province. Britain controlled the Yangtze valley. France chose the South-West. In each of these regions, the foreign powers obtained a monopoly of mining and railway concessions and the authorisation to install military and naval bases, 'leased territories', which gave their armed forces a foothold on the soil of China itself.

The 'break-up' was also a dismemberment of the Empire. The kingdoms on its borders broke loose after centuries of paying tribute and homage to the emperor. Thus Nepal and Burma passed under British control; Vietnam was annexed by France in 1885, after a war in the course of which China tried in vain to go to the aid of her neighbour; and Korea became a Japanese colony in 1910.

During the same period, the Catholic and Protestant missionaries assured of the support of the Great Powers (France in the case of the former, Britain in the case of the latter) profited openly from the political and military strength deployed by the West at the time of the 'break-up'. On more than one occasion, 'gun-boat diplomacy' worked to their advantage. They were very restless, very anxious to protect their flocks, especially when they were in disputes with non-Christians and the mandarin authorities. They were the Westerners with whom the peasants were most often in contact and they rapidly became unpopular. In 1870, in Tientsin, a dispute flared up between the mandarins and the French consul, who was without consideration taking the side of the Catholic mission. Several bloody incidents resulted, the angry Chinese crowd claiming twenty-one victims—missionaries, nuns, Chinese Christians, and the French consul himself.

On the other hand, the traditional Chinese classes of mandarins and gentry were discredited by the conciliatory nature of the imperial policy from the time of the Opium Wars onwards. It was thus the popular religious organisations—the secret societies, in other words—which were best fitted and the most ready to encourage the protest movement against Western penetration. They would not remain indifferent to the economic, political, and religious pressures of the foreigners, and it was they who were to lead the resistance by opposing, first and foremost, the Western elements closest at hand—the missionaries.

Anti-Christian Agitation

Between 1885 and 1890, in the Yangtze region—estuaries of the river in the rich province of Szechuan—there arose a wave of popular anti-Christian agitation. The Catholic and Protestant missions of Chungking, in Szechuan, were attacked in 1886. The Catholic church of Lungshui, also in Szechuan, was burned in the same year, then again in 1888 and again in 1890, when it was attacked by 30,000 people.

In 1891 the movement spread over the whole of the Yangtze Basin; the Jesuit mission of Wuhu, near Nanking, was attacked in May, as were the Catholic missions in Nanking and Yichang, the Catholic orphanage at Kiukiang, and several Protestant missions.

Public opinion immediately attributed these troubles to the secret societies. This was the point of view of a reader of the *North China Herald*, the great British weekly paper of Shanghai, who, in a letter to the editor, wrote the following:

SIR, In the course of conversations with you (as well as with a few others) during the past three years, the most recent occasion having occurred nearly a year ago, I made *(inter alia)* the following statements:—

1.   That the greater part of northern and mid-China is full of disaffection, and honeycombed with secret societies.

2.   That the provinces bordering on the river Yangtze are the most disaffected.

3. That Nanking itself is the head centre.

4. That the one object in which all the secret societies agree is the desire to destroy or drive out of China the present Manchu dynasty.

5. That the method which these societies consider to be the most likely to effect their purpose is to embroil the present government with Foreign Powers, so that if a war with a Foreign Power should occur, a favourable opportunity for a rebellion would then arise. And that even if war was not actually brought about, the state of friction would be such that no Foreign Power would be likely to sympathise with, or actively assist the government of China...

This outbreak of hostility towards the missions was, then, primarily, a political manœuvre intended to disrupt the good relations that had existed between the West and the Manchus since the repression of the T'ai P'ing rebellion, and to isolate the Manchus, who remained the number one target of the secret societies.

The Reawakening of the Elder Brothers

In September 1891, in Shanghai, the imperial police arrested a young Englishman named James Mason, a former employee of the Customs inspectorate; he had been illicitly allowing cases of arms and dynamite to get through to the Association of Elder Brothers, who were planning an insurrection in Chenkiang, an important city in Lower Yangtze. Mason admitted to being a member of the association, and the *North China Herald* described him as a 'monomaniac with the Ko-lao-hui on the brain'.

In the late spring of 1891, the situation became serious enough for the Viceroy of Nanking, Liu Kun-i, to denounce the association's activities in a proclamation, and to threaten the Elder Brothers with severe repression. He also promised to pardon those who left the organisation:

The members of the Ko-lao-hui appoint their own leaders, secretly engrave false seals, distribute pieces of cloth (as proof of membership), make recruits, and commit crimes contrary to the established laws. Their guilt cannot be expiated even by death punishment. I have taken steps to discover and arrest them in every direction. Once captured and convicted the members shall suffer instant death, in accordance with the special laws which have been framed to punish secret societies, without mercy being shown. Still in the Ko-lao Society there are plenty who are willing members but at the same time there are also many ignorant people who have been duped and misled. These joined with the expectation of being assisted with money and food and clothing, and of being backed up in cases of disputes. They trusted blindly to the society's promises, and bought the cloth ticket. It is true that to enter the society is itself a crime punishable by the laws, but taking into consideration that their original intention was excusable and that they have only stepped into a trap prepared for their destruction, I am unwilling that the jade and stone should be indiscriminately consigned to the fire (the actually and apparently guilty should be equally punished) just at this juncture of making arrests.

Therefore by this proclamation I notify you, people of all classes, to take warning. Those who have bought the cloth ticket to become Ko-lao members, should take the earliest opportunity to retreat, burn the cloth ticket, repent, turn over a new leaf, enter into some other occupation, and become good subjects, so as to save their lives, or hand the cloth ticket to the authorities who will do the burning. Anyone secretly informing the officials as to who the Ko-lao leaders are, when these are convicted, not only will be exempted from punishment, but will be rewarded. Even if the leaders should themselves truly repent and come forth, their past conduct will not be enquired into. Should they persist in their blind path from first to last then once apprehended they will know that the laws of the State will be dealt out to them to the last measure without leniency. They will then regret in vain. Let all wake up from their dreams and seriously consider this and not allow the good admonishing to be lost to them! Let the father restrain his son, the elder restrain his younger brother from falling into the clutches of the law. (2)

The Big Sword against the Christian West

There were many other cases of direct action by the

secret societies against the Christian missions. In 1894 a Church of England rest house in a hillside resort above Foochow was suddenly attacked by a group of armed men. Nine missionaries were killed. The attack, attributed to the Vegetarian Sect, was a harbinger of the Boxer Rising.

In 1897 it was the Big Sword, probably in liaison with the White Lotus, which in Shantung province led a movement of hostility towards the West and Christianity. This is how a Catholic missionary described its activities:

Beside the three great religions of China,[1] there exist numerous religious sects, like the Golden Elixir, the Eight Diagrams, the Nine Palaces, the Observance Sect, the *Hao-li* Sect, the Incense-Stick Sect, the Half Incense-Stick Sect, the Vegetarians, the Society of Elder Brothers, the Central Door, the *Tai-ji-tu* Society, the *Dunkia* Sect, the White Lotus Sect... It is impossible to list them all: there are 3,600. All of them are pagan, many are confined to one village, and are not worth mentioning.

Recently at Ch'aohsien, in Shantung province, and in various districts in the eastern part of Honan province, as well as in districts of Kiangsu such as Hsoochow, the Big Sword Society began to manifest its activities. I heard it spoken of in the spring of last year. At that time I did not believe it. But last autumn very many people were talking about it, and I could no longer dream of denying its existence.

In the spring of this year, when I was away on a preaching tour, I noticed that people walking to and fro in the streets often had spears with two red ribbons on them. This was the Big Sword's sign of recognition. The society's members dared to hold a general assembly lasting four days in public at Tanhsien, and to put on a play. More then 100,000 people attended.

How and why did this sect make such rapid progress?

They spread about a rumour that by manipulating a certain talisman, reciting incantations, swallowing an amulet in a drink, it is possible to become invulnerable to knives and bricks—to be protected from all forms of attack. They said that everything would be accomplished in a single night

---

[1] Confucianism, Buddhism, and Taoism.

without any one needing to fear gunshots, cannon-fire, or sword thrusts, because their charms would protect the people. That is why they got the nicknames of *Kin-chung-chao* (golden clock). *Tie-pu-shan* (clothing and tissue of iron), and *Wu-ying-bian* (shadowless whip).

Simple folk are afraid of robbers and bandits and cannot face them. They told themselves that the Big Sword could protect them and their families from gunfire; so they rushed to receive the teaching of this sect, without regard for the expense.

The rich families who had been won over to these magic practices were very numerous, too. There must have been several thousand. If this sect had really been able to put an end to the activities of robbers, they would have deserved nothing but praise; but in the event things turned out very differently. It was in the spring of this year that the society began to show its true face.

Members of the Big Sword used any pretext to start disputes and they attacked in a body certain people who had been unwilling to follow them. If soldiers happened to insult them, they gathered their men together and set out to attack.

As the Catholic Church denied that they had the power to be invulnerable to knives and guns, believing that story to be nothing but lies, the Big Sword members became enemies of the Catholic Church. They wanted to destroy all the churches and kill all the converted. They gathered together tens of thousands of people and destroyed a large number of churches in Ch'aohsien, Chengwu, Tanhsien, Fenghsien, Peixian, Hsiaohsien, Tangshan, Kaocheng, and Lanyi. They killed a number of priests.

By that time, Catholics no longer dared to stay at home. Many took refuge in Jining Cathedral; the rest hid and did not risk showing themselves.

The Catholic Church appealed to the local authorities, who immediately sent fresh supplies of troops to attack the Big Sword's hideout. The principal leaders were captured and executed on the spot. The rest were ordered to go home and forbidden to continue their practices. Each one had to report to the local authorities after six months, on pain of being arrested at home by soldiers and punished in the same way as the leaders.

What became of their alleged power to escape gunfire? Simple people, in their ignorance, had allowed themselves to be wrongly persuaded: today they regret it infinitely.

When I reflect upon the rise and fall of the Big Swords, I believe more and more firmly in what the Bible says: 'All that is not planted by God will be pulled up by the roots... that which comes from man cannot succeed'. But how will China compensate the Catholic Church for all the burned churches and all the murdered Catholics? I will continue this report when negotiations are complete. (3)

The action of the secret societies against the missionaries and Chinese Christians had the paradoxical result of giving the West a greater pretext for intervening and obtaining new advantages after the Boxer Rising had been put down by the 'eight-nation army'.

The Boxer Rising

The term 'Righteous Harmony Fists' (*I Ho Ch'üan*), vouched for from the beginning of the nineteenth century, designated yet another offshoot of the White Lotus. About 1898, the organisation began to attract notice in North China by attacking the missions and then attacking other foreign establishments (for example, the telegraph lines). Sacred boxing played an important part in its activities.

In 1898-99, the Boxer groups seem to have identified themselves more and more with the militias (*t'uan*: corps) which had been in existence for a long time in the villages with the agreement of the authorities. From then on, the rebels tended to be referred to by the name *I Ho T'uan*, 'Righteous Harmony Corps'. This change makes it apparent that certain high-level imperial civil servants, like the governor of Shantung province, Yu Hsien, had regarded the popular organisations not unkindly, thinking that he might use them against the West, at least as a means of putting pressure on them. In the spring of 1898, the West's drive had in fact been sharply intensified. Within a few weeks Germany, Russia, Britain, and France had successively obtained, through threats, the cession of military bases in—respectively—Shantung, the tip of the Liaotung Peninsula, Shantung again, and opposite the island of Hainan.

The following accounts show well the vigour with which the movement had been propagated and the favourable reception it had from the people.

Some of them come from mandarins, others from missionaries.

Sacred Boxing and Magic Practices

Since the first month of this year, there have been in the neighbourhood of Yingfou what are known as 'Righteous Harmony Militias', which do nothing but deceive people by the teaching of their doctrine; their influence has now become so strong that the power of the bandits has spread far and wide.

According to particular circumstances, their magic practices consist of several kinds of incantation, comprising from eight to twelve or from sixteen to twenty characters and capable of going up to ten sentences. They persuade boys of about ten years old or so to recite incantations with their eyes closed, and to bow three times towards the south. Then they lie down on their backs on the ground and after a moment they jump up and announce their surnames and first names, which are usually those of the heroes of previous dynasties. They make the gestures of boxing, move forward, and fall back, dancing with their hands and feet. Some of them hold bamboo rods, millet stems, wooden poles, etc., of which the long ones represent spears and lances, and the short ones two-handed sabres or ordinary swords. Going out in little groups through the gates and along the paths, they jostle each other impulsively; their violence is extreme, their gallantry almost irresistible. Every time they do these exercises, they must gather together several dozen boys in order to be able to play in this particular way.

On the first and second days, at the beginning of their studies, they lie down on their backs; then they leap up, keeping their eyes closed while they gesticulate and jump about. If men or things are placed in their way, they never collide with them. When their dance is finished and they are going to depart, they bow three times towards the south, saying: '*Lao-shi-fu* (Old Master-Father), I ask permission to leave'. Then they return to their normal state.

When they have been in training for a few days at least, they no longer lie down on their backs and no longer keep their eyes closed. During the boxing practice, they no longer recite incantations more than once, and they immediately start gesticulating and leaping about; they become extraordinarily skilled at it. As they leave, they bow once and it is over.

No one knows how this perverse doctrine was spread. Their name is 'Righteous Harmony Boxers'. At Yingfou there are countless young men who go to practise these exercises, and when they are asked why they do it, they all unanimously answer that it is in preparation for killing and hunting down foreigners. They say too that this sort of cut-throat fighters' boxing is only part of the exercise. In future they will have to become proficient in the magical methods by which the wind and the rain are summoned, clouds are made to disperse, and mists to disappear, etc.

The higher civil servants of the local administration have already introduced severe prohibitions. Informed sources said that these processes represent one of the eight methods of the White Lotus's religion. As for the reason why they recruit young boys especially, it is because by being trained from a young age they are sure to become very proficient in the long term; in a few years, when the power of the Boxers has spread further, the young boys will be men and their faith will inevitably have been strengthened. Thus, a single appeal will evoke a hundred responses, and the people will rise up brandishing their rods. It is an indescribable calamity. (4)

The Mandarins' Version of the Beginnings of the Boxers
In the fifth lunar month, at the start of the rising of the Boxer bandits in the town of Towlin, there were at first no leaders. At that time, there was in the Baigow region a certain Chang Te-cheng, who up to then had been a boatman on the Baigow river, loading and transporting goods for shops and traders. Putting in at Towlin, he went to the shops to settle the freight accounts. On the way, he met three boys who were just doing some boxing exercises. Chang looked at them and said: 'Your boxing is not the true kind. I, by moving one finger, will immobilise you.' They put him to the test and he did indeed succeed.

There were then in the town certain characters named Sun, Liu, Chow, and others, who liked telling stories. Their habitual way of life was that of good-for-nothings, and there was no mischief that they did not commit. They hailed Chang, saying: 'Would you not be the immortal master of such a sacred area?'[1] Chang stuck out his neck and answered: 'Yes'. Sun and Chow announced this to the inhabitants of the entire town, praising his merits for all they were worth.

After communal deliberation they set up a sacred area of which Chang was elected master. At the beginning, they pitilessly collected subscriptions from among the inhabitants to meet the expenses. Subsequently, as the organisation grew in all directions, they set up illegal customs barriers on the river to extort money from all the boats which passed. In case of refusal, under the pretext of looking for traitors, they looted unscrupulously. One day, Chang, arriving outside the city walls at the head of a crowd, examined the lie of the land all round; then, reciting incantations, he traced a line in the air and began to indoctrinate the crowd, saying:'Here there is already a rampart; why should we fear the enemy?' After this, there was no lack of enthusiastic followers, and in this way the whole town took up his refrain in chorus. Chang sent men secretly to invite the Boxer bandits of the region to come to the town and pay homage at his court, saying: 'All nations come to the court'. The town fell deeper and deeper into a state of extraordinary seditious madness; they felt no scruples at doing evil. Such is the origin of the Towlin Boxer-bandits. From what local people have heard and observed, the two bandits, Sun and Chow, who had taken precautions long before, fled by boat after the recapture of the town by the imperial troops. (5)

The Attack Denounced by the Missionaries
15th September 1899. Renewed antagonism of the 'Boxers'. We are having another struggle with the 'Boxers'. Our poor people are suffering bitterly, and we have all been in danger. I am hoping that this new outburst will soon pass away, but it is most detrimental to our work, not to say anything of the anxiety regarding our personal safety, when these reckless men combine to attack our converts and threaten to destroy us and our homes.—Our work is at a standstill, and the Romanists suffer with us.

16th December 1899. Just a short note to say that the rebellion is spreading like a prairie fire. Over the borders in Shantung, American Congregationalists, American Presbyterians,

---

[1]The Boxers were organised into *dan* (sacred areas), which they used as meeting places.

French Catholics and others have suffered severely. Many churches and chapels have been destroyed and hundreds of converts have been looted, and some names have been added to the long and ever growing roll of martyrs.

In our district a preacher has been captured and ransomed by the officials. One of our chapels has been cleared of all its furniture, but not destroyed as the enemy's drilling place is next door. A few of our converts have been looted, animals and grain taken away and all furniture smashed. One preacher has been hiding for a long time, but has at last managed to escape to us. Very many Catholic chapels have been destroyed, and Catholic gentry ransomed and have paid ransom money. About 30 counties are involved, and the officials are helpless now. They are to blame for not nipping the thing in the bud, and they blundered seriously when they paid ransom money. This only aggravated matters, and made the Boxers more arrogant and insolent. 1500 foreign drilled soldiers have arrived in Shantung and there must be a desperate battle soon in that region. The Governor of Shantung[1] has been dismissed and his place taken by the well-known Yuan Shih-k'ai,[2] Resident in Korea at the time of the war. We have appealed for protection, and have 10 soldiers and about 20 opium sots known as Yamen[3] runners. The Consul telegraphed that the Viceroy is sending soldiers. We trust that they will soon be here, as the enemy is in strong force 6 miles away, and we hear from various quarters that he is to be attacked within 2 days. We have a number of Christians here as a guard, fairly well equipped, but we can never hope to drive off the hundreds of fanatical scoundrels, whose flags have characters *Mieh Yang* (extermination of foreigners) inscribed upon them...

23rd. Dec. Since writing the foregoing, we have felt the full force of the storm. Our compound has today over 80

---

[1]Yu Hsien, Governor of Shantung in 1898-9, known for his favourable attitude to the Boxers. At the end of 1899, faced with renewed outbreaks of killings and fire-raising, the West complained to the Chinese government and Yu Hsien was dismissed.

[2]The future President of the Chinese Republic after the 1911 Revolution. He had played an important rôle in the struggle for influence between Russia and China in Korea, a struggle which led to the Sino-Japanese War of 1894-95.

[3]Official administrative buildings of a Chinese village.

refugees, who have lost all their earthly possessions—including grain, clothing, bedding, animals, etc., and 5 of our chapels are of no use any longer. Battle fought last week. 70 killed and 100 captured of the enemy. 70 soldiers here now and more expected on Monday. It will be a sad Xmas for us all... (6)

The Boxers' Syncretism

In common (as we have seen) with all the secret societies, the Boxer movement, in so far as its religious aspects were concerned, was of a distinctly syncretistic character.

Sacred boxing, a means of promoting perfect physical fitness and spiritual progress at the same time, also played a large part in its practices; so did the consulting of mediums. Young boys of about fifteen took part in sessions of hypnotic trances and possession, and were regarded with particular respect.

Charms, prophecies, magic formulae assuring the invulnerability of the faithful and of the leaders destroyed or claimed to destroy the military potential of the enemy and promised the control of the elements, particularly the rain (the years preceding the rising had been marked by catastrophic droughts).

Here is the prophecy announcing the imminence of ten calamities:

First worry:	The Empire will not have peace;
Second worry:	The people of Shantung will be wiped out;
Third worry:	In Hupei and Hunan there will be floods;
Fourth worry:	There will be fighting in Szechuan;
Fifth worry:	South of the Yangze will be thrown into chaos;
Sixth worry:	More than half the population will perish;
Seventh worry:	The Boxers will be too weak to deal with these catastrophes;
Eighth worry:	Foreigners will devastate Chihli;
Ninth worry:	More clothes than people to wear them;
Tenth worry:	More food than people to consume it. (7)

Charm against the consequences of drought:

Rain does not and will not fall and very soon there will be fighting and killing. If you do not pass on this message from Buddha you will not be able to escape unnatural death. If, on the other hand, you copy this once and give it to another man, your family will be safe. If you can copy this ten times and give the copies to others, your whole village will be safe... If you use Kerosene,[1] you will be punished by the gods... The recipe to nullify the effects of poison: dry plums 7, *Eucommia Ulmordes*[2] 0.5 taels,[3] reed-ears 5, and green lentils 49.

Charm against the Christians:
The heresy has no respect for either gods or Buddha. It does not allow the burning of joss-sticks; nor does it obey the Buddha precepts. Its followers are arrogant to our great Ch'ing Empire. They preach a heresy of Jesus and God in Heaven. There is no need to give the details of their blasphemous deeds. But the Celestial Court is angered by them and sent down Chao Yun[4] and eight million celestial troops to destroy them. Before long, there will be fierce battles in which soldiers and civilians will suffer. The Buddhist *I-ho-t'uan* (on the other hand) can defend the country and deliver our people from suffering. When you see this notice, you should make out three copies in order to save your family. If you can make out ten copies, you will be able to save your neighbours as well. If you do not copy, you will be killed.

The Social Framework of the Boxers
The Boxer movement drew its support mainly from the poor peasantry of North China, particularly the agricultural workers who had been victims of the drought of the preceding years. It had an equally strong appeal among the boatmen who had been ruined by the recent falling-off of traffic on the Imperial Canal now that goods were transported by sea; and among disbanded soldiers, of whom there were many in the area.

Of the two principal Boxer leaders, one, Chang Te-cheng (see page 117), was a former boatman, and the

---

[1]The sale of American paraffin, which competed with the locally produced oil, in the villages was for the peasants the most blatant sign of foreign penetration.
[2]This plant—in Chinese, *du*—is a shrub of the spurge family; its bark has medicinal uses.
[3]The tael *(liang)* was a unit of weight used in monetary dealings and corresponding to a weight of money.
[4]Legendary hero of the period of the 'Three Kingdoms'.

other, Ch'ao Fu-tien, was a former soldier. Thus the
Boxers were no exception to the rule we have already
observed; their administrators came from marginal
elements of rural society, not directly engaged in agricultural production.

The place held by women in the movement is equally
significant. Special units of young girls from 12 to 18
years old, the Red Lanterns and the Blue Lanterns,
operated alongside the male units. They were led by a
woman named Huang-lian Sheng-mu, the 'Sacred Mother
of the Yellow Lotus', who was claimed to possess great
magical powers; she, too, came from a family of boatmen.

But the Boxer movement does not seem to have been
preoccupied with social upheaval, even in the primitive
way that, for example, the Nien had been ('Strike at
the rich and help the poor'). The password 'Protect
the people', one of the three great Boxer slogans, only
appeared belatedly, probably to make the simple
peasants more willing to supply the rebels with provisions. The two other slogans were entirely political:
'Support the Ch'ing dynasty' and 'Hound out the
foreigners'.

Much has been written and discussed about the
problem of the Boxers' failure to conform to the general
rule of the secret societies (which was to support the
Ming and oppose the Ch'ing) in defending the Manchu
dynasty.

It appears that at first the movement accused the
Manchus of betraying China and handing the country
over the foreigners. Some of the early Boxer leaders
even claimed to be descendants of the Ming. But in
1898–99, for little-known reasons, but probably as a
result of advances made by certain elements in the
Court, they allied themselves to the Ch'ing dynasty,
in spite of its Manchu origins, and appealed to the people
to support it as a symbol of Chinese independence in
the face of the ambitions of the foreigners.

This political *volte-face* brought about a complete
break between the Boxers and the other secret societies,

particularly the White Lotus, to the common traditions of which they were originally closely linked. There were even, in a number of instances, bloody engagements between members of the two societies.

National Objectives

It is very significant that, from the start, the Boxers had concentrated on the struggle against foreigners, by attacking, for example, telegraph and other technical installations introduced by the West.

In this connection G. Dunstheimer has aptly compared them with the 'machine-breakers' or luddites of the early industrial revolution in Europe. But in China, it was a luddism of a national, rather than a social kind, which attacked modern technical realities because they served the foreign enemy, and not the class enemy as in England in the late-eighteenth century.

It has been observed that the hostility of the Boxers towards Christianity has no meaning except in this nationalist perspective. The Boxers were thus the precursors of the modern Chinese national movement of the twentieth century, as such expert commentators as V. Purcell, J. Chen, and G. Dunstheimer have stressed. Whilst remaining an archaic organisation (it has been described as 'the last great historical manifestation of the Chinese Middle Ages'), the Boxer movement was nonetheless very modern.

The following text provides an illustration of the close connection between their reaction to the 'break-up' and their religious preoccupations.

...Where Modernity and Archaism Mingle

During the reign of the emperor Hsien Feng (1851–60), the Catholic Church and the West plotted together against China. They squandered our country's money, demolished our temples and the effigies of Buddha, took over—as burial grounds for their familes—the land belonging to our people: thousands of men hated them. The very fruit-trees and buds were struck every year by scourges—insects or drought. The nation was troubled, the people anxious, and anger had risen sky-high.

Today let us be thankful for the mercy of the Great Lord of the Heavens in sending gods to our altars to teach our brothers the sacred boxing which will help us to 'strengthen the Ch'ing dynasty, annihilate Western power, and promote heavenly righteousness'. In bringing ourselves to help our country, we are strengthening our community and protecting our people in the fields and villages. At the height of the crisis, that is a sign foretelling the coming of happiness.

Yet we fear the fools and scoundrels who would profit from our influence to act unscrupulously and oppress the weak with the aid of the strong. That is why we beg the village leaders and the organisers of the Boxer Corps to act justly according to the law and not to seek personal gain. If they were to allow themselves to be corrupted,they would be struck down by a withering glance from the gods, and condemned without partiality or pity in accordance with the gravity of the case.

Belief in a foreign religion and the use of sorcery have aroused the anger of Heaven, which sends the saints to earth to teach *I-ho* boxing to our brothers. *I* means righteousness and *ho*, concord. With righteousness and concord, harmony and understanding will reign in the villages. Virtue is our principle, agriculture our employment; we obey Buddhism. We do not admit personal vengeance in the name of common justice, the oppression of the poor by the rich, the humiliation of the weak by the strong, or the inversion of true and false. (10)

To Expel the Blue-Eyed Devils

When the devils[1] troubled our country, the gods came to the aid of the Boxers of *I Ho Tuan*. To be converted to Christianity is to disobey Heaven, to refuse to worship our gods and Buddhas, and to forget our ancestors.

If people act in this way, the morality of men and the chastity of women will disappear. To be convinced of this, one has only to look at their eyes, which are completely blue. If the rain does not fall and the land dries up, it is because the churches stand in the way of Heaven. The gods are angry and they come down from the mountains to preach *Tao*.[2]

---

[1] i.e. Westerners.
[2] The Sacred Way, the basis of the Taoist religion.

It has nothing to do with lying or with the White Lotus.[1]

To pronounce magic words is to learn to speak the truth; the 'yellow letters'[2] go up to heaven; incense is burned to summon the gods and the angels. The latter come out of the caves, the former come down from the mountains and come to help mortals by teaching them sacred boxing.

Our military strategy is simple: boxing must be learned so that we can expel the devils effortlessly; the railways must be destroyed, the electric wires severed, and the ships demolished. All this will frighten France and demoralise Britain and Russia. The devils must be suppressed so that the Ch'ing empire may unite and celebrate peace. (11)

In 1900 the Boxers occupied Peking and beseiged the diplomatic quarter, where the foreigners had taken refuge. It was the Powers who were themselves to suppress the insurrection, relieve Peking by an international expedition, and impose a very severe treaty on China. The latter comprised the payment of a large indemnity (450 million taels) and other measures advantageous to the West (from that time, for example, the revenue of the Chinese customs had to be paid directly into the big Western banks). In spite of their determination, the Righteous Harmony Corps had only succeeded in increasing their country's dependence on the foreigner. Their movement had remained localized in the north of the country, limited to certain social strata, and oriented exclusively towards the past.

Against France in Indo-China

When, in 1883, France suddenly attacked independant Vietnam — or what remained of it, since the south of the country, the future Cochin-China, had been annexed by Napoleon III twenty years before—the Chinese imperial government went to the help of this land which, in its intellectual, political, and religious traditions, was closely linked with China. But it was not alone.

---

[1] As we have seen, the Boxers and the White Lotus, originally linked, separated when the former decided to support the Manchu dynasty.
[2] Sheets of yellow paper on which votive characters were written. They were burned during public worship.

A popular Chinese organisation connected with the secret societies, the Black Flags, which was strong in Kwangsi province in the region bordering on Tonking, put itself at the service of Vietnam and fought the aggressors tooth and nail. It struggled on until, in 1885, the imperial Vietnamese government had to give in and accept the status of a French protectorate.

At the beginning of 1885, a French warship, the *La Galissonière,* damaged during the French attack on Taiwan, came to Hong Kong for repairs. The Triad, which—according to the estimate of the British governor himself—had more than 20,000 members on the island, then called all the dock workers out on strike. The governor, rather than clash with this underground force, advised the French ship to try its luck in Japan.

It is worth noting that when—for the first time in its history—the Chinese industrial proletariat took the initiative and staged a truly political strike, which was successful, it was a secret society that gave the call to action.

For Monarchic Restoration

In the south of Vietnam, around Saigon, there were at the beginning of the twentieth century numerous secret societies, undoubtedly close relatives of those existing in China. They were called: *Nghia Hoa* (the equivalent in Vietnamese of *I-ho,* 'righteous harmony', as with the Boxers); *Thien-dia-hoi* (Heaven and Earth Society, one of the names of the Triad); *Luong-Huu-hoi* (Society of Friends); and *Nhon-hoa-duong* (Virtue and Equity Group).

Like the societies in China, they had a religious element; a medium either directed their activities or was influential. A sense of solidarity between members was strengthened by secret initiation rites, and amulets of invulnerability were distributed to members. Meetings were held at night, in pagodas, with the connivance of Buddhist priests; the societies' beliefs contained Buddhist and Taoist elements. Recruitment took place in the same milieux as in China—urban and rural outcasts—

but the societies were also supported in some cases by wealthy people if not by 'proto-capitalists'.

As in China, these societies too had clearly defined political objectives—in this case, the ending of French domination.

However, there already existed at that time a group of Vietnamese intellectuals who felt the need to substitute a progressive ideology for the old Confucianism; the anti-French secret societies displayed a very traditional patriotism and aimed only at restoring to Vietnam an independent monarchy founded solely upon the 'Mandate of Heaven'.

What they opposed to French domination was the cult of earth spirits, of fundamental importance in the old Vietnam, or respect for harmonious social relations as defined by Confucian morality. Their patriotic ideology was thus entirely backward-looking.

The Anti-French Oath

All those who have taken the oath must be devoted and faithful to their mutual obligations as brothers of the same blood.

Between comrades, they must help each other, prevent each other from failing in their duties, succour each other in misfortune, and never abandon one another, even in danger.

Concord must reign; the disciple must obey his master, love his country and think of his king, do his duty (by coming to the aid of the oppressed), speak respectfully, behave temperately, correct his faults, not drink alcoholic beverages, not be greedy, know how to take advantage of circumstances, not betray his leaders or his masters, not take other men's wives, not compete with his neighbours, not steal, not mock at people behind their backs, not say the opposite of what he thinks, take vengeance on his enemies, and not be ungrateful.

If your family is destitute and rebellion reigns in the land, remain good sons and good subjects. Do not be afraid of confronting difficulties and fatigue. Do not fear evil men.

If you die carrying out your duty you will be heroes; if the opposite is the case, Heaven and Earth will kill you:

you will be drowned, burned, or bitten by snakes, or pierced with arrows in battle; your body will be decimated.

This oath is as vast and important as the mountains and the seas; you must not fail to keep it.

If you speak to others in secret, the Saints and Spirits will be there, watching you.

O Almighty Haû-De (King of Heaven)...

In the year Dan,[1] the gods met and decided to create men and beasts.

In every reign faithful subjects and virtuous men have existed; alas! they are no longer of this world.

Furthermore, the spirits will come to the aid of the royal family; thanks to their supernatural powers, they will re-organise everything according to the will of heaven and they will have pity on those who joined together, in the interests of their country, to help their King'[2] to overthrow the French and recapture Annam.

We who, in an assembly of heroes, have of common accord drunk the cup of blood, shall give all our devotion to aiding and succouring our fatherland that it may recover its unity.

We shall do everything possible, all our duty; we shall all have one goal and we shall pray that we may be altogether united and that peace will come.

When the kingdom flourishes, the nation will be rich, the citizens powerful; they will benefit from the advantages of peace, and our former dignitaries will from that time keep their positions for a long time.

We shall meet with sincerity in the garden of immortality and all make our vows that everything may turn out according to our wishes. People will gather in every home to pray that the King may have a long life, and we shall come together beneath his independent sceptre as in the days of Kings Nghieu and Thuen.[3]

---

[1]'The year Dan' (the year of the Tiger) was adopted by the Vietnamese from the old Chinese mythological tradition: it is the year of the creation of the world.

[2]The emperor of Annam was then the young Duy-tan, who in May 1916, just after the Saigon prison attack, fled to try and call the people to rebel. It is probable that the secret societies of Cochin-china were in contact with him.

[3]Mythical sovereigns whose names evoke for the Vietnamese a golden age of prosperity.

We shall never forget the glass of blood we drank as we took the oath.

If we meet with difficult times, they will be changed into pleasant ones. Difficulties will change and become easy. All will go well. Let us pray and wait! (12)

The Anti-French Prayer

May the clemency of Heaven and Earth grant us its protection; the light of the sun and moon is reflected upon us; we receive all these benefits.

It is a misfortune for us to meet the Europeans who have been in possession of our land for many years; they have oppressed us together with our King. The sages stay in the rice-fields but worthless men become civil servants.[1] The methods of governing and the sentences inflicted are becoming more and more severe. Morals are degenerating; Heaven and Earth are sad to see the people in such misery.

We swear today to join together for the sake of our country and our people; we shall fight against the guilty ones. All whose heart is as ours will be at peace, but those whose will opposes ours will be killed and cut into a thousand pieces, along with all their families.

After taking the oath, we must be loyal to our fatherland, or Heaven and Earth will kill us all.

Let us rely on the blessings of Heaven and Earth, and of all the Spirits. Let us prostrate ourselves for this prayer. (13)

In Cochin-china, in the years 1910-15, when the resistance of the cadres of the former Vietnamese monarchy and of the Confucian scholars had died out and the modern nationalist organisations had not yet taken up the cause, the secret societies were very active.

In 1913, for example, eight bombs exploded in Saigon and Cholon. Six hundred peasants, dressed in white and wearing amulets, attacked Saigon in the hope of seeing their leader Phan Xich-long descend from the sky. (A soothsayer and pretender to the imperial throne, he claimed to be the son of Ham-nghi, the young emperor

---

[1]The French had indeed only been able to recruit dubious subjects as colonial administrators. Before a parliamentary commission of enquiry at the time, Vice-Admiral Rieunier had declared: 'We have at our service only Christians or scoundrels.'

who, in 1885, had refused to accept the protectorate and had kept the French troops fighting for three years.)

Phan Xich-long was arrested, and on 15th February 1916 at 3 a.m. his supporters attacked the Saigon prison in which he had been detained for three years. One hundred and seventy-two were caught carrying arms.

The attack failed, but in a small town not far away, Bienhoa, more fortunate rebels succeeded in storming the prison and freeing all the prisoners.

The Attack on Saigon Prison

The following passages are extracts from the dossiers of the French military tribunal which tried the assailants of 1916. Here is the cross-examination of a witness:

> The sorcerer Nguyen-van-Mui explained: 'On the 12th of the 1st Annamite month (14th February 1916), a man named Dang (who is among the accused) came to the house of a neighbour, Huong-truong-Ho; not finding him at home, Dang came to my house, bringing me four or five amulets which he said were from his relative, the sorcerer Ba-My, with instructions to burn them and swallow the ashes in order to be made invulnerable.'
>
> 'These amulets,' continued Mui, 'had been distributed by They Ba-My to his supporters. One of them was intended to be simply swallowed in order to double one's strength and courage. The other two had to be burned first, then the ashes had to be mixed with alcohol, the mixtures, when absorbed, giving strength and success in the case of the first, and protection from spirits in the case of the second. As for the last one, it is intended to give protection from epidemics when it is burned and its ashes are scattered in the wind outside one's house.' (14)

And here is the government commissioner's indictment to the first War Council in Saigon:

> At Phuoc-Long, in Cholon province, the three brothers Nguyen-van-Dai, Nguyen-van-Bong, and Nguyen-van-Hanh are unrepentantly anti-French and ardent revolutionaries.

All three, with their family, belong to the *Phat-te*[1] secret society,˙ which regards Phan-xich-Long and Tu-Mat as princes, and the president of which was Nguyen-huu-Tri. This society has quite large groups of members in every village.

For Tan-Kieu (Cho-lon), Hanh is the leader of one of these groups. It was he who called the weekly meetings. It was he who distributed the amulets. Dai, already arrested on 20th June 1913 for plotting against state security, was released on 1st September 1913, but he continued nonetheless to be a zealous member of the *Phat-te*.

The whole of this family took part in the attack on the central prison with the exception of young Bo, the son of Bong, the third brother, who stayed behind in Tan-kieu to guard the straw huts.

At about midnight on 14th February, Dai and his men landed at Cau-Kho. There were a large number of boats there which brought the rebels. A group of 300 men, all armed with sabres and spears, made their way towards the prison. Among those present were Bong, Hanh (Dai remaining at Cau-Kho to guard the boats), Nguyen van-Tran, son of Bong, Nguyen-van-Manh, son of Hanh, Nguyen-van-Dang, son of Bong, and Nguyen-van-Chieu, son of Dai.

Nguyen-van-Chieu managed to get only as far as the rue Mac-Mahon before˙ meeting the police, from whom he fled. He threw his weapons into the Cau-Kho stream.

Nguyen-van-Manh almost reached the prison, where he was killed. Nguyen-van-Tran, though wounded in the arm, face, and side, managed to get back to the boats. On the 15th, at 6 a.m., Dai took him back to Tan-Kieu. He was carried in a hammock from the bank to the paternal hut. He died on the 16th February. They told the registry office that he had died from the after-effects of the plague. Vo-van-tung, Bong's neighbour, acted as second witness to the declaration. The same Tung and Pham-van-Meo, a coolie in Hanh's service, buried Tran 150 metres from the hut.

Bong and Hanh reached home safe and sound, together with a dozen rioters who rested at Tan-Kieu before going

---

[1]'Society for the distribution of aid'; the name stresses the function of mutual help which existed in addition to its political and religious functions.

home. Three days later, Hanh cycled to Saigon to keep a watch on events.

Thus, although the family was cruelly tried by the loss of two of its number, it keeps up its revolutionary and anti-French feelings more violently than ever, and is only waiting for an opportunity to start again. Dai, who had taken part in the 1913 conspiracy, played an active rôle in last February's plot. And three days after the crime, Bong went to Saigon to see what had been achieved. Witnesses are positive. The various enquiries have been fruitful. At Hanh's house, two pairs of white trousers[1] with suspicious stains on them and a long-handled sabre, rebel clothing and weapons, were found. Dai had judged it prudent to disappear from Phuoc-Long after 15th February, and it was only possible to arrest him on 4th March. At Bong's house were found two long-handed sabres, a complete rebel outfit, the hammock used to carry Tran when he was wounded, a basket of inscribed amulets and two personal tax receipts in the names of Nguyen-van-Loi, of the village of Long-hau-Tay, and Le-van-Hieu of Tan-Kieu, hidden behind the altar of Buddha. From all the evidence, the whole of this family—though they naturally persist in denying it—took an active and violent part in the attack on the prison. (15)

Against the Russians in Manchuria

At the other extremity of the Chinese world, on the mountainous borders of North Manchuria, a popular organisation with numerous affinities to the secret societies, the Red Beards *(Hung-hu-zi)*, opposed penetration by Tsarist Russia.

We saw in Chapter 3 their 'code of honour', which underlined the 'justiciary brigand' character of these groups.

At the end of the nineteenth century, the Red Beards even tried to constitute a stable political formation both independent and highly democratic—an extremely rare instance in the history of the secret societies. In a sort of no man's land which escaped the control of either the

---

[1]The members of secret societies who attacked Saigon in February 1916 to free the emperor Phan-xich-Long wore white clothes, as we have seen.

Russian or the Chinese authorities, the district of Jeltuga, miners, gold-diggers, and trappers formed the 'Republic of Jeltuga'. At the time it aroused great interest among anarchist intellectuals in Western Europe. Articles full of its praise were included in the *Revue Blanche,* the *Correspondant,* etc. However it did not survive the combined operations of the Russian and Chinese armies.

But groups of Red Beards did withstand the Russian troops for a long time, and made life difficult for the quasi-colonial enterprises which Russia had been forced to undertake in Manchuria (in particular the Trans-Manchurian Railway).

A Russian encyclopedia of the period devoted an article to the Red Beards and this text, partisan as it is, reflects the prestige these outlaws had, even in the eyes of their Tsarist opponents.

In Manchuria, North China, and Korea in the Amur region and the Maritime Province, vagabonds and nomadic elements of the Chinese population who have fled from justice or from the despotism of the Chinese authorities and who secure the means of subsistence by looting and brigandry (in most cases, solely out of necessity) are known by the name of Red Beards. They show evidence of great solidarity one with another.

They direct their criminal activities primarily against the well-off of the towns and villages. It is only in extreme cases that they attack the small farmers.

In the majority of cases the Red Beards, having decided to make an attack on the fortune of a well-to-do Chinaman, kidnap him and demand a ransom. To attain their objectives they make use of numerous agents among the ordinary population, from which they come and with which they frequently maintain overt or secret contacts. It is to the ordinary population that they return once their operations are over.

Certain Chinese villages are entirely made up of settlements of former Red Beards who maintain contacts with their comrades who still practise brigandry.

Until the arrival of the Russians in Manchuria,[1] there had even been special insurance societies which entered into business relations with the Red Beards and guaranteed traders, in return for a payment, the completely safe passage and transport of goods.

In recent years, in Manchuria, the Red Beards have drawn attention to themselves by acts of brigandry against the population. The pretext for this was our troops' hunting down of the bandits. The Russian occupation of the country had indeed forced the Red Beards out into wilder and more isolated regions, away from the trade routes. Since they had for several years been increasing the number of acts of aggression committed against the East China Railway,[2] its employees and peoples along the route, the new situation created by the action of our troops could only irritate the outlaws.

In the winter of 1900, a revival of their activities was recorded. They gathered together in huge bands which hid in the largely unexplored gorges of the Changpai Shan mountains, and carried out a series of bold attacks against the railway and the population.

The military expedition led by Generals Kaul'bars, Verbitski, Fock, and Miscenko was crowned with success, but it was not until the autumn of 1907 that the most important gang leaders were captured.

The experience of the past few years has shown that the Chinese authorities are in no state to get rid of the Hunggu-zi; and Chinese troops are powerless, since for the most part they are recruited from former Red Beards, and they are moreover continually beaten by the rebels. This problem remains quite serious on our territory and in Manchuria, for in recent times, with the departure of the Russian troops,[3] the Red Beards have resumed their activities and are doing their utmost, at the expense of the population, to avenge their past failures. (16)

---

[1] The Russians had been in Manchuria since 1897. In December of that year, the Tsarist government had sent a squadron to occupy the roadstead of Port Arthur. Subsequently a Sino-Russian convention ceded the southern part of the Liaotung Peninsula to Russia on a 25-year lease.

[2] Or Trans-Manchurian, which connected Irkutsk and Vladivostok. It was constructed by Russia from 1896 onwards.

[3] In the Sino-Russian agreement of April 1902, Russia agreed to withdraw her troops from Manchuria.

CHAPTER SIX

In the Service of the Republican Cause

Under the Republican Banner

At the beginning of the twentieth century, modern universities appeared in China. Furthermore many young Chinese intellectuals went to study in Hong Kong or Japan. Certain professional soldiers of the 'New Army' formed by the imperial government on the Western model, and certain layers of the bourgeoisie, particularly the wealthy tradesmen who had emigrated to the Western colonies of South-East Asia and the whole Pacific coastline, began to join with the new intelligentsia in thinking that the struggle against the Manchus could no longer be sustained simply by nostalgia for former dynasties. China must look to the future, must adapt to the modern world. From now on when the Manchus were attacked it was certainly because they symbolised foreign domination but it was equally because they represented reactionary power.

The Kuomintang and the 'Three Principles of the People'

These new ideas were advocated by—for example — Sun Yat-sen, brother of a Chinese planter in Honolulu and a former student of the Hong Kong College of Medicine. In 1895 he founded an 'Association for the Rebirth of China' *(Hsing-chung-hui)*. Another anti-Manchu group was founded by Huang Hsing, a native of Honan, who, together with his Chinese fellow-students at Tokyo University, constituted an embryonic republican movement.

Henceforward, all the activity of these militants was to be directed towards the Republic. In 1905, the various groups combined to form the *T'ung-meng-hui* (Sworn League), which in 1912 became the Kuomintang, with Sun Yat-sen and Huang Hsing as the principal leaders.

The programme of the *T'ung-meng-hui*, formulated by Sun Yat-sen, is summed up in his famous 'Three Principles of the People' (or 'Triple Demism'):

—independence (and therefore the overthrow of the
Manchus);
—sovereignty (by the setting-up of a Western-style
parliamentary democracy);
—well-being (a vague formula implying in particular
an 'equalisation of rights on earth' which Sun
Yat-sen derived from the American socially-oriented
economist Henry George).

From then on the anti-Manchu struggle was thus
inseparable from the struggle for political and social
progress.

Very quickly, the T'ung-meng-hui had numerous
sections and numerous affiliated organisations, in China
as well as among Chinese émigrés overseas.

This new political orientation was not, moreover,
limited to old China. In these crucial years at the end
of the nineteenth and beginning of the twentieth century,
the whole of Asia was seething with similar new ideas.
The 'Young Turks' and the 'Young Persians' made no
division between national rebirth and progress. To
Japan, still elated from its victory over Russia in 1905,
came Philippine and Vietnamese revolutionaries. In
Tokyo itself, a whole group of radical intellectuals,
advocates of a pan-Asiatic policy of expansion which
would at the same time free other Asian peoples from the
Whites, supported the young revolutionaries of East Asia.

It is to one of these Japanese pioneers of revolutionary
pan-Asianism, half-secret agent, half-adventurer, Hirayama Amane, that we owe the earliest work available
on the secret societies in modern times. His book,[1]
published first in Japan and then in Shanghai in 1912,
immediately after the Republican Revolution, was the
fruit of the long-standing contacts he maintained with
the secret societies through militant Chinese revolutionaries he met in the course of journeys he made in
South-East Asia.

_____

[1]See the Bibliography at the end of this book.

A Great Revolutionary Potential

For the T'ung-meng-hui as for the other anti-Manchu republican groups, the secret societies were a considerable supporting force. They had long experience of the struggle against the imperial régime; they had cadres established and exerted a great influence on both the peasants and the urban poor.

'The potential revolutionary strength of the lower social strata was very great', declared Wu Yu-chang, one of the veterans of the revolutionary movement, in his recent autobiographical work on the 1911 Revolution and the republican movement in his native province of Szechuan. (1)

'I have compiled my *Study of the Origins and Diffusion of Sects and Societies* in order to provide elements of information for those who wish to save the country', wrote the militant republican, Tao Cheng-chang,[1] at the time. (2)

The desire to enrol the secret societies under the banner of the Republican Revolution is evident in the very rare 'Supplement on the Chinese Revolution' published in 1908 by *La Guerre Sociale*, organ of the Parisian socialist revolutionaries. This text is pseudonymously signed 'Keming-tan' (the Revolutionary Party), and was probably compiled by one of the young Chinese anarchists who then formed a very active group in Paris.

The feeling of solidarity is developed to the extreme in the Chinese, to the detriment, it is true, of individual initiative, and it is in that, above all, that they differ from Europeans. Because of it, associations have developed in China to an extraordinary extent, that the more individualistic West is far from having achieved. They are of all kinds: religious fraternities, family groups, mutual or corporate aid societies, among which the strangest are those of the beggars and bandits; they are infinite in number, have the most diverse aims, and encompass all interests. But alongside these more-

---

[1] Author of a previous article on the secret societies at the beginning of the twentieth century, originally presented in the form of a lecture given to members of the T'ung-men-hui living in the Dutch East Indies. See the bibliography.

or-less recognised or tolerated organisations, there exist secret revolutionary associations whose importance in the history of China has been great and whose activity in the contemporary movement is considerable.

Among these associations, which are extremely numerous, the most powerful are unquestionably the Elder Brothers and the Association of the Tree Dots, or Triads. They are also the oldest. They are both more than two hundred years old, and were founded at the beginning of the Manchu domination to combat it with a national programme. Their members are great in number and are to be found in every part of the Empire, but especially in the Yangtze region, in the case of the Elder Brothers, and in the South, in the case of the Triads... The Association of the Three Dots is closely involved in the present revolutionary movement.

These societies recruit their members from every class of Chinese society, but especially from among farmers, workers, and tradesmen. A great solidarity unites the members, who have an obligation of mutual aid. Strikes have often been started by them. If one of the members suffers an injustice, all the others are expected to get it avenged, and to this end the secret societies have on many occasions made use of terrorism. Mandarins have been victims of their attacks, an exceptional occurrence among the Chinese who oppose despotism with passive resignation rather than with boldness and revolt.[1]

These societies thus keep alive, in spite of the somnolence of Chinese life, a revolutionary tradition which the present revolutionaries have been able to put to good use; but, by themselves, they would not have been able to determine the the course of this movement which is so new in every way and which is turning contemporary China upside down. Patriots, nationalists, chauvinists even, faithful to the memory of the native dynasties, enemies of the detested Manchus, they aimed no higher than hounding the usurpers off the imperial throne. Nevertheless, forced to appeal to the people, using as their propaganda the hatred aroused by the mandarins, by their inevitable opposition to the established social order they took on a democratic colouring. The T'ai P'ing

---

[1] A rather bald assertion, typical enough of the state of mind of a young intellectual taking refuge in Paris. The risings and popular movements so important throughout the history of China continued, as we have seen, to play a fundamental rôle in the nineteenth century.

Kingdom of the Great Peace had tried to realise these new aspirations. Nevertheless, so as to give them real body, it was necessary for today's revolutionaries to penetrate this army which was all prepared for revolt and inculcate it with their propaganda and ideas, to give it a new life and a new programme of action. (3)

Close Co-operation

All the available documents do indeed confirm that, during the ten or fifteen years leading up to the Revolution of 1911, co-operation between the secret societies and the republican groups was very close, whether it was a question of organic co-operation or of joint action.

In many cases, the founders and militants of the revolutionary groups came from the secret societies or had been members previously. This was undoubtedly the case with Sun Yat-sen himself, who—according to a tradition still alive in Hong Kong which is reported by W.P. Morgan in his study of the Triad—was a member of that sect or at least of one of its offshoots in Honolulu. It was certainly true also of Cheng Shi-liang, friend and close collaborator of Sun Yat-sen, who was in 1885, with him, founder of the Association for the Rebirth of China. In the same way, the leaders of the secret societies participated, in 1907, in the foundation of the *Kung-chin-hui* (Society for Mutual Progress), a more or less dissident offshoot of the *Tung-meng-hui*, whose activities spread as far as Szechuan and throughout the middle basin of the Yangtze.

Apropos a discussion between militant revolutionaries in refuge in Tokyo about their co-operation with the secret societies, Wu Yu-chang wrote:

> From 1906 to 1908, owing to the fact that all the armed uprisings launched by the Revolutionary League had failed, certain people who were unsteady became disheartened. At that time the Revolutionary League in Japan was loosely organised. Sun Yat-sen, Huang Hsing and other leaders did not visit Japan very often, and without leadership the league was like a heap of sand. I decided to make frequent contacts with the league members from various provinces and often

held meetings with them. In this way real contact was maintained among the responsible league members of the various provinces, which prevented the league from dissolution and enabled it to persist in revolutionary struggle. Owing to the increasingly critical situation in China many revolutionaries in secret societies including my eldest brother fled the country and went to Japan. One day I had a talk with Chiao Ta-feng and some other members of the League.'The League recently,' I said, 'has been busying itself with preparations for uprisings and has practically forgotten the secret societies. Since many members of the secret societies from various provinces are now in Japan why not merge the secret societies of the whole country?' This suggestion was gladly accepted by all those League members who in the past had connections with the secret societies...

My eldest brother, who had a high standing in the Society of [Elder] Brothers in Szechuan, now on my recommendation became a member of the Revolutionary League. He was very pleased with my idea of merge. In the latter half of 1907, through the assiduous efforts of the League members, the leaders of the secret societies—the Society of Brothers, the Society of Filial Piety and Fraternity, the Triple Society, and the Triad Society— organised in Japan the *Kung Chin Hui* or the Society for Mutual Progress. Chang Pai-hsiang, leader of the Society of Filial Piety and Fraternity, was elected president of the new society, because as a senior member of the secret society, he was familiar with its responsible personnel in many places and had a big following in eastern Szechuan. Besides Chang, Chiao Ta-feng and Sun Wu were also leaders of the Society of Mutual Progress. At a later date they did well in establishing close relations with the secret societies in Hupeh and Hunan Provinces. The Society for Mutual Progress stood for the same principles as those of the Revolutionary League but it laid more stress on anti-Manchu propaganda. Considering that many of the top leaders of the secret societies came from landlord families or had close ties with the landlord class, the Society for Mutual Progress changed the slogan of 'equalisation of landownership' into 'equalisation of human rights' so that it might be easily accepted by all of them. Later, certain leaders of the Society for Mutual Progress, in defending this change, said that the latter slogan has a much broader concept and that it was much more suitable for propaganda among members

of secret societies. But facts proved that because the society
abandoned the original slogan, it was impossible to agitate
the broad masses of peasants. Therefore, in making the change
the society had really committed a mistake of far-reaching
consequences. The society's programme had serious defects.
Its organisation was loose and its component societies carried
out activities in their own way without following any central,
unified leadership. In spite of this, however, it succeeded in
rallying most of the secret societies in southern China under
the banner of opposition to the Manchus. This gave the
Revolutionary League a front organisation with a comparatively broad popular basis and helped to spread the revolutionary movement. (4)

Today, Wu Yu-chang is one of the doyens of the
Central Committee of the Communist Party. He has
come a long way since the time when he was elected
'Great Elder' of a secret society in Szechuan.

It was in Szechuan, too, that Chu Teh, future Commander-in-Chief of the Chinese People's Army, made his
political debut, when he joined the Society of Elder
Brothers with the aim of rallying its members to fight
for the Republic. He gave an account of this in his autobiography, taken down from his dictation by the American journalist Agnes Smedley in 1937-38.

The Political Début of General Chu Teh

Over a decade later, foreign and Chinese reactionaries
charged that the cell system of the Chinese Communist Party
was an alien idea imported by the Russian Bolsheviks. When
I mentioned this,[1] General Chu dismissed it as stupid if not
a deliberate fabrication. Or, he added, it was based on the
foreign imperialist assumption that the Chinese people were
a subhuman race without intelligence. The cell system, he
said, was as old as Chinese secret societies, and the Tung Meng
Hui had taken it over from the ancient Ko Lao Hui.

With no publication of its own in Yunnan, the Tung Meng
Hui smuggled literature into the interior from the coast.
Cadets[2] made copies and circulated important articles further.

---

[1] The speaker is Agnes Smedley, American Communist journalist.

[2] Chu Teh was at this time an officer cadet in the modern army ('New
Army') created by the Manchus early in the twentieth century.

'In our secret cell meetings we talked eternally about military uprisings. Theoretical political discussions were either feeble or non-existent. We were followers of the God of War. We were forced only by national developments to broaden our ideas.'

Class Prejudices

'These were times of great suffering for our people. There were floods, droughts, and famine, and of all calamities the dynasty was the greatest. Struggles of desperation began to break out. Starving peasants arose under the leadership of the Ko Lao Hui in many places, attacked landlords, tax collectors, government institutions, and seized food. The uprisings were mercilessly crushed by the government and the heads of the leaders were stuck on high poles before towns and villages. The Tung Meng Hui led sporadic revolutionary uprisings.

'The two streams of struggle never mingled.[1] The peasants fought their desperate battles alone, the Tung Meng Hui did the same. The Tung Meng Hui membership consisted primarily of intellectuals, with a sprinkling of merchants and other middle-class elements, whom class prejudices kept from uniting with the peasants. The result was that everyone was crushed...

It was the use of the Reform Armies against the revolutionary movement which forced the Tung Meng Hui, under orders from Dr. Sun Yat-sen, to begin secret political work among the troops of the Reform Armies. Chu Teh learned about the orders when he was assigned work by the Tung Meng Hui, in the Szechuan Regiment. This was dangerous work because the new viceroy of Yunnan, Li Ching-hsi, had organised an extensive espionage network against revolutionaries.

Chuh Teh Is Initiated

Chuh Teh began his new task by looking up the three soldiers with whom he had been friendly while serving as a private in the Szechuan Regiment, and whom he had suspected of

---

[1] These recollections which Agnes Smedley reports do not seem to correspond to reality on this point, at least as regards other provinces of China (see the preceding text).

being members of the Ko Lao Hui. The system of work which he developed became the pattern which the Chinese Communists used in later years. Sitting with these men in an isolated spot, he talked with them about their personal and economic problems and wrote letters for them to their families. From this, he went on to discuss national problems.

It wasn't long before they invited him to join the old Ko Lao Hui. He accepted and his initiation took place before many soldier members who gathered in an isolated temple in the hills. There he went through the ancient ritual, which included much kowtowing and drinking the blood oath of brotherhood. This oath was carried out in the following manner: first, Chuh Teh and the members giving the oath cut a vein in their wrists and allowed a few drops of their blood to fall into a bowl of wine. The bowl was then passed around and each of the principals in the ceremony drank a little. As this was done, Chu pledged deathless loyalty to the society's principles of brotherhood, equality, and mutual aid. He then learned the signs and passwords by which society members can, to the present day, identify one another anywhere. (5)

Inter-Penetration: a Success

In Kweichow province, the same formula was used to facilitate organic co-operation between the Republicans and the secret societies. Offshoots, satellite organisations, connected with the Republicans but fairly autonomous, allowed secret societies to feel more at home in them. One of these offshoots, in the little town of Chenchow, was well known. It was called the 'Mutual Aid Community' (*Tung-chi-kung*), a name which appealed to the tradition of solidarity which was so alive in the secret societies.

As an old man, Hu Show-shan, one of the veterans of the *T'ung-meng-hui*, wrote the following account:

At the end of the Manchu dynasty, the organisation and activities of the Society of Elder Brothers had become very important in this region of Kweichow. In 1902, when I was serving in the army, a militant from the north of Szechuan called Huang Shi-cheng received from the Association for the Rebirth of China, then directed by Sun Yat-sen in Hong Kong, the order to go to the Chenchow district to carry out an enquiry, make contacts, and get the movement going. Huang held an official position in the Society of Elder Brothers, and he used this to make friends and serve the revolutionary cause. The result of this work was the foundation in March 1905, in Chenchow, of the 'Mutual Aid Community'. Over 150 people attended the inaugural meeting.

As their 'mountain name' *(shan)*, the new group chose that of Sun Yat-sen; as 'lodge name' *(tang)*, that of the first Ming emperor; as 'river name' *(shui)*, that of Ch'eng-kung;[1] as 'perfume name' *(hsiang)* the slogan, 'Liquidate the Ch'ing'.[2] According to the membership register, there were 250 members at the start, but the number quickly increased to 14,000. I know that there were among them many members of the Society of Elder Brothers, and the work of liaison and organisation was carried out by members of that society. The new association was itself connected with the Society for the Study of Independence, which represented the Tung-meng-hui in Kwei-chow province. It can be assumed that the majority of the members of the Society for the Study of Independence were members of the Society of Elder Brothers. Otherwise it would have been difficult for such a society to get as many as 14,000 members.

The success of the 1911 Revolution in Kweichow was certainly the result of the wide contacts that the Society for the Study of Independence had in the province, and came too from the ardour and valour of the members of the Society of Elder Brothers, organised under the direction of the revolutionaries.

In the revolutionary struggles, nearly all the dangerous and perilous tasks were carried out by members of the Society of Elder Brothers. (6)

A Setback among the Émigrés

However, the Republicans' efforts to secure the help of the old anti-Manchu secret societies did not always meet with the same success.

---

[1]Cheng Ch'eng-kung or Koxinga, a Ming supporter who, in the seventeenth century, refused to ally himself with the Manchus. He set up an autonomous principality in Taiwan and probably belonged to the Triad.

[2]As we saw in Chapter 1, it was the custom of the Triad lodges to have four names. It was the same with the Elder Brothers, a fact which confirms that there were connections between the two organisations.

Sun Yat-sen, in his autobiography, writes, for example, that on his first trip to California in 1896, he was unable to dispel the apathy of sections of the Triad established among the Chinese of San Francisco:

Amongst the Chinese emigrants in America I found an even more sleepy atmosphere than in the Philippines. I crossed the continent from San Francisco to New York. On my way I stopped at various places for a few days—for ten days at the most—everywhere preaching that to save our mother-country from threatening destruction we must overthrow the Ch'ing dynasty, and that the duty of every Chinese citizen was to help to reconstruct China on a new democratic basis.

Although I spared no effort in this propaganda, the people to whom it was directed remained apathetic and little responsive to the ideas of the Chinese Revolution. At that time, however, there were fairly widespread amongst the Chinese emigrants the so-called 'Hung-men' societies, although by my time they had been reduced to little more than mutual aid clubs. Their history is as follows. The supporters of the Ming dynasty raised several rebellions against the Ch'ing dynasty, but always suffered defeat at the hands of the Imperial troops, and when, during the rule of K'ang Hsi, the Manchu dynasty reached the height of its strength, all the efforts of the supporters of the Ming dynasty proved to be doomed to failure. Some of them paid for their audacity with their lives, others managed to escape. Seeing the impossibility of overthrowing the Ch'ing, they seized then upon the idea of nationalism and began preaching it, handing it down from generation to generation. Their main object in organising the 'Hung-men' societies was the overthrow of the Ch'ing dynasty and the restoration of the Ming dynasty. The idea of nationalism was for them an auxiliary. They carried on all their affairs in profound secret, avoiding Government officials and hiding also from the Chinese intellectuals whom they looked upon as the eyes and ears of the Chinese government. Knowing the pyschology of the masses, the 'Hung-men' societies spread their nationalist ideas by means of various ploys, which had a great effect amongst the people. In the ideas they spread abroad, everything was based on arousing discontent with one's position and with existing inequality, and preaching the necessity for revenge.

Their passwords and watchwords were dirty and vulgar phrases, and Chinese intellectuals avoided them in disgust.

Party solidarity, which afforded them help when in trouble, and a certain co-ordination in their activities proved very helpful for wanderers and for various Chinese prodigal sons. Their nationalist ideas helped them in their struggle against the hated Ch'ing dynasty, and consequently fed their hopes of a restoration of the Ming dynasty.

The Chinese people were in constant conflict with the Imperial officials, and never abandoned their opposition to the Ch'ing dynasty. The watchwords: 'Down with Ch'ing!' and 'Long live Ming!' were near and dear to many Chinese. But the same cannot be said of our many Chinese emigrants, as they, being abroad in free country, had no necessity to organise societies of fighting character. Therefore in America the 'Hung-men' societies naturally lost their political colour, and became benefit clubs. Many members of the 'Hung-men' societies did not rightly understand the meaning and exact aims which their society pursued. When I approached them, during my stay in America, and asked them why did they want to overthrow the Ch'ing dynasty and restore the Ming dynasty, very many were not able to give me any positive reply. Later, when our comrades had carried on a protracted revolutionary propaganda in America for several years members of the 'Hung-men' societies at last realised they were old nationalist revolutionaries. (7)

A Common Cause: the Example of Ma Fu-yi

Over and over again, tirelessly, the Republicans attempted a series of unsuccessful attacks on the Manchus. Official Republican historiography lists eleven, of which only the last, that at Wuchang in central China (October 1911) was to succeed. In actual fact these attempts were far more numerous, and it was nearly always the case that they were combined actions of the revolutionaries and the secret societies.

The figure of Ma Fu-yi, a Triad leader in Hunan province who was soon to be a martyr of the Republican cause, symbolises this joint action. The account of his earlier activities, given recently by one of his old companions in arms, showed what ascendancy a secret society leader could have at that time among the people, and particularly with what authority he was capable of enforcing order among his fellow citizens. In this way he acted as a substitute for the weakened local administration.

Ma Fu-yi was born about 1865. His family were natives of the Village of the South, in the Siantang district of Hunan. His clan[1] was well known in the region, and had 20,000 members over an area of several dozen li. . . Among their number were rich merchants, land-owners, and members of the gentry; altogether they represented an important force.

Alone in the clan, Ma's relatives had been farmers for several generations, and they were looked down on by the rest. At Siantang Ma's father worked the land of one of the members of the clan, but after a quarrel he had left. He and his family had then found themselves without a roof over their heads or any land to farm and they had fallen into the greatest poverty.

One of their relations, a certain Liu, from Liling, presented him as a tenant to the landowner called Fu in the district. . . Ma took his wife and children, and, as Fu was a good man, the family settled at Liling.

Ma Fu-yi went to school for several years. He was able to write flowing letters and to put together short, simple compositions. As he grew up, he became courageous and resourceful. He was a fine talker and was capable of making his own decisions. If there were disputes or injustices in the village, he intervened informally and pronounced an equitable judgement. The people respected him for that. Complaints were often brought to him and he dealt with them at once, even to the detriment of his farm work. But his brothers and his father had had enough of seeing him behave like this. They gave him some money and asked him to leave with his family. So Ma went to the next town, Lookow.

It was a big prosperous commercial town with more than 10,000 inhabitants. Every year at the time of the festivities of the 1st, 5th, and 8th months there were very lively religious processions. On these occasions the big merchants from afar frequented the gambling-houses. They sometimes staked up

---

[1]In South China at this time clans were still very active social groups. They contained all those descended from the same ancestor and possessed temples, land, etc.

to tens of thousands of *yuans*.[1] These games lasted three, four—even ten days. The prosperity of the district depended on the gambling and on the sums spent on it, so when vagrants, bandits, and brigands came into the town and started scuffles, the trading community took fright.

A large number of the gaming houses had been opened by secret society leaders. Ma had already enrolled in a society in his village and had been its chief. The other leaders knew that Ma was very poor, and to help him out they contemplated deducting a certain percentage from the profits of the gaming houses. The tradesmen, anxious to maintain order in the town, knew that Ma had always been a good man and that he held a high position in the secret societies. The head of the merchants' guild, a certain Ma—from the same clan as Ma Fu-yi had a conversation with him, and asked for his help and co-operation. Ma Fu-yi accepted very willingly. One day, he invited the leaders of the secret societies to a banquet in the biggest tavern in the town. Once they were seated he said: 'Gambling is one of the sources of the development of trade at Lookow. The government has not banned it, and we benefit from its magnanimity. But gambling attracts good-for-nothings like thieves, kidnappers, and even bandits who add violence to theft. These men torment the travelling merchants and the local population. This is a dangerous situation; we must look for ways of remedying it.'

Together they prepared the following secret clauses, which they decided to apply exactly as they stood: no cheating, no fighting, no kidnapping, brigands forbidden to come nearer than 20 li from the town, etc...

The application of these regulations brought peace back to the town and Ma's republic became even better.[2] Many inhabitants of Lookow joined him; his prestige spread to the districts of Lilang, Siantang, and Liuyang, and even as far as the Yangtze, Hupeh, and other provinces. The number of his followers reached 10,000.

---

[1] The *yuan*, or Chinese silver dollar, was worth about the same as an American dollar.

[2] This episode is typical of the secret societies' tendency to oppose the official order and replace it by a fairer social order, brought about by their quasi-official arbitration.

The society to which Ma belonged was a branch of the Triad, which had no uniform internal rules. Each leader could open lodges as he thought fit. The different lodges of the society had each to carry the four names corresponding to the four symbolic categories *(biao-chi)*: *shan, tang, hsiang,* and *shui*. Each leader was free to choose his four names. The *shan* (mountain) name of the lodge organised by Ma was *K'un Lun shan* (K'un Lun Mountain[1]); its *tang* (lodge) name was *chung-yi-tang* (Loyalty and Justice Lodge;)[2] its *hsiang* (perfume) name was *lai-ju-hsiang* (perfume which comes thus); and its *shui* (water) name was *tsz-ju-shui* (water which goes away thus).

Leidashi and Yuanchow are separated only by a river and are not far from each other. The local product was lime, for which more than twenty kilns had been constructed, three quarters of which belonged to a certain Huang, of Majiahe. A thousand workers worked in these kilns, and many belonged to secret societies. Vagrants, local good-for-nothings, and bandits had also found their way in, and this mixture of good and bad men was the cause of constant difficulties. Huang, after discussing the matter with the foremen, asked Ma to become foreman-in-chief of all the kilns...

And once more, Ma restored law and order.

At the beginning, Ma had recruited peasants, workers, and small tradesmen. In time, rich men and members of the gentry joined him. Although this association was very mixed, it went from strength to strength.

In February 1904; Huang Hsing[3] and others organised at Changsha the *Hua-hsing-hui* (Society for the Renewal of China.)[4] They decided to contact the secret societies to plan an uprising. They had heard Ma talked about and they would have liked to ally themselves with him. (8)

---

[1]Great chain of mountains in Central Asia, long believed by the Chinese to be the centre of the earth.

[2]This is the name of one of the main meeting-halls of the fortress where the justiciary-brigands, heroes of the famous medieval romance, the *Shui-hu,* used to meet.

[3]One of the leaders of the Republican Party (see above, page 135).

[4]In 1905, the *Hua-hsing-hui* joined with a society run by Sun Yat-sen and other anti-Manchu movements to form the *Tung-meng-hui* (see above, page 135) which was to organise the 1911 Revolution and to become the Kuomintang.

The preparations for joint action did in fact go quite a long way. Members of Ma Fu-yi's secret society on the one hand, and Huang Hsing and his friends on the other, planned for 1904 a general uprising of the whole province of Hunan. The scheme envisaged five simultaneous points of attack. Huang Hsing kept Changsha, the provincial capital, for himself, and entrusted the action in the local areas to Ma Fu-yi. But the police uncovered the plot. The following year, Ma Fu-yi organised another plot, which the police again got wind of. He was captured and executed.

This episode has remained particularly well known in China, and Ma Fu-yi's memory is still venerated in Hunan. But his was not an isolated case.

In 1906, the coal-miners' insurrection at Pingsiang in central China was organised by the T'ung-meng-hui and the Society of Elder Brothers.

In 1908, the attack carried out by Huang Hsing and Sun Yat-sen against the little town of Hokow, on the borders of Tonking, only succeeded (for a few days at least) thanks to the intervention of the 300 members of a local secret society, whose chief organised the assault and for a time managed to make himself master of the town.

Many similar cases could be cited.

Difficulties of a 'United Front'

In spite of their determination and their efforts to work out a political ideology, the modernist intellectuals and young officers could not bring about victory on their own. There were only a handful of them, and they were regarded favourably only in a social stratum which was itself little developed—the bourgeoisie. They needed the support of the millions of humble town-dwellers, of the tens of millions of peasants, whose mass risings had so often in the past brought about the fall of dynasties and 'kings of perdition'. But this broad 'united front' against the Manchus was not easy to attain. The civil and military officials of the revolutionary party were for the most part sons of rich bourgeois, literati, wholesale traders, and

landowners; very few came from the people, as did Sun
Yat-sen and Chu Teh.

Leaders in Exile; a little-changed Base

Furthermore, many of the leaders of the modern political groups were not even on Chinese soil, but were in
Japan or the overseas émigré colonies. This was the case
with Sun Yat-sen, Huang Hsing, and Wu Yu-chang.

The secret societies had a firm-based hierarchy at their
disposal; they exercised a considerable influence over the
people; the prestige conferred on them by 250 years of
uninterrupted struggle against the Manchus was intact;
and they had immense experience of underground
activity. They, alone, were in a position to secure popular
support for the young intellectuals. As we have seen, they
did in fact—in the fifteen years which preceded the 1911
Revolution—play an indispensable part as 'half-way
house' between the militant revolutionaries and the
people.

But if study of the texts shows clearly the importance of
their contribution to the Republican cause, it still leaves
many problems unsolved.

As we have seen from the text by Wu Yu-chang and
from the example of Kweichow, the formula chosen for
co-operation had been not the direct affiliation of secret
members to a Republican organisation but the creation'
of 'sub-branches', more or less linked to the T'ung-meng-
hui and other modern revolutionary parties.

Thus the grades of the Society of Common Progress
were the same as those of the Elder Brothers; and the
Mutual Aid Community of Kweichow had the same
four-name system (mountain, lodge, river, perfume) as
the Triad.

In these sub-branches, the atmosphere remained similar to that of the old secret societies, and the existence
of these transitional groups suggests that people's feelings
had evolved less quickly than the objective content of
their political activity.

It is of this intellectual evolution, this ideological muta-
tion, that one would like to know more. In placing them-

selves at the service of the Republican Revolution, had the members of the secret societies really abandoned their platform of restoring the Ming? Did they clearly envisage the prospect of a renewal of China through the establishment of a modern republic! Probably not all of them, nor even most of them did. But it would be interesting to know the intellectual route taken by a man like Ma Fu-yi.

The Secret Societies' Influence on the Republican Movement

This influence was not one-way. The secret societies certainly left their mark upon the T'ung-meng-hui and then on the Kuomintang. Was it not they who contributed, for example, the taste for passwords and 'stage-managed' effects, the feeling for hierarchy and for the prestige of the leader, the faith in the virtue of blows?

In 1914, Sun Yat-sen tried to impose upon all the members of the revolutionary party an oath of personal allegiance, confirmed by the impressing of finger prints. A certain very clear *blanquisme* in the whole career of Sun Yat-sen up till his co-operation with the Communists in 1923 could very well be a reflection of his long and intimate association with the secret societies.

In other respects, the influence of the secret societies seems to have tended in the direction of political moderation.

The real revolutionary 'kernel' of the Tung-meng-hui was probably composed of only a handful of militants grouped around Sun Yat-sen. The other Republican societies—Society for Mutual Progress in the Yangtze region, Society for the Study of Independence in Kwei-chow—were only loosely joined to this kernel. But their range of influence in China itself was probably far greater than that of the little group of exiles in Tokyo. It was these other groups—part satellites, part rivals of the Tung-meng-hui—which were in touch with the secret societies. The programme of these parallel groups was more moderate than that of the Tung-meng-hui itself, for example on the agrarian question (of which the programme of the Society for Mutual Progress made no mention).

But the secret societies were too complex, socially and ideologically, and too ambiguous, to have been able to play an unequivocally 'progressive' rôle. They co-operated with the advanced Republicans, certainly, but it appears that they were also in touch with their bitter rivals, the constitutional monarchists. The leaders of that movement, K'ang Yu-wei and Liang Ch'i-ch'ao, dreamt of a authoritarian monarchy on the Japanese pattern, which would remain faithful to Confucianism while adapting itself to the modern world. They too had had to go into exile in Japan after trying in vain in the summer of 1898 to carry out their programme of modern reform. They too were very active until 1911, as much among the Chinese abroad as in China itself, where they had many sympathisers among the gentry.

They too were to try to secure the support of the secret societies by making use of the influence exercised over them by certain elements of the land-owning class.

The story is told, for example, of one of the leading reformists, Tang Cai-chang, who received from a rich Chinese trader in Singapore a large sum (300,000 taels) intended to buy arms for an Elder Brothers uprising in the Yangtze region. He spent most of the money in the pleasure-houses of Shanghai, and the planned uprisings could not take place.

In a more general way, it appears that, from Tokyo, K'ang Yu-wei and Liang Ch'i-ch'ao were in regular contact with the secret societies and were even members.

However, their efforts to separate these organisations from the advanced Republicans had only limited success. In the main, the co-operation between secret societies and Republicans was firmly established; it was to continue during the 1911 Revolution.

The 1911 Revolution

In October 1911, after so many vain attempts, the Republican insurrection in Wuchang was successful. The success can only be explained by that summer's change of camp on the part of the moderate gentry, who had decided to break with the Manchus once and for all. This adjustment of the equilibrium of the political forces was precipitated by the 'railways affair', in which the gentry vigorously opposed the Manchu government's takeover of the railways then under construction in central China from private provincial funds. What was feared was that these railways would be mortgaged with foreign banks.

Thus reformists and revolutionaries found themselves temporarily in the same camp. Manchu power could not hold out against this double pressure. A local Republican success at Wuchang, in central China, set off a chain reaction in all the provinces. Popular risings liquidated Manchu power almost everywhere.

The secret societies made an active contribution to victory. In several cases their leaders formed part of the temporary provincial governments which set themselves up spontaneously. In Hunan, for example, the following account shows both the rôle of the secret societies and the gentry's refusal to tolerate this popular alliance for long.

On 22nd October 1911, a bill was posted with the heading: '*Yamen*[1] of the Head of the Military Government of Hunan, Republic of China.' It announced that the head of the military government *(Dudu)* was Jiao Ta-feng, and his assistant Chen Tsuo-hsin.

At the time this new provincial administration was set up, nothing was beyond the preliminary stage; no laws had been prepared; everything seemed to be happening at once... A group of young student volunteers looked after things, each dealing with a particular field.

Civil servants of the former régime found the system an excuse for veiled sarcasm; ambitious men jumped at the opportunity to write to the leaders and to try to influence the offices of the new governor.

---

[1] Group of official buildings of a town or administrative area.

The *Changsha Journal*, which was in the hands of the former ruling party,[1] fulminated against those who 'carry out their civic duties as best they can', criticised the improvised administration, and declared that in their view the whole thing was nothing but 'the staging of an opera'. . . This sort of reasoning finally prevailed, and after a long period of silence cliques of the gentry again raised their heads. Former civil servants shook the dust from their mandarin caps and congratulated themselves on their criticism, whilst the young people left the *Yamen* to work elsewhere.

Jiao Ta-feng was originally the chief of a secret society which had succeeded in assembling people and maintaining contacts everywhere on a huge scale.[2] At the time of the armed rising at Liuyuang (1906), he had been supported by all the forces of his secret society, and very many of them sacrificed their lives on that occasion.

When Jiao was chosen as governor, his comrades in arms arrived in Changsha en masse. They milled freely around the *Yamen*, creating an excited atmosphere.

The Changsha *Yamen* was an administrative centre in the grand style, an imposing and magnificent building. Jiao was not the right man for a place. His informality surprised everyone. With such an unsophisticated governor, relations between great and small could not help being good, but it was precisely in that, in the eyes of the gentry, that the scandal consisted. Rumours circulated according to which the governor's *Yamen* had become the Liangshanpo Forest,[3] and that the work done there was like the Wu-Kang-sai.[4] Jiao Ta-feng and Chen Tsuo-hsin were compared to Chen She and Wu-Kuang.[5] They were accused of demagogy and of planning a *coup d'état*.

Mei Hsing, an opponent of the revolutionaries, ordered several dubious characters who were under his command to

---

[1]i.e. of supporters of the monarchy which had just been overthrown by the revolutionaries.

[2]Wu Yu-chang, in the text quoted previously, suggests that Jiao Ta-feng had the rank of 'grand master' in the Elder Brothers.

[3]Forest where the brigand-heroes of the *Shui-hu* romance had established their hideout.

[4]Uprising which took place in Hunan province at the end of the Sui period (A.D. 598-618).

[5]Rebels who rose up against the Ch'in emperor Shih Huang Ti (221-209 B.C.)

gather together a few vagrants of the district and to take them to the Heh-feng match factory, in the northern part of the town, to provoke a riot and burn and loot the houses. Subsequently they persuaded the men of the conservative party to throw out warnings to the governor himself that if he did not take the situation in hand the riot would continue.

Chen Tsuo-hsin, Jiao's assistant, did not shirk his duty. He hurried to quell the riot. The moment he arrived at the factory, he was killed. The crowd, led by one of the bandits, forced their way into the governor's *Yamen*. Jiao did not yet know that Chen had been murdered. He came out to speak to the workers in a friendly way, and was immediately killed. (9)

This was not an isolated case. In the autumn of 1911, the advanced revolutionaries had been able to seize power equally in the provinces and at the level of the central government set up in Nanking. Sun Yat-sen had been elected temporary president of the Republic. But the moderate gentry, once rid of the Manchus, intended to avoid being over-run.

Early in 1912 Sun Yat-sen was ousted and replaced by Yüan Shih-K'ai, a general and high Mandarin, Confucian in outlook—clearly a man of the *ancien régime*. Events in Nanking followed the same pattern as those in Changsha. The modernist Republicans' success had been fragile and ephemeral. China was about to enter a period of military dictatorship which made it a Republic only in name.

The 'Second Revolution'

During the summer of 1913, the Left made a final attempt. This was the 'second revolution' in the course of which Sun Yat-sen tried to raise against Yüan Shih K'ai certain provinces of the South whose armies had remained faithful to him. He failed again, and once more had to go into exile. However, he had been able to count on a peasant rising which, at the same moment, was trying to attack Yüan Shih K'ai from the rear in the North-West provinces: the Pai Lang insurrection, from the name of one of its leaders.[1] Once again, the Association of Elder Brothers provided the best troops.

---

[1] It is inexact to call this rising (as do many Western and even Chi-

Pai Lang demanded the departure of Yüan Shih K'ai, called for the formation of a 'good government', and took once more the traditional slogan of the secret societies: 'strike at the rich and aid the poor'.

Even this hostile account left by a British consul bears witness to the vigour of this movement which Yüan took almost two years to quell.

'White Wolf is Recruiting'.

The number of burnt-out ruins of hamlets, farmsteads, and huts' along the trail we had just traversed could not fail to attract one's notice, and enquiries elicited the fact that they were the result of the passage of the terrible 'White Wolf' rebels, who passed in and out of Shenshi in scattered bands by these out-of-the-way mountain trails in 1914. During our wanderings through Shenshi and Kansu we often found ourselves travelling in the footsteps of this devastating horde, whose trail of desolation could be traced in the ruins of farms, villages, and towns from the border of Honan to the confines of the Kokonor. Their lootings, burnings, and killings recall the depradations of the T'ai P'ing and Mahomedan rebels who devastated N.W. China, south and north of the Ch'inling Shan respectively, fifty years ago.[2]

This terrible horde of bandits or rebels was an aftermath of the rebellion of 1913. It consisted of an organised and well-equipped nucleus of a few thousand fighting men, disbanded soldiery from the Yangtze Valley and Secret Society men from Honan, together with many thousands of local adherents drawn from amongst the brigands, soldiers, and bad characters of the provinces through which they passed. The four words 'Pai Lang Chao Liang' (White Wolf is recruiting) passed secretly up and down the Han Valley, and recruits from all quarters flocked to join the band. After 30,000 of Yüan

---

nese historians) 'the White Wolf Movement'. As recent Soviet works have shown, the rebel leader was called Pai Lang. *Pai* is a common family name (though it can also mean 'white'); this first name, Lang, was written with a character meaning 'pale'. It was to discredit him, and to create around him an atmosphere of terror, that his government opponents replaced the ideogram *Lang* by another pronounced in the same way but meaning 'wolf'. The author of the text here quoted thus uses the expression 'White Wolf' wrongly. See *Voprosy Istorii* (Historical Questions), 1960, no. 2.

[2] An allusion to the great revolt of Chinese Muslims in Kansu and Shenshi provinces in the years 1865-75.

Shih-k'ai's best Northern troops had failed to crush these rebels in Honan, they burst through into the Han Valley via the rich mart of Laoho K'ou, where a foreign missionary was murdered in the sacking of the city, and early in 1914 worked through the mountains into Central Shenshi. Hsian, with its mighty walls,[1] withstood the raiders as it had withstood the Mahomedans fifty years earlier, and the horde drove on almost unopposed through Western Shenshi into Southern Kansu, looting, burning, and killing. The massacres of Chinese non-combatants were appalling, and the raiders, many of them mere youths, richly dressed in looted silks and jewellery and armed with modern rifles and Mauser pistols, rivalled in their cruelty and lust for indiscriminate slaughter the most terrible of Chinese rebels of days gone by. The object of the raid into the North West seems to have been the stocks of opium in Shenshi and Kansu. The resistance they met with and the measures taken to deal with them reflect no credit on the Chinese Government of the time and it is a common rumour that many high officials were privy to the raid and shared in the loot which was brought back to Honan. It was not until they reached the Mohomedan districts of Kansu near the Kokonor border that they suffered any serious loss, and that was mainly at the hands of the Mahomedan population of those parts, who are not accustomed to permit themselves to be looted and killed without showing fight, and from the hardships of the long forced marches through that wild region, rather than owing to the action of any Government troops. Eventually the survivors straggled back with their loot through Shenshi to their homes in Honan and Anhui. The Chinese officials assert that the White Wolf himself, who appears to have been an ex-military officer from the Yangtze armies,[2] was captured and executed.

The failure of the Shenshi troops, mostly revolutionary levies of Ko Lao Hui men and ex-brigands, of much the same type as the raiders, to deal with the White Wolf rebels was to be expected; but the failure of the Northern Army opposed to them in Honan in the winter of 1913–14 seems at first sight difficult to account for. The rebels were of course much more mobile than the Government troops, as they

[1] Principal city of North China, ancient capital of the T'ang (A.D. 618- 905).
[2] i.e. the Republican army which rose up against Yüan Shih-k'ai in 1913.

lived on the country by taking what they wanted and impressed men and animals everywhere to carry their transport. Then again, their lives being at stake, they could be depended on to fight when cornered, whereas it is difficult to induce the Chinese soldier to close with his enemy in a fight of this kind in which he has no interest. Where not an ex-brigand, the Chinese soldier is often a good fellow in most respects, but he is apt to be too sensible to be willing to run the risk of getting killed without adequate reason. Hence battles between rebels and Government troops in China usually consist in the discharge of large quantities of ammunition at a safe distance from one another. It is the civilian inhabitant of the raided towns and villages who gets killed if he does not manage to escape in time to his *chaitzu*[1] in the mountains. (10)

It is thus clear that the historic dynamism of these archaic groups was far from being exhausted at the time of the Republican Revolution, even if all aspects of their intervention in Chinese politics in this period are not precisely known.

On the day after his election as first president of the Chinese Republic, Sun Yat-sen celebrated in Nanking, the new capital of China freed from the Manchus, a solemn quasi-religious service to salute the spirits of the great Ming emperors who, in the fourteenth century, after the expulsion of the Mongols, had established their capital in the city. All contemporaries interpreted this ceremony as homage paid to the secret societies' 250 years of struggle against the foreign Ch'ing dynasty. History had taken a step forward; a new political system had replaced the Empire, and there was no longer any question of restoring the old Ming dynasty. The historical mission of the Chinese secret societies had thus come to an end.

---

[1]Refuge.

CHAPTER SEVEN

The Chinese Revolution (1919–1949)

In thirty years, the Chinese political scene was utterly transformed.

New social forces came into the foreground: there was the modern commercial bourgeoisie which had already played a major rôle in the 1911 Revolution and whose vigour was far from exhausted; there was the young intelligentsia, avid for knowledge and political action, patriotic, and fundamentally hostile to the traditional Chinese past; and in addition there was the industrial proletariat, still not large in numbers but concentrated in a few large cities and holding key positions in the economy (railways, ports, mines).

New ideologies gained ground: modern nationalism, sympathy for Western democracy, but more widely Marxism and socialism.

Then again, new forms of political action replaced the peasant risings and petitions to the emperor. Political parties were organised: the Kuomintang, the party of the bourgeoisie though for a while it figured as the great national party; and, above all, the Communist Party.

Over and over again, the entire country was shaken by violent waves of unrest, the 'movements' (*yün-tung*) which combined, in a novel fashion, street demonstrations, worker or student riots , and the boycotting of foreign goods. One such was the '4th May Movement' of 1919, in protest against the decision of the Versailles Conference to hand over to Japan the former German rights and possessions in China, instead of restoring them to China. Another was the '30th May Movement' of 1925, in protest against the shooting of unarmed demonstrators by the British police in Shanghai, which claimed several dozen victims. The city was immobilised for three months and 500,000 workers all over China came out on strike in sympathy.

After 1927, above all, another kind of political struggle appeared: revolutionary war, supported mainly by the peasantry, but altogether different from former risings in that it combined armed combat with a new political theory, and in that it was also directed by a political party.

These new forces, new ideas, and new forms of political struggle were to bring about the Chinese Revolution in five clearly defined stages:

1. *The Movement of 4th May 1919,* which was in effect the radical intellectuals' declaration of war on the old China. In its wake, some turned to Marxism (the Communist Party was founded in 1921).

2. *The Revolution of 1924-27,* directed against the 'war-lords', heirs of Yüan Shih-k'ai. Sun Yat-sen's Kuomintang accepted Communists as members and with their help led a military expedition against the feudal North, made itself master of almost the entire country, but—in the spring of 1927—abruptly broke with its Communist allies as soon as their dynamism seemed to threaten the propertied classes.

3. *The Civil War of 1927-35,* in the course of which the revolution's centre of gravity moved from the towns out into the country. It was between the Kuomintang, which had by then become master of China, and the Communists. The Communists tried to establish a soviet régime among the poor peasants of South China. They were finally defeated and had to retreat, in 1935, to the other end of the country. It was the famous and historic Long March.

4. *The War of Resistance against Japan (1937-45),* in the course of which the passivity of the Kuomintang, now withdrawn to Chungking in the south-west, contrasted with the activity of the Communists and peasant guerrillas whom the latter encouraged behind enemy lines.

5. *The Renewal of the Civil War between the Kuomintang and the Communists,* after the Second World War; the collapse of the régime of Chiang Kai-shek and the coming of the People's Republic of China.

The Secret Societies at the Beginning of the Workers' Struggles

Even this very brief resumé serves to indicate that from then on the secret societies appeared as archaic and outmoded groups. Their dynamism seemed exhausted; their historic mission accomplished. They had to make way for other groups waging social and political struggles by more modern methods. But were things as simple in reality?

In the cities their rôle was indeed completed. At the very beginning of the history of the workers' struggles they had certainly exercised a powerful influence: this was true of the Hong Kong strike of 1885 against French intervention (Triad); insurrectional strikes by the Pingsiang miners in 1906 and 1915 (Triad); the Han-yang arsenal strike in 1913 (Lao-jun Society, from the name of a Taoist divinity); the Shanghai carpenters' strike in 1918 (Green Band); the Shanghai strike in support of the 4th May Movement (Triad – more and more often known as the Red Band, or Green Band); etc.

The first militant trade-unionists – about 1920 at the time of the founding of the Communist Party – were interested in the secret societies' influence in the sphere of labour. One of the first Communists assigned to trade-union work, the young student Li Chi-han, was said to have joined the Red Band so as to get in closer touch with the workers.

Teng Chung-hsia, another Communist intellectual and one of the founders of the modern workers' movement in the 1920s, was struck by the secret societies' capacity for struggle:

> Among the lower classes of Chinese society, there exist organisations of the 'secret society' type, like, for example, the Green Band, the Red Band, the Elder Brothers, the Triad, etc. The history of these organisations is too long to be told here. They are much more highly developed than the associations of a provincial nature.[1] They have a leader, an ordered system, secret signs and passwords... Those who enter these organisations have to undergo secret trials.

[1]The writer has just been speaking of workers' guilds organised on the basis of common provincial origin.

The rootless life caused by unemployment and insolvency makes the lower classes of society seek to form this sort of organisation to help one another, resist government persecution, and protect their personal existence. They are also used by the capitalists and the gentry to combat their personal enemies.

These societies frequently use military combat methods both in hand-to-hand fighting and in the use of arms. In the majority of cases the leaders are professional criminals...

As regards their internal organisation, they are constructed on the model of clan societies: 'Grand Dragon', 'Second Dragon'... The divisions between masters and disciples are very clear and discipline is very strict. These societies of the lower classes imitate all the monarchic and patriarchal principles of the upper classes.

Naturally, the great mass of members of these societies soon become cannon-fodder in the battles between the different leaders and instruments for the making of their profits...
(1)

At all events, the appearance of modern workers' organisations, the impetus of the labour movement, the development of a working-class consciousness, and the influence of the Chinese Communists among the workers were to mean the redundancy of the secret societies. They played no part in the big strikes such as the Hong Kong seamen's strike of 1922, nor, for stronger reasons, in the pan-Chinese Work Congresses held regularly between 1922 and 1927.

Deprived of their mass support, they were rapidly to degenerate into an occult force, greedy for clandestine profits, for influence and intrigue, ready to attach themselves to the forces of social reaction.

From Alliance with Reactionary Forces to Gangsterism

In Shanghai – a great industrial centre, principal home of the conservative bourgeoisie, and international vice capital – Chiang Kai-shek and the right-wing of the Kuomintang decided, in 1927, to get rid of workers' organisations and Communist cadres, and this in spite of the fact that it was thanks to the insurrectional strike

fomented by these elements that Chiang and his movement had been able to occupy the city.[1] They made
approaches to secret societies, the Green Band and Red
Band. This collusion was strongly denounced at the time.
For example, in the *China Forum*, a left-wing Shanghai
review, the American journalist Harold Isaacs wrote, in
1932, about the support which the secret societies
continued to give to the Kuomintang after 1927 to help
it keep control of the working classes:

Shanghai: Trafficking, Smuggling, and Crime
Chief among the instruments of the Kuomintang used to
keep the reaction firmly in the saddle have been the notorious
gangs of Shanghai, with their affiliations in other big cities of
China. To understand the character of the Shanghai gangs,
it is necessary to combine the characteristics of the Society
of December Tenth as utilised by Louis Bonaparte, the Russian Black Hundred, and the modern Chicago variety of
racketeers and criminal gunmen.

Shanghai's foremost organisation, known as the Green
Circle, has an unknown membership, estimates of which
range from 20,000 to upwards of 100,000 with the probabili-
ties in favour of the smaller figure. The gangs deal in human
slaves, opium traffic, kidnappings, blackmailing, gambling,
gun-running, protection rackets, and plain, everyday murder.

The rank and file of these gangs include riff-raff of the
slum proletariat, most of the detectives and policemen of the
French Concession, International Settlement, and Chinese
municipality, military officers in the local garrison commander's headquarters, officers of the Bureau of Public
Safety, minor politicians and jobholders, most factory foremen and labour contractors, Kuomintang 'labour leaders'
(trade union officials)[2] as well as many petty merchants. The
lower strata of the gangs carry on all the remunerative activities listed above. Because these gangs are also politically
utilized on behalf of the reaction by its leaders they have also
drawn into their membership bankers, rich businessmen,
highly placed politicians, and Kuomintang officials.

---

[1] It is these events that serve as a backcloth to Andre Malraux' novel,
La Condition Humaine.

[2] The trade unions had passed under the direct control of the Kuomintang and Chiang Kai-shek since the latter's break with the
Communists in 1927.

At the head of these oganisations, with their widespread ramifications (as to the Red Circle in Hankow), are three men: Tu Yueh-sen, Hwang Ching-yung, and Chang Siao-ling. The 'Big Three', as they are not infrequently referred to in the Chinese press, are the lords and masters of the societies, which are in feudal, patriarchal form, organised in 'layers' or 'generations'. They are also the supreme rulers of the French Concession, in which all their activities centre. As a matter of fact the French authorities derive tremendous wealth from the activities of the Gangs and in return the administration is turned over to them. Tu Yueh-sen is a leading member of the French Municipal Council.

The three leaders, up to about a year ago, divided Shanghai among themselves and worked more or less in harmonious conjunction. But an internal struggle, begun over opium spoils, resulted in a strengthening of Tu Yueh-sen at the expense of Hwang Ching-yung. Tu emerged from the fight as the virtual uncrowned Tsar of Shanghai...

The 'White Terror'

Prior to 1927 the gangs of Shanghai generally confined their activities to opium and slave traffic, working in conjunction with the then-overlord, Sun Chuan-fang, a feudal militarist of the old type. It was not until the reaction set in against the rising Revolution in April 1927 that the gangs emerged as a political instrument of the first order.

With the Nationalist Armies still far from Shanghai, the workers of the city had risen, armed, and driven the forces of Sun Chuan-fang from the city. When Pei Chung-hsi, the Kwangsi general, arrived in Shanghai on 22nd March, 1927, most of the workers who then controlled the city were still unaware of what was going on behind the scene and were still under the delusion that the 'Nationalist' Armies had come to liberate them and that Chiang Kai-shek was their leader. Most of them therefore laid down their arms and turned the city over to the 'properly constituted Nationalist authorities'.

Two days later, following the Nanking incident,[1] Chiang came down to Nanking, and held his conferences, with the

---

[1] On 26th March 1927, Nanking had been bombarded by the British fleet following incidents in which Nationalist soldiers who had just arrived in the city had been involved.

bankers of the city. As a result of the rapprochement there effected, the reign of terror against the revolutionary workers was immediately launched. Those who had not surrendered their arms were promptly hunted down and slaughtered—not by Chiang's soldiers, however, who still thought they were for, and not against, the masses. Nor could the foreign soldiers be given the job since the echoes of 30th May, 1925[1] were still too sharp to be ignored. So the job of slaughter was turned over to the gangs, in whom the bourgeoisie found a ready tool.

At the head of the execution squads were Chang Siao-ling, then No. 1 gangster, and Yang Hu, today a member of the C.E.C. of the Kuomintang in Nanking, who was then Shanghai Garrison Commander, appointed by Chiang Kai-shek. Associated with these White Terror chiefs at that time was a man named Chen Chuen, secretary to Chang Siao-ling and private secretary to Tu Yueh-sen.

Working in close co-operation with the foreign police forces in Shanghai, the gangs hunted down and butchered thousands of revolutionary workers and intellectuals in all sections of the city. That first wave of terror is estimated to have cost the lives of at least 4,000 young men and women. It is interesting to note that when Chiang retired momentarily from the scene in August and some of the leaders had to efface themselves temporarily, Chen Chuen became Professor of Religion in Chinan University! He combined this job with his duties as Tu's private secretary up to the time of the Japanese invasion.

From 1927 onwards, the gangs became increasingly an important arm of the Kuomintang, used chiefly to keep the lid down on the workers' mass movement, to smash strike action through intimidation and control of all the so-called labour organisations. With the smashing of the revolutionary labour unions and the establishment of 'respectable' trade unions, the gangs assumed full leadership and have functioned in that capacity ever since...

Working Class Cells

Gangsters are used as spies among the workers. Militants are thus detected and subsequently butchered. Gangsters are the direct instrument of native and foreign exploiters who use them as foremen and labour contractors. Every labour

[1]See above, page 160.

union, every factory, every working-class district is shot through with agents of the gangs who have proved an able supplement to the legalised organs of repression which have helped shatter the working-class movement in the last five years.

Under these conditions truly militant leaders of strike movements are arrested, sentenced to long jail terms or imprisoned, or killed and the strike smashed. There was, for example, in September, 1931 the case of Zih Ah-mei, leader of the workers of the French Concession Tramways who were on strike. He was not a gangster but an able and intelligent labour organiser.

He was of course arrested, charged with being a Communist, and although there was no proof against him, a detective was obliging enough to produce a Communist leaflet which he said he found in Zih's home. Zih denied ever having seen it, charged it had been planted. Without lawyer or any defence but his own voice, Zih was sentenced to ten years' hard labour and deprived of all civil rights (whatever they are in China) for twelve years additional after a trial that lasted ten minutes.

The filtering of gangsters through the ranks has had a demoralising effect on the rank and file itself in many districts. An anonymous worker correspondent wrote (*China Forum*, January 20th, 1932):

'If they (the gangsters) only stand right opposite to the workers, harshly oppressing the workers, that would not increase our difficulties so much. We would know then that they will always be confederates of the capitalists. If we want to fight capitalism we must have a hand-to-hand fight with its servants.

'What is our most difficult task is that the influence of the Red and Green gangs has penetrated right to the midst of the workers to demoralise them. In our factory ALL the powerful workers are members of the gangs. The reason is that if they join the gangs, they are sure of their jobs. The gangsters are not afraid of any unemployment.

'They have no reasonable principles, no future aims. Their organisation centres around one man. A strong-willed man with thirty to fifty disciples can work within his territory. They are afraid of nobody but the ruling class, the capitalists.

'It seems to me that if the vanguard of the working class could cause their penetration to within the worker masses to be as effective as the gangsters, our victory will come even sooner.'

The Kuomintang-controlled trade unions are placed entirely in the hands of the gangsters, who as officials can act in labour disputes independent of the rank and file. These 'labour leaders' frequently live in comfortable houses whose monthly rental amounts to more than a worker can earn in a year.

They get a rake-off from workers' wages, from every job given a worker, from the 'squeeze' manipulated by foremen and contractors, from direct subsidies provided by grateful factory-owners, from selling opium to workers, and from buying their children as slaves. At Chinese banquets it is not uncommon to hear a pudgy-faced, fat-fingered capitalist remark: 'Yes, much that is bad can be said about the gangsters, but they have served one good purpose—keeping down the workers.'. . .

Gangsters against Strikers

One of the most glaring examples of their 'mediation' occurred during the large-scale strike of China Merchants Steam Navigation Company seamen in January of this year. More than 1,000 seamen walked out on 7th January, tying up thirteen vessels. They demanded: (1) Grant of the same double-pay bonus given other government employees and office employees of the same company; (2) Recognition of the Seamen's Union; (3) Equal treatment with office employees; (4) No dismissals without cause; (5) Permanency of double-pay bonus for the final month of the year.

The seamen charged government corruption as the cause of non-payment of wages and other deprivations. On 9th January Tu Yueh-sen and Li Ching-wu of the Green Gang stepped in as arbitrators. They wheedled the seamen into letting just one ship through. The S/S Kiangyu sailed that night transporting the 4th Division to Hankow for Red Suppression work![1] On 11th January Tu and Li told the strikers that the first three of their demands would be granted and the last two 'taken under advisement'. Work was resumed the next day. . .

---

[1] The Kuomintang was at that time engaged in operations against the Communist armies of south China.

In Shanghai and China generally, where oppressed, exploited workers are forbidden to organise or hold a single demonstration without meeting machine-gun bullets, gangsters are organised in a great secret society for vice and crime and utilisation by the Shanghai bourgeoisie and the Kuomintang against the revolutionary working class. As in the big cities of the United States, so in Shanghai, social and political decadence has brought gangsters to the top and they are used to keep the productive proletariat in a state of slavery. (2)

In the Country: he Red Spears

In rural areas, however, the secret societies kept their authentically popular character well into the twentieth century, and continued to play a certain part in the revolutionary movement.

They were behind some rudimentary peasant risings analogous to those organised by the White Lotus, the Nien, or the Golden Coins in the nineteenth century. These movements were directed against the landowners, but also against public power, represented since the end of the Empire by the 'war-lords', provincial potentates detested by the peasants, and finally against the bandits, whose resumed criminal activities profited from the state's weakness.

In 1924, in Szechuan, the Will of Heaven sect *(Shun-tian-jiao)* became prominent. Its members wore red trousers (the traditional colour of the secret societies) and – stripped to the waist – fought the bandits who attacked the villages. They were convinced that they were invulnerable.

In 1920, in Hopei and Szechuan, a peasant movement directed by Taoist priests attacked the town of Wang-sian. Each new member received a fluid of immunity, and their leader proclaimed himself emperor by promulgating an edict hostile to the merchants, militarists, and missionaries. These sects of the 1920s reverted to names and expressions charged with history and glamour: the 'Great Peace' *(T'ai P'ing)*, 'Righteous Harmony' *(I Ho* – the Boxers' title).

This concern to protect the villages from the depredations of the militarists and bandits was very marked among the Red Spears of North China in about 1925. Here is a description that appeared in a Shanghai review in 1927:

The name of 'Red Spear Society' must have existed five or six years ago. There was a group of gymnastic people who had the useful and necessary habit of defending themselves and their villages by long and red-tasselled spears. As an institution it may be just the remnant of the 'Boxers'.

But as a movement the Red Spear Society began early in the spring of 1925 when numerous conflicts broke out among the militarists.[1] War broke out between Kiangsu and Shantung, between Shantung and Honan, etc.

A System of Village Self-Defence
At that time Chang Tsung-chan formed an alliance with Li Ching-lin who formed the so-called Chihli-Shantung Allied Army. To recruit this army they practically denuded the rural districts of the available armed forces, with the result that villages were left defenceless against the ravages of the bandits who infested the districts. The farmers therefore were obliged to organise their own means of self-defence and to do this they organised village alliances.

In Chinese these alliances are called *Lien Tsuan Hwei*, meaning literally 'joint village societies'. In one locality Red Spear Society is the nucleus of such a village alliance, in another Big Knife Society, in another Black Spear Society, in still another Yellow Spear Society. While the outsiders fancifully call these open alliances by different names of secret societies, the members of these alliances keep for themselves the title of *Lien Tsuan Hwei*.

As a system of village self-defence *Lien Tsuan Hwei* was imitated in Honan to resist the militaristic administration, or to protest against the lack of any administration, when Yueh Wei-chun was in that province.

Yueh Wei-chun professed liberalism and toleration, and yet permitted his troops to devastate the villages. Naturally the peasant movement of self-defence was greatly fostered by this self-contradictory policy. Just as in Shantung, it had

---

[1]Since the death of Yüan Shih-k'ai in 1916, China had been in the grip of military anarchy, and armed conflicts broke out incessantly between different provincial armies.

various names. In western Honan, where the Red Spear Society is very strong, there is also a White Spear Society. In southern Honan, besides the Red Spear Society, there is a Yellow Spear Society and a Green Spear Society. Recently the movement has extended to Shensi, where Liu Chen-hua inaugurated a rule of militaristic terror. The Shensi village alliances for self-defence have also assumed different names: Red Spear Society, White Spear Society, and League of Hard Bellies, etc.

The present peasant movement was originated from Shantung, has flourished in Honan and Shensi, and is now spreading into the neighbouring provinces of Hupeh, Anhui, Kiangsu, and Chihli; and because of its popularity, the name of 'Red Spear Society' has been taken to cover nearly all the diversified organs of the same general movement...

Combining Superstition and Physical Training...

The ancient tribal discipline takes the place of modern equipment, and superstition accompanies the physical preparation. Every new member must have a tutor. The daily lesson consists of kneeling naked and praying, of drinking cold water in which several written spells have been immersed, and of submitting to hard blows to stiffen the muscles. At least one hundred days are required to graduate from this elementary training. No doubt strong muscular bodies are a great asset. When the Red Spears capture firearms from the soldiers or from the bandits, as so often happens, they represent a real force not to be despised. In Honanfu in western Honan alone there are no less than one hundred thousand Red Spears.

Organised, Disciplined, Effective...

The Red Spears of Honanfu are divided into nine divisions; each has its own chief commanding two thousand members. They have a regular system of fines and punishment, a director-general of discipline, and a general staff composed of experienced advisers. Other localities have almost the same sort of organisation. Usually each division covers an area of several villages, each village claims a sub-chief, and above all the divisions there is the commander-in-chief. He who has been tutor to all the division chiefs can aspire to that highest post. The burden of finance is shared by all well-to-do members; often there is assessment according to the possession of lands.

Certainly the Red Spears have demonstrated their capability. At one time they guarded several Shantung cities for over half a year. They lived in temples and vacant public buildings, and prepared food all by themselves.[1] In Honan they have defeated hundreds of thousands of the Shensi army; and the Red Spears of Shensi are now subduing the invaders from Honan...On 29th May of this year, four thousand Red Spears in Shensi carrying rifles, spears, knives, and farming implements attacked the city occupied by a militarist. They presented two demands: the abolition of all illegal and excessive excises and assessments, and the prohibition of soldiers to enter their villages. Only when the militarist made a definite promise according to these demands, was his life spared and the seige lifted. This strongly recalls the English peasant movement in June 1381, which brought the simple country-folk headed by Jack Straw and John Ball face to face with King Richard.

...A Certain Political Idea

Besides the resistance against brigands and militarists, the Red Spears are imbued with a vague political idea. This idea has been developed from territorial separation and feudalistic sectionalism. It is a wish to realise true self-government: that the administration, the military defence, and the public taxation of a province be carried on by and for the people of that same province...

Then there is a really sincere desire on the part of those peasants to see a peaceful rule and the liberation from foreign Powers. Their hatred against oppression and domination must form a healthy though merely instructive opposition to militarism and imperialism...

What is the Red Spear Society? Originally it was a spontaneous movement of self-defence. Owing to the process of proletarisation, many of its members have become bandits and militarists.

But this process of demoralisation may be arrested by the peasants joining with the proletarians employed on the railways and linking up with the city workers and by their

---

[1] In other words, they did not live at the expense of the civilian population, a fact which contributed to their popularity.

adopting a political programme. A tendency towards this is already observed. (3)

The Communists Become Interested in the Red Spears

In the years 1925-27 the fundamental question of Chinese politics was the conflict between the Nationalist government of Canton, directed by the Kuomintang and supported by the Communists, and the 'war-lords' who controlled Central and Northern China.

At the same time, the workers' movement, extremely active in Canton, Shanghai, and Wuhan, was becoming confusedly aware of the need to draw more support from the peasantry, which had up to that time hardly been involved in the revolutionary struggle.

So it was that the Communist Party, as well as the Communist International, struck by the importance of the Red Spears movement, came to feel it right to give them a place in their political strategy. For the Communists, indeed, they represented both an ally with peasant strength, and a movement localised in North China and therefore likely to be able to take the enemy from the rear.

In 1926, a work on the Red Spears appeared in Moscow,[1] and in December of that year the Executive Committee of the Comintern wrote to the Central Committee of the Chinese Communist Party saying that the Red Spears 'are directed by reactionaries but are objectively revolutionary in character by reason of their mass nature.'

In the same year, the Communist leader Li Ta-chao published a long article on the Red Spears which was the earliest attempt in China at a Marxist analysis of the secret societies. He tries to explain their primitive beliefs:

> As for their superstitions, these too are the natural manifestation of an objective reality. Since modern weapons have found their way into the villages, together with the disorder of military banditry, the peasants have begun in a general

---

[1] A.Ivine, *Krasnye Piki*, 158pp.

way to practise self-defence. For this they needed weapons. But they had nothing in the way of arms except bamboo canes, clubs, knives, spears, swords, lances, shovels, forks, or scythes. They realised, however, that this was not enough, and that is why they asked the boxers and acrobats, traditional figures in rural society, to teach them boxing and breathing techniques in order to supplement this insufficiency of knives, swords, canes, and clubs. But this was still not enough. So they appealed to all the familiar elements of village life: the Confucius painted on the school sign, the divinities Kuan-ti and Kuan-ying,[1] whose image is in the local pagoda, the Lao-jun invoked by itinerant Taoist priests, the patron-saint of the local temple, the heroes of the Epic of the Three Kingdoms—Chang Fei and Chao Yun, the characters of the popular romance, 'Pilgrimage to the West', like Chu Ba-jie and Sun Wu-kong,[2] bonesetters' talismans, divination by sand, *yin* and *yang* jargon, the eight diagrams, the five elements, etc., thinking they could scare their enemies thereby.

But with talismans and tricks on one side and machine-guns and rifles on the other, it was bound to be an unequal battle, from which they learned some painful lessons. In the villages, some peasants had been enrolled in the militarist forces, and so they knew how to use machine-guns and rifles, which made them progress rapidly and made them resolutely reject belief in divinities in favour of the adoption of modern weapons. Once they have machine-guns and rifles they no longer need Chu Ba-jie and Sun Wu-kong, or talismans. Once they have modern weapons in their possession their belief in the five elements and the eight diagrams progressively loses its force.

Li Ta-chao ended this analysis with an appeal addressed to the Communists to help the Red Spears to become a modern, democratic peasant movement, rid of its archaic characteristics and capable of co-operation with China's other revolutionary forces.

In June 1927, the break between Chiang Kai-shek and the Communists was already complete, but there continued to exist in Wuhan, Central China, a 'govern-

---

[1]Buddhist divinities.

[2]Chu Ba-jie is a pig of considerable strength, Sun Wu-kong a monkey full of ingenious tricks.

ment of the Kuomintang Left' supported by the Communists. That government's political weekly published an article appealing once more for co-operation between the Red Spears and the revolutionary forces:

'The Red Spears Have Taken the Wrong Road...'
    The Red Spears organisation is a resistance movement of simple peasants who have been deeply affected by the oppression of rotten political power and the havoc which has resulted from it: devastation of the fields, the very heavy burden of farm rents and taxes, looting and disorder from soldiers and bandits...

    If we study the Red Spears—who form a certain proportion of the peasantry—in detail, we find that their spirit of resistance corresponds almost exactly to the intentions of our peasant movement. Differently expressed, the central claims of the Red Spears are those for which we think the people of the Peasant Unions must strive. But the childishness of the Red Spears and the mistakes they make stem primarily from their extreme political innocence, and not from the fact that the squireens and rural despots make use of them. All of which comes back to saying that they have gone the wrong way and that it is very regrettable.

    They are incapable of finding a means of realising their true aspirations, they are prisoners of their feudal customs. Such was the principal cause of the defeat of the Boxers. Such, I think, is the destiny of the Red Spears, too.

    They have no basic organisation. When an incident occurs they beat drums in all the villages to gather the men together (at least in Shantung—I do not know about the recent progress and development of the Honan Red Spears).

    The members obey the orders of their leaders unconditionally, and grant them dictatorial powers. They can sometimes hold small assemblies which appear democratic, but this has nothing in common with centralised democracy. In battle, their ardour is strengthened by superstitious slogans and passwords; they brandish wooden lances decorated with red pennons, and charge forward, bare-chested. Their battle tactics are in fact extremely fierce, but they are not up to organising the problems of communications or transport and are therefore incapable of carrying on a lengthy struggle. Thus their affairs always appear to have a tiger's head and a serpent's tail.

Their Enemies...

Their enemies, certainly, are the squireens, the evil-minded local magistrates, the soldiers, and the bandits. They have recently realised that, among their enemies, there were also the high-ranking 'war-lords' like Chang Tsung-chang. But their knowledge is too limited for them to be able to distinguish clearly which are the gentry and which the oppressors. That is why, recently, certain groups of Red Spears have been used by the reactionaries.

In general there are two categories of reactionary forces using the Red Spears: on the one hand, the squireens; on the other, the militarists and politicians. The first category hopes to use the traditional militia methods[1] to defend its interests and keep the villages under control. The second seeks to seize arms, horses, and men from the Red Spears for military reinforcements.

The Red Spear groups used in this way have a feudal character and are completely opposed to the authentic revolutionary forces. We should pay a great deal of attention to the influence of the reactionary forces within the Red Spears.

'This Phenomenon is Explicable...'

In China, at a time when the feudal régime is disintegrating and modern industry is not fully developed, the peasants engaged in agriculture undoubtedly retain their feudal ideology. For a long time, modern industry has belonged to foreigners, and the foreigners do what they like. The peasants' political consciousness is primitive; they cannot understand that the upsurge of modern industry demands the disappearance of feudal relations in agriculture; furthermore, from xenophobia there comes a reaction which tends to preserve

---

[1]Traditionally, in periods of insecurity, villagers were authorised to form their own armed militias to defend themselves against soldiers, bandits, vagabonds, etc. These village militias were often used by the ruling classes. But as we have seen in connection with the Nien and the Boxers, the secret societies also made use of them to officer the peasantry.

the backward character of agriculture and feudal social relations. The Red Spears are part of this process. In appearance their activities aimed at putting an end to the extortions of the bureaucrats and the squireens, obtaining the abolition of arbitrary taxes, and ending the peasants' political and economic trials are very reasonable. But if they wish to preserve for ever the old type of agricultural production and the feudal relationships which are characteristic of it, to oppose everything foreign including modern industrial relations, this from the point of view of social evolution can be called nothing else but a contradictory phenomenon on the road leading to the salvation of the peasants.

I recall that during the 4th May Movement well-meaning people formed in the villages *bu-yi-hui* (societies for material and clothes) whose members swore not to use foreign materials or other products: that was a glorious manifestation of the breakdown of the feudal system. I have heard it said that most of the peasants, because the Kuomintang uses a strange terminology, quite different from the gentry's way of speaking, are full of suspicion of the party and its 'Western' habits;[1] that is an example of the feudal outlook.

To Win Over the Red Spears.....

All things considered, to win over the Red Spears, we must:

1. help them to realize their objectives (for example, rid them of corrupt civil-servants and squireens); put an end to the extortions they suffer;

2. frequently discuss with them the course to follow to satisfy their demands, so as to gain their confidence;

3. spread among them political knowledge and the practice of democracy, in order to rid them of their feudal ideology (by, for example, setting up libraries and clubs, giving lectures, and showing them films...);

4. not make a direct attack on their superstitious beliefs, but encourage them gradually to free themselves from them;

5. not pontificate upon such-and-such an 'ism' by way of propaganda, but reinforce their class consciousness and

---

[1] It is a fact that many of the Kuomintang leaders were young intellectuals who had received a Western-style university education in China and were fairly cut off from the peasant masses.

orient them towards the struggle against the squireens and the oppressors;

6. have as final objective the transformation of the Red Spears groups into true Peasant Unions, of which poor peasants and labourers will be the nucleus.

All this is only a brief outline of work to be done in connection with the Red Spears, and not a detailed plan of action. Today, at the time of the second Northern expedition,[1] the battlefields are in the very heart of the Red Spears' territory, which means that this issue is of extreme importance.

I am convinced that the more we can solve the Red Spears problem, the less need there will be for concern over the fate of the peasants in Chihli, Shantung, and Honan.

I myself consider this article very elementary, but if it serves to stimulate discussion it will be of value to the revolutionary movement. Let us therefore concern ourselves with this question. (5)

The Communist Party and the Secret Societies

From the summer of 1927 onwards, then, the Kuomintang government in Wuhan allied itself in its turn to Chiang Kai-shek. Moscow and the Chinese Communists were losing all hope of triumphing in China by means of a nationalist revolution based on the cities. The revolution was to move out into the country – under Mao's influence in particular, and in spite of elements of resistance within the Communist movement in China as well as Moscow.

---

[1]From July 1926 to March 1927, the revolutionary armies of the Canton government had launched a 'Northern expedition', and the Kuomintang had obtained mastery of the whole of the Yangtze basin. At the time this article was written, the split was already complete between the right-wing of the Kuomintang established in Nanking (with Chiang Kai-shek), which had broken with the Communists, and the left-wing of the Kuomintang established in Wuhan, which continued to collaborate with the Communists. This Wuhan government, known as the 'Kuomintang Left', was then preparing its 'second Northern expedition' in the direction of Peking, still held by the war-lords. It collapsed in July 1927 and most of its leaders joined Chiang Kai-shek.

The question of the secret societies now took on even more importance. It is interesting to note that it was already on the programme of the Institute for the Setting-Up of Cadres in the Peasant Movement established in Canton in the period of co-operation between the Kuomintang and the Communists, with Mao as director. Now that the Communists, with the support of the poor peasants, were engaged in a merciless struggle against the Kuomintang, they could not remain indifferent to the influence that the secret societies continued to exert in the country.

A figure like Liu Chi-tan provides a good illustration of the *rapprochements* which took place in the early 1930s between the Communists and certain rival secret societies.

Liu Chi-tan was a peasant who belonged to the Association of Elder Brothers. Over and over again, he had directed peasant uprisings against the landowners of his native province of Shensi. At the time of the Long March, when the defeated Communists were approaching that area, he joined them, became a member of the Party, and saw himself entrusted with important political responsibilities. He fell soon after and was honoured as a martyr of the revolution among the anti-Japanese guerrillas in the following years.

Guerrillas against the Japanese

From 1937 onwards, indeed, in the war against Japan, the Communist Party organised peasant guerillas behind enemy lines. The secret societies—or some of them, at least—were still active against the invader in North China, and the Communists could not ignore this fact.

An independent observer stressed their importance in Shantung:

> The local forces of the people are generally led by the middle peasants, but their ranks are filled by the poor. Their form of organisation is rather backward and has many medieval traits. They have numerous names and each is independent of the other. Superstition is the bond that all use

to bind their members together. The groups are divided according to the different god each worships and the different method each uses to train its members. The particular god each worships and the rituals it performs are as a rule kept secret. The eating of meat and garlic, and sexual intercourse are forbidden by all the sects. Such are the peculiar traits of these semi-medieval superstitious peasant organisations.

The Kung (Palace), where training and the worshipping of the god takes place, is the unit of these peasant organisations. Ordinarily, there is only one *Kung* in each village. Whenever ten members are recruited in a village, they have the right to establish a *Kung*. Those villages that have less than ten members are affiliated to a neighbouring *Kung*. Before the *Kung* is officially recognised, the members are led to the mother *Kung* by the master, a well-trained veteran member of the sect, to perform an initiation ceremony. The members then elect two *Kung* chairmen, of whom one is the real chief and the other his assistant. Among the rest of the members there are no differences in rank, and they address each other as Brother. Above the *Kung*, there is a General *Kung* in each *hsien*[1] with jurisdiction over all the local *Kungs*. The oldest of all the General *Kungs* acts as the Senior General *Kung* and is placed in charge of relations between *hsiens*.

After a *Kung* is set up, its members gather together every evening to receive training from the master. At dawn, the group is dismissed. This continues until the training is finished. The main activities in which the members are trained are worshipping and boxing, and each sect has its own rules, methods, and specialities. For instance, the Red Spear Society specialises in boxing and the use of the spear, and permits its members to participate in battles only after a month of training; whereas the Kang Feng Tao[2] and others practise rifle shooting in addition, and allow their members to take part in fighting as soon as they join the organisation. During the training period both the Red Spear Society and the Kang Feng Tao absolutely forbid their members to have any contact with women, while the Chung Yang Tao[2] recruits women members.

As to the doctrines of the various sects, both the Red Spear Society and the Kang Feng Tao emphasise resistance

---

[1]District.

[2]The author has been unable to trace the original Chinese characters of these names, and considers it unsafe to try to translate them.

to the Japanese. But the Chung Yang Tao still advocates restoration of the emperor and believes that a 'Son of Heaven' will descend to save China. It is, in fact, a very reactionary group. In the areas where it has a stronghold, efforts have been made to resist the government authorities in the collection of taxes for the maintenance of the army.

The above-mentioned peasant organisations are of great importance in South Shantung. The most influential are the Red Spear Society and the Chung Yang Tao, both of which are antagonistic to General Sun,[1] but friendly to the Fourth Brigade of the Eighth Route Army[2] and the Sixty-ninth Army.[3] The Fourth Brigade has, of course, helped them in every way possible. But the best results in the development of the political and military understanding of the Red Spear Society were achieved by the Sixty-ninth Army. This is shown by the fact that members of the Red Spear Society were not only eager to enlist in the training class established for them by General Shih,[4] but after receiving some training, had actually learned enough to issue manifestoes and plan for political action. In one of its manifestoes, the Red Spear Society showed its political maturity by condemning the lawlessness of Sun's army and advocating the purging of reactionary forces and opportunist careerists. It proclaimed itself to be the armed force of the people, and, therefore, to be willing to do its best to assist other Chinese forces in resisting the Japanese. In another manifesto, the Red Spear Society appealed for the co-operation of other sects and proposed the establishment of a joint office of all the sects to facilitate collaboration. Thanks to its continuous efforts, an Associated Committee of All Sects was formed. This step was of great importance in the development of the anti-Japanese movement in South Shantung. (6)

The Communist Party therefore directed more and

---

[1] Commander of the Kuomintang units fighting the Japanese in that area.

[2] The Communist forces of North China had—since the agreement between the Communists and the Kuomintang in 1937—been integrated by the Kuomintang general staff under the name of Eighth Army.

[3] The Kuomintang army operating in that region.

[4] The general commanding the Sixty-ninth Army.

more initiatives towards the secret societies in the guerrilla areas.

In July 1936, when general war had not yet broken out but appeared imminent to all informed observers, Mao Tse-tung had issued, in the name of the Central Committee of the Communist Party, an 'appeal to the Brothers of the *Ko Lao Hui* (Association of Elder Brothers)'.

Mao Tse-tung's Appeal to the Elder Brothers

After stressing the seriousness of the Japanese peril, he proposed to this venerable association a real pact of unity of action:

> Formerly, following its principles—'Restore the Han and exterminate the Ch'ing', 'Strike at the rich and aid the poor'—the *Ko-lao-hui* participated actively in the anti-Manchu revolutionary movement of 1911. The revolution in northern Shensi has also benefited from the considerable aid, support, and active participation of comrades from the *Ko-lao-hui*. Comrades such as Hsieh Tzu-ch'ang or Liu Chih-tan are not only leaders of the Red Army; they are also exemplary members of the *Ko-lao-hui*. This revolutionary spirit, these glorious feats, must be manifested even more widely in today's heroic struggle to save the country and save ourselves.
>
> The Central Chinese People's Soviet Government[1] has many times in the past proclaimed its views about resisting Japan and saving the country, and called upon all those who are unwilling to be slaves without a country to unite, without distinction of party or class, and go and fight together against our common enemies—the Japanese imperialists and the traitors who are selling out their country—in order to secure the independence and liberation of the Chinese nation.
>
> ### *What We Have in Common*
> The *Ko-lao-hui* has always been representative of the organisations of the resolute men of our nation, and of the broad masses of peasants and toilers. It has constantly been the

----

[1] i.e. the Chinese Communist authorities established in North China after the Long March.

victim of the oppression of the militarists and the bureaucrats; its members have been considered as 'inferior people' or calumnied as 'bandits', and it was denied a legal existence. The treatment inflicted on the *Ko-lao-hui* by the ruling class is really almost identical with that inflicted on us![1] In the past, you supported the restoration of the Han and the extermination of the Manchus; today, we support resistance to Japan and saving the country. You support striking at the rich and helping the poor; we support striking at the local bullies and dividing up the land. You despise wealth and defend justice, and you gather together all the heroes and brave fellows in the world; we do not spare ourselves to save China and the world, we unite the oppressed and exploited peoples and social strata of the whole world.

'A Close and Intimate Alliance...'

Our views and our positions are therefore quite close; there is even more complete correspondence as regards our enemies and the road towards salvation. Consequently, we once more make a special and very sincere appeal to all our brothers of the *Ko-lao-hui* throughout the whole country. Regardless of our past subjects of discord or mutual grievances, we must now forget them in order to unite under the slogan of resisting Japan and saving the country. Let us constitute a close and intimate alliance of brothers, let us together defend righteousness and come to the aid of our country in its need. This is your sacred duty, and the sacred duty of the whole Chinese people!

The Soviet Government is the government of the oppressed people of China. We have the responsibility to receive and to protect all those who are persecuted and threatened with arrest by the Kuomintang Government. Consequently, the *Ko-lao-hui* can exist legally under the Chinese Soviet Government. Moreover, we have instituted a reception bureau for the *Ko-lao-hui* for receiving all the heroes, brave fellows, and courageous fighters for upright causes who are unable to maintain themselves in the white areas. We hope and request that the lodge masters and grand masters of the various lodges in all parts of the country, and our brothers among the brave fellows on every hand, will send representatives or

---

[1] Mao Tse-tung is certainly alluding here to repressive measures taken by the Kuomintang against the Elder Brothers; detailed research is needed on this point.

come themselves to discuss with us plans for saving the country. We await them with enthusiasm, and will give them a
hearty welcome! We proclaim loudly:

Show the revolutionary spirit that characterised the
Ko-lao-hui in the past!

Let the *Ko-lao-hui* and the whole of the Chinese people
unite to strike at Japan and to restore China!

Long live the liberation of the Chinese people!

The Chairman of the Central Government of the
Chinese People's Soviet Republic:

MAO TSE-TUNG
15th July, 1936.

Relations Sometimes Difficult

A manual for cadres of the New Fourth Army (one of
the principal Communist armies operating in the guerrilla
territory of North China against the Japanese), drawn
up in 1941, devotes a very interesting section — *à propos*
of political work among the peasants — to difficulties
encountered by the Communist armies in their dealings
with the armed units of secret societies which controlled
certain areas before the guerrillas were established:

The Red Spears, Big Swords, United Village Associations,
etc., are all simple, armed, self-defence organisations of the
peasants, and they have a very long history in peasant villages.
Since the Incident,[1] they have undergone rapid development
and commonly exist in all parts of the guerrilla areas. Their
main objectives are the forcible collection of taxes and
opposition to disturbances caused by troops or bandits. Therefore, they are opposed to Japanese imperialist aggression,
but if they are not encroached upon by the enemy, they offer
no resistance and fight only if attacked. Politically, they are
neutral, and they are led, for the most part, by rich peasants...

The strongest force in these groups is a kind of superstition,
and as a result their conservatism is particularly intense...

Do not insult their religious beliefs and superstitions, but
respect their creeds and leaders. (8)

Some Pro-Japanese Secret Societies

Several secret societies, as we have seen, maintained

---
[1] i.e. the beginning of the war.

their traditional links with the peasant masses and were naturally impelled with them to resist the invader. Others, on the contrary, chose to collaborate with the Japanese. For example, the Way of Fundamental Unity (see Chapter 2), a rather esoteric sect influential in the big cities of the North and East such as Tientsin and Nanking, which until then had hardly concerned itself with politics—not openly, at least—came out in open support of the Japanese.

The pro-Japanese Chinese government formed in Nanking in 1940 by Wang Ching-wei, the Chinese Laval—opposed to Chiang Kai-shek through a very old rivalry—relied on various secret societies with similar tendencies; Wang Ching-wei himself supported a 'Hung Society of the Five Continents' (*Wu-chow-Hung-men*), which claimed the celebrated name of the Triad (*Hung*) and sought to rally the Chinese émigrés in Japan among whom the Triad had previously been very influential.

W.P. Morgan reports in his study of the Triad in Hong Kong that when the colony was occupied by the Japanese, many Triad leaders allied themselves to them, (cf. Chapter I).

How does one set about differentiating between pro- and anti-Japanese secret societies? The significant distinction here—as with the revolutionary movement of the 1920s and after—could be that between the mainly peasant, hence patriotic organisations, and the urban secret societies, more cut off from the masses and ready for pragmatic 'political operations'.

We must limit ourselves simply to raising the question, since the political behaviour of the secret societies during the Sino-Japanese War of 1937-45 has scarcely begun to be studied.

It is even more difficult to do more than hint at the problem of the secret societies from 1949 onwards. The establishment of the Chinese People's Republic and all its economic, political, and social consequences was bound to leave these archaic groups high and dry. They petered out or went over to the reactionary forces which, since 1949, have kept up in Taiwan their claims to return to power.

For this reason the authorities of the Chinese People's Republic in the years following the Liberation (*chieh-fang*), denounced over and over again the collusion between the counter-revolutionary groups linked with Taiwan and certain elements in the old secret societies. There have been a number of mentions in provincial news-papers of the Big Sword, Red Lamps, White Cloud, and especially the Way of Fundamental Unity (which seems to have been the most active and stubborn).

On 15th March 1952 the *Yangtze Journal*, published in Wuhan, denounced a counter-revolutionary sect, 'The Altar of the Woman with the Bushel' (*tow-mu-tan*), for practising medicine as a blind and for claiming to be bringing to power a child of eight called Chu and reputed to be a direct descendant of the former Ming emperors.

This final appearance on the historical scene of the old Ming legitimism which for centuries, up to 1911, had been so strongly identified with popular aspirations and hostility to established power is perhaps symbolic of the destiny of Chinese secret societies in the contemporary world.

For them, as for the whole of China since 1949, history has moved on.

CHAPTER EIGHT

An Interim Conclusion

How may one define a Chinese secret society in modern times? Is it no more than a picturesque expression provoking curiosity and imagination? Or have we here a genuine historical category rich in content and with unique significance in the socio-political dynamics of nineteenth- and twentieth-century China?

The sixty or so original documents presented in this volume are certainly not enough to provide an answer to these questions. Historical research on this subject is only just beginning.

Of course, as certain experts have pointed out, the very term 'secret society' as it exists in modern Chinese (*pi-mi chieh-shih, pi-mi hui-shih*) is a neologism which is probably merely a re-translation into Chinese of the corresponding European expression, perhaps via Japanese. A study of this point from the point of view of historical philology would be useful. But even if there were a foreign loan, linguistically speaking, it would at the most prove that, until the nineteenth century, the Chinese did not feel the need to stress the secret nature of these occult organisations, perhaps because it went without saying. Would it mean that these organisations did not exist in their own right? Rather the opposite.

In China, people were content to call them *hui* (associations) or *chiao* (sects), and those frequently varied terms—of which a short list was given in Chapter 3—indisputably designated a strongly defined political and social reality. Our examination of their records, cursory as it has had to be, during this hundred-year period, has nevertheless been sufficient to reveal their nature as a total opposition force: political and religious, social and ideological. There is none of the dualism which, in the West, traditionally divides such matters into spiritual and temporal. Chinese secret societies (let us provisionally retain this term established by usage) took the diametrically opposite view to the established order, while at the same time, by a curiously mimetic process, drawing from it their inspiration to define their own, 'parallel' order.

At this point, any false comparison with the West must be abandoned. Chinese secret societies were neither essentially philosophico-religious like the Rosicrucians, the Vehmgericht, or Freemasonry, nor essentially political and social like the Mafia or the Carbonari. They were deeply rooted in Chinese historical reality; they cannot be defined except in connection with the traditional Confucian conception of man, the world, and society.

What, then, is their 'historical weight'? If it is true that every historian runs the risk of exaggerating the importance of his subject, conversely it must be noted that many authors—and not necessarily the least famous —have often tended to underestimate (deliberately, it would seem) the *hui* and the *chiao*, even when it is known that they had close connections with them. Such was the case with Hung Hsiu-ch'üan, the T'ai P'ing emperor with his hostile declarations to the Triad; it was the case with Sun Yat-sen, asserting that the societies were no longer active when the Republicans took over; and it was the case with Wu Yu-chang, one of the veterans of the 1911 Revolution. It is rather as if the secret societies seemed risky allies, unworthy of acknowledgement, about whom it was best to say as little as possible. Field-Marshall Chu Teh is without doubt one of the few twentieth-century Chinese statesmen to acknowledge openly that he was a member. This general silence is another problem.

Yet the secret societies constantly threatened the imperial régime in the nineteenth century, formed a powerful part of the tidal wave which finally overwhelmed it in 1911, and reacted strongly to foreign penetration at the end of the nineteenth century as they did to the Japanese invasion in the twentieth. They were not just marginal forces, relics of the past. Their historical dynamism was far from being exhausted, at least up till 1911, and the modernisation of the economy, the opening-up of the ports, the migrations of industrial workers, on the contrary widened their social basis, at least for a time.

It is, however, far less easy to define their historical rôle correctly than to retrace the broad outlines of their activity. Did it, in the final analysis, serve the forces of progress or those of social reaction? Was their intervention positive or negative?

Throughout this brief enquiry one has been especially struck by their positive aspect. As we have seen, they threatened the power of the Manchus and contributed to their downfall; they caused real anxiety to the West and then to Japan. The unexpected size of the Boxer Rising, for example, made a strong impression on the West, and was one of the factors which led it to give up its plans for the complete partition of China – plans which were well under way at the end of the nineteenth century.

This positive role, as much social as national, is inseparable from their popular character. The secret societies relied for support primarily upon the oppressed classes of the old China – the poor peasants, itinerant workmen, disbanded troops, unskilled labourers, coolies, and street porters. They were the authentic expression of popular hostility to China's *ancien régime* and the foreign menace, and they represented its original form of organisation.

However, their activity remained restricted within narrow limits, and thus has undoubted negative aspects. Their backward-looking ideology and primitive superstitions prevented them from tackling what was perhaps the most important problem facing nineteenth – and twentieth-century China – that of progress: of technical and scientific progress, but of political and social progress, too. Right up to the Liberation they remained exclusively oriented towards the past. They were incapable of helping the masses to raise and resolve this problem; what is more, they may actually have prevented it, by contributing to the survival of outdated ideas and beliefs: the eight diagrams, the *yin* and the *yang*, amulets of invulnerability, the deified heroes of the popular pantheon. We have noted, too, that their connection with the poor had never excluded a certain dependance on the propertied classes and the goodwill of the gentry, whose intrigues they frequently served; their opposition to the political and social *ancien régime* was therefore far from being absolute and unshakeable. Finally, they had never constituted more than a partial solution to the problems and aspirations of the masses, a minority formula. They had never taken in more than an active minority, anxious to defend its own interests by any means, legal or otherwise, but taking for granted its dissociation from the rest of the hardworking population, and, if the need arose, living at its expense. One thinks of the description by the heroes of Mérimée's *La Jacquerie* of the wolves which fight against the shepherds and the dogs but scorn the sheep and devour them at a suitable moment. This minority situation was almost a condition of the secret societies' existence.

Fundamentally they were not detached from the Chinese *ancien régime*. They were an opposition force but within the established order: they were an integral part of it, stamped with the same defects and prisoners of the same limitations. Thus, until 1911, their untiring activity achieved nothing more than repeated failures. It could be said that they were an aspect of the functioning of the *ancien régime* rather than a fundamental alternative to it.

The 'unclamping' of Chinese political life came from the outside, from social forces and new ideas which collided with old China: modern intelligentsia, bourgeoisie, proletariat, modernist Republican movement; then Marxism, *T'ung-meng-hui*, Kuomintang, Communist Party. The secret societies only 'backed the right horse' in cases where they were associated with movements initiated by these new forces: the Republican anti-Manchu organisation, and then, in the country at least, national anti-Japanese resistance. By contrast, when they acted alone, the Small Sword, the White Lotus, and the Nien failed against the imperial authorities, the Boxers against the West. All of which underlines the fact that the secret societies only achieved real success as contributory forces, supporting the new forces of Chinese politics.

These new forces asserted themselves only gradually, the major turning-point coming between 1911 and 1919, with the Republican Revolution and the 4th May Movement. But it would be an over-simplification to suggest that after this turning-point the secret societies suddenly lost all their authentically popular character, all their capacity to play a positive role. They undoubtedly degenerated quickly in the cities from the 1920s onwards, and they no longer exist except as gangs for dubious trafficking, or in the service of social reaction. But in the country the secret societies' decline and replacement by the new forces has been much slower. In the 1920s the Communists had no doubt about the popular character of the Red Spears, and again in 1936 their Central Committee considered it useful to offer the Elder Brothers a pact of unity of action against the Japanese.

In the nineteenth as in the twentieth century, the secret societies showed themselves incapable of making history on their own. But they were closely linked to the struggles which the Chinese people tirelessly waged throughout this period against their internal and external adversaries.

References

CHAPTER 1: A Secret Society; The Triad

1. 'Account of the Malay Abdullah, Secretary to Sir Stamford Raffles, Governor of Singapore', (A. Wylie, 'Secret Societies in China', *Chinese Almanack for 1853*, Shanghai 1854, pp. 327-329

2. 'Extracts from the Triad initiation ritual'. From G. Schlegel, *Thian Ti Hwui, the Hung League*, Batavia 1866

3. 'Oath taken by members of the Triad Society and notices of its origin' (*The Chinese Repository*, vol. XVIII, June 1849, no.6, pp. 282-287)

4. Leon Comber, *Chinese Secret Societies in Malaya*, New York 1959, pp. 284-286

5. Plan of a Triad lodge, from W.P. Morgan, *Triad Societies in Hong Kong*, Hong Kong 1960, p. 106

CHAPTER 2: A Few Other Societies

1. Letter from J. Leboucq S.J., 27 February 1875 (*Etudes* November 1875, 5th series, vol. VII, pp. 208-209)

2. D.H. Porter, 'Secret Societies in Shantung' *(Chinese Recorder*, vol. XVII, January-February 1886, pp. 64-65

3. See note 1 above

4. An article appearing in the Tientsin newspaper Ta-Kung-pao, November 1930, reproduced in B. Faver, *Les Sociétiés Secrètes en Chine*, Paris 1933, pp. 178-182

5. Chung-kuo Lao-tung yün-tung shih (History of the Chinese Workers' Movement), Chungking 1942, pp. 74-77

6. W.A. Grootaers, 'Une société secrète moderne', Annotated bibliography (*Folklore Studies*, vol. V, Peking 1946, p. 340)

CHAPTER 3: Secret Societies and Chinese Society

1. 'Qin-fei ji-lue' (Dossier on the bandits of the Golden Coins Society reproduced in *Chin-tai shih tzu-liao* (Materials of modern history) no.3, Peking 1955, p. 147

2. See chapter 2, note 1, pp. 205–206

3. Ibid, p. 203

4. Ku Kang, 'Hung-hu-tzu' (The Red Beards), an article from the review *Tung-fang tsa-chih*, Shanghai, July 1927, pp. 73–77

5. Quoted by Chiang Siang-Tseh, *The Nien Rebellion*, p. 15

6. See chapter 2, note 2, p. 68

7. Sun Yat-sen, *San Min Chu I, The Three Principles of the People*, ed, L.T. Chen, Shanghai 1927, Lecture 3, pp. 57–60

8. Mao Tse-tung: *The Political Thoughts of Mao Tse-tung*, p. 176

9. T'an Ssu-t'ung ch'uan chi *(Complete Works of Tan si-tong)*, Peking 1954, pp. 63-64

10. From an article in *Li-shi yan-jiu*, quoted in the Bibliography

11. *Ta-Tsing-leu-lee ou les lois fondamentales du Code pénal de la Chine avec le choix des statuts supplémentaires*, translated into French by Staunton and Renouard de Sainte-Croix, Paris 1812, vol.11, pp. 456–461

12. See above note 7, pp. 618–619

CHAPTER 4: Against Imperial Power

1. Report of the Mandarin Wang Yang-yan, reproduced in G.W. Cooke, *China, being the Times special correspondence from China in the years 1857–58*, London 1859, pp. 436–441

2. *Chinese Almanack for 1853,* Shanghai 1854, p. 332

3. Article in *North China Herald*, Shanghai, 10 September 1853

4. Ibid

5. Ibid

6. Theodore Hamberg, *The Visions of Hung Siu-Tshuen*, Hong Kong 1854, pp.54–56

7. 'Xing-lie ri-ji hui-yao' (Daily reports of Xing Lie) reproduced in the *Nian Jun* series, Shanghai 1953 vol.1 p.309 et seq

8. See Chapter 2, note 1 pp.211–212

9. Letter from Rev. Father Palâtre (*Les Missions catholiques*, 13, 20, 27 September 1878)

10. *Anti-foreign riots in China in 1891*, Shanghai 1892 pp.74–75

11. Quoted by Wang Tian-jiang (article in *Li-shi yan-jiu* mentioned in the Bibliography)

CHAPTER 5: Against Foreign Penetration

1. See chapter 4, note 9, p.81

2. Ibid, pp.229–230

3. Article published on 5 August 1897 in the Chinese Catholic newspaper *Shantung shi-bao*, reproduced in *Shantung li-shi zi liao* (Shantung historical material), Peking 1959, vol.1, pp.52–53

4. Document of 1901, reprinted in *I Ho T'uan* (The Righteous Harmony Militia), Shanghai 1953, vol.1, pp.239, 4–14. After G.G.H. Dunstheimer *Réligion et magie dans le mouvement des Boxeurs d'après les textes chinois*, T'oung Pao, vol.XLVII, books 3–5, pp. 358–359

5. Ibid

6. Missionaries' Letters, reproduced by V. Purcell, in *The Boxer Uprising, a Background Study, 1963*, pp. 288–289

7. *I Ho T'uan* (The Righteous Harmony Militia), Shanghai 1953, vol. IV, pp. 148–152. From the English version by J. Chen, 'The nature and characteristics of the Boxer Movement', *Bulletin of the School of Oriental and African Studies*, London 1960, p. 305

8. Ibid, p. 295, note 3

9. Ibid, p. 301

10. Yang-song, *Zhong-guo jin-dai-shi zi-liao* (Collection of documents in Chinese contemporary history), Peking 1954, pp. 506–509

11. Ibid

12. G. Coulet, *Les Sociétés secrètes en Terre d'Annam*, Saigon 1926, pp. 106–108

13. Ibid, pp. 114–115

14. Ibid, pp. 51–55

15. Ibid, pp. 88–89

16. L. Borodovskij, 'Hunhuzi' (The Red Beards), *Encyclopedia Slovarg*, vol. 37a, book 74, St Petersburg 1903, p. 778

CHAPTER 6: In the Service of the Republican Cause

1. Wu Yu-chang, *The Revolution of 1911*, Peking 1962, p. 94

2. Tao Cheng-chang, *Liao-hui yuan-liu-kao* (Study of the origin and spread of sects and societies), reprinted in the *Xin-hai ge-ming* series (The 1911 Revolution), Shanghai 1957, vol. III, p. 100

3. 'Les Sociétés Secrètes', Kemington and Harmel, 'La Révolution Chinoise', supplement to *La Guerre Sociale*, May 1908, pp. 6–7

4. Wu Yu-chang, op. cit. pp. 93–95, Peking 1962

5. Agnes Smedley, *The Great Road, the life and times of Chu Teh*, New York 1966, pp. 87–89

6. *Xin-hai ge-ming hui-yi-lu* (Memories of the 1911 Revolution), Peking 1962, vol.III, pp. 466 et seq

7. Sun Yat-sen, *Memories of a Chinese Revolutionary,* Taipeh 1933, pp. 164–166

8. See above, note 6, vol.II, pp. 239 et seq

9. Ibid, vol.II, pp. 204 et seq

10. E. Teichmann, *Travels of a Consular Officer in Northern China,* Cambridge 1921, pp. 22–24

CHAPTER 7: The Chinese Revolution (1919–1949)

1. Deng Zhong-xia, *Zhong-guo zhi-gong yun-dong jian-shi* (Short history of the Chinese Workers' Movement), Peking 1953, pp. 3–4

2. 'Gang rule in Shanghai', extract from *Five Years of Kuomintang Reaction.* Edited by H.R. Isaacs, re-edited from the special issue of *China Forum,* May 1932, Shanghai, pp. 1–7

3. 'Red Spears in China' (*China Weekly Review,* 19 March 1927), article reproduced from *Chinese Student Monthly* (published by the Chinese Students of the U.S.A.)

4. 'Lu-Yu-Shen deng sheng-di Hong-jiang-hui' (The Red Spears of Shantung, Honan, Shensi and other provinces), an article reprinted in *Li-Ta-chao xuan-ji* (Selected works of Li Ta-chao), Peking 1959, pp. 564–570

5. 'Hong-xiang-hui gong-zui zhi li-lun yu shi-ji' (The theory and practice of work among the Red Spears), Shen Lan-sheng, *Zhong-yong fu-gan* (Central Bulletin), Wuhan, no.69, 1st June 1927

6. Wang Yu-chuang, 'The Organisation of a typical guerilla area in South Shantung', reproduced in E.F. Carlson, *The Chinese Army, its organisation and military efficiency,* New York 1940, pp. 104–106

7. Mao Tse-Tung, 'The Chinese Soviet Government's Appeal to the Association of Elder Brothers', published in *Douzheng* (The Struggle), 12 July 1936, pp. 3–5

8. 'The Fourth Army's Guide to work among the masses', 15 June 1941, reproduced in C.A. Johnson, *Peasant Nationalism and Communist Power*, Stanford 1962, pp. 88–89

Bibliography

General works on contemporary China

J.K. Fairbank, E.O. Reischauer, A.M. Craig: *East Asia. The Modern Transformation*, Houghton Mifflin Company 1965, pp.955

Ho Kan-shih: *A History of the Modern Chinese Revolution*, Editions en langues étrangères, Peking 1959, pp.627

Li Chien-nung: *The Political History of China, 1840 – 1928*, Van Nostrand Company Inc., Princeton 1956, pp. 545

Wu Yu-tchang: *La revolution de 1911*, Editions en langues étrangères, Peking 1963, pp.143

R. Pelissier: *La Chine entre en scène*, Julliard, Paris 1963, pp. 413

J. Chesneaux, J. Lust: *Introduction aux études d'histoire contemporaine de Chine*, Mouton, Paris 1964, pp.148

Chinese Works on the Secret Societies

Wang Tian-jian: 'Shi-jiu shi-ji xia-ban ji zhong-guo de bi-mi hui-she' (Chinese Secret Societies in the second half of the 19th century), article from *Li-shi yan-jiu* (Historical Studies), 1963, no. 2, pp.83–100

Hirayama Amane: *Zhong-guo bi-mi she-hui shi* (History of Chinese Secret Societies), translated from Japanese, Shanghai 1912, pp.98

Tao Cheng-chang: 'Jiao-hui yuan liu kao' (Study of the origin of the Secret Societies), reprinted in Xin-hai ge-ming (1911 Revolution), Shanghai 1957, vol.3, pp. 99–111

Western Works on the Secret Societies

G. Schlegel: *Thian ti Hwui, The Hung League*, Batavia 1866

B. Favre: *Les Sociétés Secrètes en Chine*, Paris 1933, pp. 322

G.G.H. Dunstheimer: 'Le Mouvement des Boxeurs· Documents et études publiés depuis la deuxième guerre mondiale', article in *La Revue Historique*, No. 470 Paris 1964, pp.387–416

Siang-tseh Chiang: *The Nien Rebellion*, Seattle 1954, pp. 159

S.Y. Teng: *The Nien Army and their Guerrilla Warfare*, Paris 1964

W.P. Morgan: *Triad Societies in Hong-Kong*, Hong Kong 1960, pp. 306

G. Coulet: *Les Sociétés Secrètes en Terre d'Annam*, Saigon 1926, pp. 425

L. Comber: *Chinese Secret Societies in Malaya, a Survey of the Triad Society from 1800–1900*, New York 1959, pp. 324

V. Purcell: *The Boxer Uprising, a Background Study*, Cambridge 1963, pp. 349

H. Cordier: 'Les Sociétés Secrètes chinoises', article in *La Revue d'Ethnographie*, vol.VII, no.1–2, Paris 1888

A. Wylie: 'Secret Societies in China', article in the *Chinese Almanack for 1853*, Shanghai 1854, pp. 325–333

Chinese Character Index

An-ch'ing-hui 安靜會
An-ch'ing-pang 安靜幫
An-ch'ing-too-yu 安靜道友
Anhui 安徽

Baigow River 白溝河
pei-shi 臂使
Ben-ming-chi 本命師

h'u-ju-shui 去如水
Chai-chiao 齋教
Chai Li-hui 齋理會 or 齋禮會

Chan-dao-shi 傳道師
Ch'angchow 常州
hang 長
Chang Fu (Chang Fei) 張飛
Chang-kuo
Chang Luo-hsing 張洛行
Chang Pai-ma 長白馬
Changsha 長沙
  (capital of Honan)
Chang Te-cheng 張德成
huo-chu 棹主
Chao Yun 趙雲
Chen Shi-yi 陳十一
Chen Tsuo-hsin 陳作新
Ch'eng 成
Cheng Ch'eng-kung 鄭成功
heng-peng 鎮棚
Cheng Shi-liang 鄭士良
Chekiang 浙江
Chia Ch'ing 嘉慶
Chia Li 假理
Chian 錢
Chiancang 錢倉
Chian Jian 錢堅
Chiang Kai-shek 蔣介石
hiao-fei 教匪
chiao-men 教門
Chiao Ta-feng 焦達峯
Ch'ien Lung 乾隆
Chih 智
Chihli 直隸
Ch'in 秦
Chin-ch'ien-hui 金錢會
chin tai 近代
chin-fei 金匪
Chin-tan-hui 金丹會

Ch'ing 清
Ch'ing-ch'a-hui 清茶會
Ch'ing Hung Pang 青紅幫
Ch'ing Pang 青
Ching 精
Chiu Kung 九宮
Chou 周
Chou-chia-tsi 仇家子
Chu 朱
Chu Ba-jie 豬八戒
Chu Teh 朱德
chung-yi-tang 忠義堂

Da-mo 達摩
Deng Guang-jiao
Dun-kia Society 迅甲
Dudu 都督

Fa 法
fa-shih 法師
Fan Ch'ing Fu Ming 反清復明
Fo 佛
Fo Fa Seng 佛法僧
fu-shan-chu 副山主
Fukien 福建

Ghee Hin 義興
Ghee Hok 義福

Han 漢
Hao-li Sect 好禮師
hao-shih 好
hsiong 雄
Hua-hsing-hui 華興會
Huang Hsing 黃興
Ho Long 龍
Honan 河南
Hopei 河北
Hokow 河口
Hsia 夏
hsiang-chu 香主堂
Hsiao-hsiang-t'ang 小香堂
Hsiao-tao-hui 小刀會
Hsieh-chiao 邪教
hsien feng 先
Hsien Feng 咸豐
hsien tai 現代
Hsin-cheng-t'ung-chiao-pu 新正通交部

Hsing 行
Hsing-chung-hui 興中會
Hsueh 學
Huai 准
Huang-ho 黃河
Huang Hsiu-jin 黃秀金
Huang-lian Sheng-mu 黃蓮聖母
Huang Shi-cheng 黃士誠
hui-t'ang 會堂
Huguang 湖廣
hui 會
Hun-chia-zi 混家子
Hunan 湖南
Hung 洪
Hung (red) 紅
Hung-ch'iang 紅槍
Hung Hsiu-ch'üan 洪秀全
Hung Hu-tzu 紅鬍子
Hung-men 洪門
Hung pan 紅幫
Hung-shun 洪順
Hung-Pang 紅幫
Hung Wu 洪武
Hung Chia 洪家
Hung Men 洪門
Hung Pang 洪幫
huo-hu 活虎
Hupeh 湖北

i 義
I Ching 易經
I Ho T'üan 義和團
I Ho Ch'üan 義和拳

Jen 仁
Ju (River) 汝

K'ang Hsi 康熙
K'ang Yu-wei 康有爲
Kansu 甘肅
ke ming 革命
Kiangsi 江西
Kiangsu 江蘇
Kien Teck 建德
Kin-chung-chao 金鐘罩
Kin Lan (Chin Lan) 金蘭
Kiukiang 九江
Ko-lao-hui 哥老會
k'ou-li 叩禮
Kuan-ti 關帝
Kuan-yin 觀音
Kuan Yu (Kuan Yü) 關羽
Kuang Hsü 光緒

kuang-ming 光明
K'un Lun shan 崑崙山
Kung 宮
Kung-chin-hui 共進會
kung suo 公所
Kuomintang 國民黨
Kwangsi 廣西
Lai
lai-ru-hsiang 來如香
Lai Wen-kuang 賴文光
Lao-jun Society 老君
Lao-jun 老君
Lao-shi-fu 老師父
lao-ta 老大
Li 李
Li Chi-han 李啓漢
Li Ching-wu
Li Ta-chao 李大釗
liang
Liang Ch'i-ch'ao 梁啓超
Liang-shan-po 梁山泊
Liu Chi-tan 劉志丹
Liu Kun-i 劉坤一
Liu Li-chu'an 劉麗川
Liu Pi (Liu Pei) 劉備
Lo Tai-kang 羅大綱
Lookow 淥口
Lun

Ma Chao-jun 馬超俊
Ma Fu-yi 馬福益
Mabao 馬保
Mao Tse-tung 毛澤東
Mei Hsing 梅興
Mengzhou 孟州
Mieh Yang 滅洋
Ming 明
Mien Shan, Mi Shan 麵山米山
ming-yen 明
Mou
Mu Yuan 繆元
Muh-yang city 木楊城
  (Mu Yang City)

Nanking 南京
Nei-ba-tang 內八堂
Nien 捻
Nien-shou 捻首
Nien-zi 捻子

Pa-kua 八卦
pai-hua 白話
Pai Lang 白朗

Pai Lien Hui	白蓮教	ta-tung	大同
Pan	潘	Ta-tao-hui	大刀會
Pan Ching	潘清	T'ai P'ing	太平
Peking	北京	T'ai-p'ing T'ien-kuo	太平天國
Pen	本	Tai-ji-tu	太極圖
Peng	朋	T'an Ssu-t'ung	譚嗣同
Phat-Te	發濟	T'ang	唐
Pi-mi chieh-shih	秘密結社	tang	堂
Pi-mi hui-shih	秘密會社	T'ao Ch'eng-chang	陶成章
Pingyi	平邑	Tao	道
Po-hsüeh Hung-t'zu	博學鴻詞科	Tao Kuang	道光
		Te	德
San-chiao	三教	Teng Chung-hsia	鄧中夏
San-fan brigands	三藩匪	Teng Ssu-yu	鄧嗣禹
San Ho Hui	三合會	ti chu	地主
San Kuei	三規	Tie-pu-shan	鐵布衫
San tai	三代	Tien-tee-whee	天地會
San Tien Hui	三點會	T'ien Ming	天命
Song	松	T'ien Ti Hui	天地會
Shan	山	T'ien Yu-hung	天佑洪
Shan-chu	山主	Tien	典
Shan-t'ang	山堂	T'ien-te	天德
Shantung	山東	T'ien-wang	天王
Shang	商	Tientsin	天津
Shao Lin Monastery	少林寺	Tongchuan	銅船
Shi-bo	師伯	Tongting (Lake)	洞庭湖
Shi-fu	師父	topekong	太伯公
Shi-shu	師叔	Towlin	獨流
Shi-tai	師太	tow-mu-tan	斗母壇
Shi-ye	師爺	Tso Tsung-t'ang	左宗棠
Shih	師	Tu Yueh-sen	杜月笙
Shih Huang Ti	始皇帝	t'u	徒
Shih Shih-lun	施世綸	t'uan	團
Shuang Li	雙理	T'ung	通
Shuang Li p'eng-yu	雙理朋友	T'ung Chih	東治
hui	水	T'ung-chiao-ta-chuan	通交大船
Shui-hu-ch'uan	水滸傳	T'ung Chih	同知
Shun Chih	順治	T'ung-meng Hui	同盟會
Shun-tian-jiao	順天教	tung	東
Siantang	湘潭	Tzu	自
Soochow	蘇州		
Ssu Ma Chien	司馬遷	Wei	威
Sun Chuan-fang	孫傳芳	wei-chiao	僞教
Sun Yat-sen	孫逸仙	Weixian	魏具
Sun Wu	孫武	Wen	文
Sun Wu-kong	孫悟空	Wen	翁
Sung Ching-shi	宋京詩	wen-yen	文言
Sunkiang	松江	Wen Yen	翁岩
Szechuan	四川	Wo-tou-shan-shi	鵝頭禪師
Ta-fu-chih-p'in	打富支貧	Wu	悟
Ta-hsiang-t'ang	大香堂	Wu-ch'eng-fu-mu	無成父母
Ta-ke	大哥	Wu-ch'eng Lao-mu	無成老母
		Wu-chih-lao-mu	無止老母

Wu-chow-Hung-men 五洲洪門
Wu-Kang-sai 瓦岡寨
Wu-Kuang 吳廣
Wuchang 武昌
Wuhu 蕪湖
Wu-ying-bian 無影鞭
Wu Yu-chang 吳玉章
Yamen 衙門
Yang 陽
Yang Hu 楊虎
Yangtze 楊子江
yao-chiao 妖教
Yi-kuan-dao 一母道
yi-shi 頤使
Yichang 宜昌
Yin 陰
Yin-chiao 淫教

Ying (River) 潁
Ying-jin-shi 引進師
Yu Ch'eng-lung 于成龍
Yu Hsien 毓賢
yu-min 游民
Yüan 圓
Yüan (dollar) 元
Yüan Shih-k'ai 袁世凱
yüeh 月
yun-tung 運動
Yung Cheng 雍正
Yünnan 雲南

Zao Chi 趙居
Zao-da-ge 趙大哥
Zhou Hsiong 周雄
Zhu Hsiu-hsian 朱秀仙

Index

Altar of the Woman with the Bushel (tow-mu-tan), 186
Amoy, 51, 73, 84, 85, 94, 106
Anhui, 48, 71, 95, 158, 171
artisans/craftsmen, 4, 10, 68, 71, 73, 87
Associated Committee of All Sects, 181

Big Sword Society (Ta-tao-hui), 1, 40, 51, 71, 112–115, 170, 184, 186
Black Banner, 37, 77
Black Flags, 126
Black Spear Society, 170
bourgeoisie, 10, 12, 135, 150, 160, 163, 166, 169, 190
Boxers, 2, 10, 40–41, 43, 44, 59, 64, 65, 71, 104, 113, 115–125, 170, 175, 189, 190
    Chang Te-cheng, 117, 121
    Ch'ao Fu-tien, 122
    Nghia Hoa, 126
Britain, 84, 108, 109, 115, 125
bu-yi-hui, 177
Buddhism, 7, 124
    Buddha, 48, 50, 120, 121, 123, 132
    Maitreya, 37, 52, 65
Burma, 109

Canton, 5, 68, 73, 77, 81, 84, 85, 86, 91, 106, 173, 179
Carbonari, 188
Central Door Sect 113
Chang Siao-ling, 165, 166
Ch'angchow, 48, 103
Chang Luo-hsing, 101
Chang Pai-hsiang, 140
Chang Tsung-chan, 170
Chang Tsung-chang, 176
Changsha, 149, 150, 155, 156
Chekiang, 31, 48, 51, 56, 70, 94

Chen Chuen, 166
Cheng Ch'eng-kung, 144
Cheng Shi-liang, 139
Chenkiang, 111
Chia Ch'ing, 37, 95
Chiang Jian, 47, 48
Chiang Kai-shek, 161, 163, 164, 165, 166, 174, 178, 185
Chiao Ta-feng, 140
Ch'ien Lung, 45, 70
Chihli, 48, 57, 58, 59, 71, 74, 106, 120, 171, 178
Chinese Communist Party, 12, 44, 141, 160, 161, 162, 173, 178, 179, 181, 182, 190
    The Central Chinese People's Soviet Government, 182, 183, 184
    The Chinese People's Army, 141
Ch'ing Dynasty, 6, 12, 14, 15, 16, 17, 20, 22, 33, 45, 61, 80, 92, 100, 104, 121, 122, 124, 125, 144, 145, 146, 159, 182
Christianity, 5, 90, 94, 113, 123, 124
Chu Teh, 44, 141–143, 151, 188
Chung Yang Tao, 180, 181
Chungking, 35, 110, 161
Comintern, 43, 173
Common Progress, Society of, 151
Communism, 11, 90
    Communist International, 173
    Communists, 12, 43, 54, 143, 152, 161, 162, 163, 173, 174, 175, 178, 179, 191
Confucianism, 4, 6, 7, 11, 42, 64, 80, 90, 127, 153
    Confucius, 174

December Tenth, Society of, 164
Dunkia Sect, 113

East India Company, 80
Eight Diagrams, (Pa-Kua), 38–40, 42, 51, 65, 81, 113
Eighth Route Army, 181
Elder Brothers, the Association of (Ko-lao-hui), 43–47, 50, 51, 71, 77, 78, 107, 111–112, 113, 138, 140, 141, 142, 143, 144, 150, 151, 153, 156, 158, 162, 179, 182–184, 191
Eleuths, 16

Filial Piety and Fraternity Society, 140
Foochow, 84, 113
France, 108, 109, 115, 125
　Paris, 137
Franco-Chinese War (1884–85), 71, 104, 125
Freemasonry, 188
Friends, Society of, 126
Fukien, 16, 31, 33, 55, 71, 86, 87

Germany, 108, 109, 115
Ghee Hin Society, 33
Ghee Hok Society, 33
Golden Coins Society (Chin-ch'ien-hui), 51, 55–57, 70, 94, 169
Golden Elixir Society (Chin-tan-hui), 52, 113
Grand Canal, 47, 71, 121
Green Band (Ch'ing-Pang), 1, 45, 47–51, 71, 162, 164, 167, 168
Green Spear Society, 171

Hainan, 115
Half Incense-Stick Sect, 113
Ham-nghi, 129
Hamberg, Theodore (the Rev.), 91, 93
Han Dynasty, 94, 100, 182, 183
Hankow, 77, 78, 165, 168
Hanyang arsenal strike (1913), 162
Hao-li Sect, 113
Hawaii, 33
　Honolulu, 33, 135, 139

Heaven and Earth Society (Tien Ti Hui), 13, 15, 17, 22, 76
　Thien-dia-hoi, 126
Ho Long, 44
Honan, 3, 37, 40, 43, 45, 48, 59, 95, 113, 135, 157, 158, 170, 171, 172, 178
Hong Kong, 15, 33, 34, 35, 80, 84, 126, 135, 139, 143, 185
　Hong Kong dock strike (1885), 34, 162
　Hong Kong seamen's strike (1922), 163
　Hong Kong Triad, 35
Hopei, 43, 45, 53, 80, 169
Hsia, Shang and Chou, 45
Hsieh Tzu-ch'ang, 182
Hsien Feng, 55, 123
Hsing-chung-hui (Society for the Rebirth of China), 135, 139, 143
Hu Show-shan, 143
Hua-hsing-hui (Society for the Renewal of China), 149
Huai, 45, 77
Huang-ho, 95
Huang Hsing, 135, 139, 149, 150, 151
Huang Shi-cheng, 143
Hunan 71, 77, 80, 95, 103, 120, 140, 146, 147, 150, 154
Hung Hsiu-ch'üan, 3, 90, 91, 92, 93, 102, 188
　See also T'ai P'ing peasant movement
Hung-men Society, 15, 69, 79, 145, 146
　See also Triad Society
Hung Society of the Five Continents (Wu-chow-Hung-men), 185
Hupeh, 31, 71, 95, 120, 140, 148, 171
Hwang Ching-yung, 165

I Ching, 56
Incense-Stick Sect, 113
India, 7

Bengal, 80
Indo-China, 2, 33, 125
Indonesia, 2, 15, 33
intelligentsia, 11, 12, 160, 190

James, F. H. (Rev.), 36, 52
Japan, 9, 10, 44 104, 108, 109, 126, 135, 136, 139, 140, 151, 153, 160, 161, 182, 183, 184, 185, 189
   Tokyo, 139, 153
   Sino-Japanese War (1937–45), 185. 2
Jiao Ta-feng 154–156

Kang Feng Tao, 180
K'ang Hsi, 56, 68, 92, 145
K'ang Yu-wei, 153
Kansu, 31, 157, 158
Ki Ying, 83
Kiangsi, 31, 48, 78
Kiangsu, 56, 78, 95, 103, 113, 170, 171
Kiukiang, 110
Korea, 109, 119, 133
Kuan-ti, 174
Kuan-yin, 19, 65, 174
Kuang Hsu, 48, 50, 104
Kuangsi, 86, 89, 107, 126, 165
Kuantung, 71, 84
K'un Lun Mountain, 149
Kung-chin-hui (Society for Mutual Progress), 139, 140–141, 152, 153
Kuomintang, 3, 12, 35, 51, 54, 135, 152, 160, 161, 163, 164, 166, 168, 169, 173, 175, 177, 178, 183, 190
Kweichow, 71, 143, 144, 151, 152

Lai Wen-kuang, 101
landowners/landlords, 4, 5, 61, 70, 74, 90, 97, 98, 100, 104, 140, 142, 147, 151, 153, 169, 179
Lao-jun Society, 162
League of Hard Bellies, 171
Leboucq, Father 3, 59
Li Chi-han, 162

Li Ching-wu, 168
Li Chinglin, 170
Li Ta-chao, 43, 173, 174
Liang Ch'i-ch'ao, 153
Liaotung Peninsula, 115
Liberation (1949), 9, 11, 186, 189
Lien Tsuan Hwei (joint village societies), 170, 184
Lin Fu-shan, 105
Liu Chen-hua, 171
Liu Chi-tan, 179, 182
Liu Kun-i, 107, 111
Liu Li-ch'uan, 86
Liuyuang, 153
Long March, 161, 179

Ma Fu-yi, 146–150, 152
Mabao, 48
Mafia, 188
Malaysia, 2, 15, 30, 33. 58
Manchuria, 3, 9, 42, 43, 61, 62, 64, 67, 108, 132–134
Manchus, 9, 11, 12, 16, 19, 34, 44, 50, 59, 68, 69, 70, 80, 87, 90, 100, 104, 111, 122, 135, 136, 138, 141, 146, 150, 151, 154, 156, 159, 183, 189
Mandarins, 2, 7, 42, 55, 57, 61, 66, 77, 81, 87, 90, 96, 99, 102, 109, 110, 116, 117, 138
Mandate of Heaven (T'ien Ming), 6, 87, 127
Manicheanism, 37
Mao Tse-tung, 3, 4, 44, 70, 178, 179, 182–184
Market of the Great Peace, 16, 19
Marxism, 43, 160, 161, 190
Mason James, 111
May Fourth Movement (1919), 2, 9, 12, 160, 161, 162, 177, 191
May Thirtieth Movement (1925), 160, 166
Middle Ages, 7, 37, 57, 61, 67, 123
Middle Kingdom, 1, 80
Ming Dynasty, 2, 6, 8, 15, 16, 17, 18, 19, 20, 22, 23, 36, 40, 45, 51, 61, 68, 69, 80, 87, 88, 89, 90, 92, 93, 94, 100, 104, 122, 145, 146,

152, 159
missionaries, 3, 11, 37, 40, 41, 109,
    110, 113, 115, 116, 118, 169
Mongolia (Inner), 104
Muh-yang (City of Willows), 16,
    17, 19, 20, 21, 23
Munshi Abdullah, 3
Mutual Aid Community (Tung-
    chi-kung), 143–144, 151

Nanking, 5, 24, 35, 85, 86, 90, 91,
    93, 102, 103, 110, 111, 156, 159,
    165, 166, 185
    Treaty of Nanking, 84
Napoleon III, 125
    Louis Bonaparte, 164
Nepal, 109
Nien, 40, 43, 58, 70, 71, 77, 94–
    101, 104, 106, 122, 169, 190
    Chang Tuan-yang, 97
Nine Palaces, 113
Ningpo, 84

Observance Society (Chai Li-hui),
    41–42, 45, 71, 104–106, 107, 113
Opium Wars, 9, 11, 33, 73, 80,
    108, 110
    First Opium War, 1, 71, 84
    Second Opium War, 84

Pai Lang insurrection (White
    Wolf rebellion), 3, 156–159
Pan Ching, 47, 48, 50
Peace and Happiness, Society of
    (An-ch'ing pang), 45, 47–48
peasants/farmers, 4, 6, 8, 10, 11
    34, 43, 68, 70, 72, 73, 84, 90,
    100, 104, 109, 121, 122, 129,
    137, 138, 141, 142, 149, 150,
    161, 169, 172, 174, 175, 176,
    177, 178, 179, 182, 184, 189
    peasant movement, 43, 57, 94,
    95, 160, 169, 170, 171, 172, 174,
    175, 179
Pei Chung-hsi, 165
Peking, 5, 6, 24, 39, 47, 53, 77, 90,
    125
People's Republic of China, 2, 161,

185, 186
Persia, 37
Phan Xich-long, 129, 130, 131
Phat-te secret society (Society for
    the distribution of aid), 131
Philippines, 145
Pickering, 15
Pilgrimage to the West, 174
P'ing-hsiang miners, insurrection
    of (1906), 34, 150, 162
proletariat, 11, 12, 34, 126, 160,
    164, 190
Pure Tea Sect (Ch'ing-ch'a-hui),
    52

Red Band (Hung Pang), 15, 34,
    45, 48–51, 162, 164, 165, 167
Red Beards (Hung Hu-tzu), 3,
    42–43, 61–62, 64, 67, 96, 132–
    134
Red Lamps, 186
Red Spears (Hung-ch'iang), 3, 8,
    43, 46, 64, 169–178, 180, 181,
    184, 181
reform movement (1898), 2, 72
Republic of Jeltuga, 133
Republican Revolution (1911), 2,
    33, 34, 44, 48, 78, 101, 106, 136,
    137, 139, 144, 151, 152, 153–
    156, 159, 160, 182, 188, 191
    Chinese Republic, 3, 59, 135,
    141, 154, 156, 159
    Republicans, 44, 143, 144, 146,
    153, 156, 188
Revolutionary League (in Japan),
    139–141
Rosicrucians, 188
Russia, 108, 109, 115, 125, 132,
    133, 136
    Moscow, 178
    Russian Black Hundred, 164
    Russian Bolsheviks, 141

San Ho Hui, 15, 77, 91
    See also Triad Society
scholars, 10, 37, 59, 60, 67, 68,
    69, 73, 87, 101, 129
Shanghai, 2, 10, 11, 34, 35, 36, 51,

63, 71, 73, 84, 85, 86, 88, 89, 94,
102, 106, 110, 111, 136, 153,
160, 163, 164, 165, 166, 169,
170, 173
Shanghai carpenters' strike
(1918), 162
Shangsha, 89
Shantung, 36, 37, 40, 43, 45, 48,
52, 56, 66, 71, 95, 109, 113, 115,
118, 119, 120, 170, 172, 175,
178, 179, 181
Shao Lin Monastery, 16, 18, 23
Shensi, 157, 158, 171, 172, 179,
182
Shui-hu-ch'uan, 61
Liangshanpo Forest, 155
Shun Chi, 68
Sian, 77, 78
Siberia, 62
Singapore, 3, 13, 30, 33, 34, 35,
86, 153
Sinkiang, 77, 78
Small Sword Society (Hsiao-tao-
hui), 2, 51, 85–89, 94, 190
Soochow, 48, 86, 103
South-East Asia, 3, 15, 135, 136
Ssu Ma Chien, 69
Study of Independence, Society
for the, 144, 152
Sun Chuan-fang, 165
Sun Yat-sen, 3, 9, 12, 33, 44, 68,
77, 93, 101, 135, 136, 139, 142,
143, 144, 145, 150, 151, 152,
156, 159, 161, 188
Sun Wu, 140
Sung Dynasty, 52
Sung Ching-shi, 77
Sunkiang, 48
Szechuan, 31, 71, 80, 95, 107, 110,
120, 137, 139, 140, 141, 142,
143, 169

Tai-ji-tu Society, 113
T'ai P'ing peasant movement, 3,
11, 12, 33, 44, 51, 71, 89–94, 95,
100, 101, 104, 106, 111, 138,
157, 170, 188
Taiwan, 54, 108, 126, 186

T'an Ssu-t'ung, 3 71
T'ang Dynasty, 20
Tang Cai-chang, 153
Tao Kuang, 39, 81, 83
Taoism, 7
Lao-jun, 174
Teng Chung-hsia, 162
Three Kingdoms, Epic of, 65, 174
Chang Fei, 22, 174
Chao Yun, 121, 174
Kung Ming, Sun Pin and Wu
Khi, 93
Liu Pi and Kuan Yu, 22
Tientsin, 53, 107, 109, 185
Tongchuan, 48
Tonking, 126, 150
Tonking campaign, 34
tradesmen/merchants, 4, 5, 6, 10,
30, 34, 61, 68, 98, 138, 147, 148,
149, 150, 164, 169
Triad Society, 1, 2, 3, 9, Chapter
1, 36, 40, 44, 51, 57, 59, 64, 67,
68, 71, 74, 77, 80, 81–85, 90, 91,
92, 93, 126, 138, 139, 140, 145,
146, 149, 151, 162, 185, 188
Hung, 14, 15, 18, 19, 20, 21, 22,
23, 30, 185
Kau Wang-yuen, Chan Pei-kii
and Li Atwan, 83
Wan Yun-lung, 20, 23
Triple Society, 140
Tseng T'eng-fang, 105
Tso Tsung-t'ang, 77, 78
Tu Yueh-sen, 165, 166, 168
T'ung Chih, 45, 104
T'ung-meng-hui (Sworn League),
12, 135–136, 137, 139, 141, 142,
144, 150, 151, 152, 190

United States of America, 108,
109, 169
California, 33, 145
New York, 145

Vegetarians (Chai-chiao), 42, 113
Vehmgericht, 188
Versailles, Treaty of, 12
Versailles conference, 160

Victoria, Queen, 1
Vietnam, 15, 109, 125, 126, 127
   Saigon, 3, 58, 59, 65, 73, 126, 129, 130, 132
Virtue and Equity Group (Nhon-hoa-duong), 126

Wang Ching-wei, 185
Way of Fundamental Unity (Yi-Kuan-tao), 2, 52–54, 185, 186
Wen Yen, 47, 48
White Cloud, 186
White Lotus (Bai Lien Hui, White Water-Lily Society), 1, 8, 16, 36–38, 40, 41, 42, 43, 44, 51, 57, 58, 60, 64, 65, 74, 80, 94, 100, 102–103, 113, 115, 117, 123, 124, 169, 190
White Spears, 43, 171
Will of Heaven sect (Shun-tian-jiao), 169
World War, 2nd, 161

Wu Yu-chang, 44, 137, 139, 141, 151, 188
Wuchang, 146, 153, 154
Wuhan, 173, 174, 178, 186
Wuhu, 110
Wylie, A., 63, 85

Yang Hu, 166
Yangtze (river/region), 5, 31, 44, 47, 77, 89, 107, 109, 110, 111, 120, 138, 139, 148, 152, 153, 157
   Yangtze armies, 158
Yellow Spears, 43, 170
Yichang, 110
Yu Hsien, 115, 119
Yüan Shih-k'ai, 119, 156, 157, 161
Yueh Wei-chun, 170
Yung Cheng, 47
Yunnan, 31, 141, 142

Zih Ah-mei, 167